To Dana, Pamela & Jack
my new "neighbors" with
my sincere appreciation.

I hope this book will enhance
your enjoyment of your new home
in "Ruidoso Country".

Joyce W. Cox

Ruidoso Country

Frank Mangan

BOOKS by FRANK MANGAN

Bordertown
El Paso in Pictures
Bordertown Revisited
The Pipeliners
Ruidoso Country

Ruidoso Country

FRANK MANGAN

Design by the author

MANGAN BOOKS
El Paso, Texas

Published by Mangan Books
6245 Snowheights, El Paso, Texas 79912

Printed in the United States of America

Mangan, Frank.
        Ruidoso country / Frank Mangan; designed by the author.
        p. cm.
        Includes bibliographical references and index.
        ISBN 0-930208-33-1; $39.95
        1. Ruidoso Region (N.M.) —History.   I. Title.
F804.R9M36 1994
978.9′64—dc20   94-20105
                                                          CIP

For Peggy and Pancho

Rio Ruidoso in Spanish means "noisy river."
But to me, Rio Ruidoso has a more subtle
connotation. It implies a blissful, happy sound.

Antonia Otero
Capitan, New Mexico

Contents

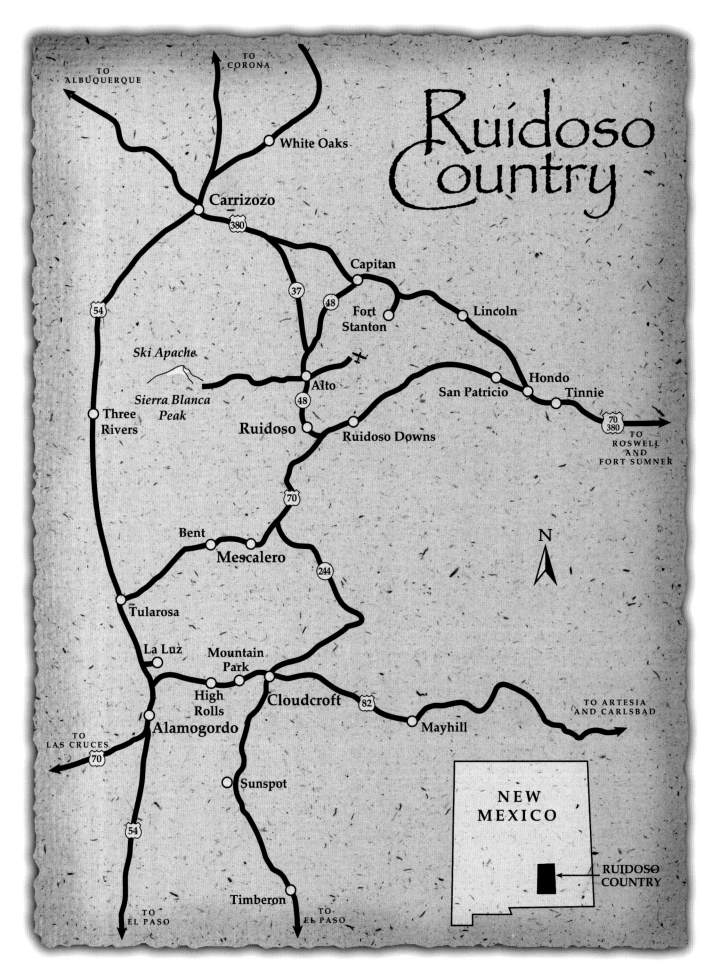

Ruidoso Country

TO ALBUQUERQUE

TO CORONA

White Oaks

Carrizozo

380

54

37

48

Capitan

Fort Stanton

Lincoln

Ski Apache

Alto

48

San Patricio

Hondo

Tinnie

Sierra Blanca Peak

Three Rivers

Ruidoso

Ruidoso Downs

70
380

TO ROSWELL AND FORT SUMNER

70

N

Bent

244

Mescalero

Tularosa

La Luz

Mountain Park

82

TO ARTESIA AND CARLSBAD

High Rolls

Cloudcroft

Mayhill

Alamogordo

TO LAS CRUCES

70

54

Sunspot

NEW MEXICO

RUIDOSO COUNTRY

Timberon

TO EL PASO

TO EL PASO

Introduction

Ruidoso Country! The name conjures up images of forested mountains, carpeted meadows, skiing, cool summers, restless rivers, spectacular silence, wild game and resort living. Add old military forts, ghost towns and state parks, and the recipe for enjoyment is "almost" complete.

What remains is the dash of historic and colorful bygone figures and events.

Mescalero Apache Indians were not the first residents of Ruidoso Country, but they dominated the land as few others have before or since. The names Geronimo, Victorio and Nana are as alive today as they were yesterday.

Spanish conquistadors with their beards and armor laid claim three hundred years ago to Ruidoso Country by virtue of the Sword and the Cross.

Cattle kings such as John Chisum and Oliver Lee controlled Ruidoso landscapes that took days to cross. Powerful figures such as Colonel Albert Jennings Fountain and Albert Bacon Fall fought titanic political struggles in Ruidoso Country. Fall's life ended in controversy; Fountain's as one of New Mexico's greatest murder mysteries.

Billy the Kid spent his most productive and dangerous years in Ruidoso Country. The towns of Lincoln, White Oaks, Tularosa and Mescalero still echo his name.

The spectre of the Lincoln County War attracts thousands of visitors annually to Ruidoso Country. You can walk the streets just as they were then. You can stand in the same courthouse where the Kid made one of the most sensational jailbreaks in southwestern history.

The legend of Susan McSween arose from the smoke and ashes of the Lincoln Country War. She became the West's best known cattle queen.

For the visitor with imagination, Sheriff Pat Garret, the tall slayer of Billy the Kid, still rides the lonesome trails. The railroads still spin steel rails across desert floor and through narrow, twisting canyons. Gold is still dug from the rusty, bottomless pits of the abandoned mining towns. Rustled cattle forever disappear over the foothills. The din of past military battles echo sprightly on suitable, quiet days.

Frank Mangan, an El Paso native, writer and publisher, not only understands Ruidoso Country history, he has watched recent portions of it develop. Frank climbed the dominant Sierra Blanca Peak when it was still primitive, before it became a famous ski resort. Frank lived as a boy in Ruidoso Country when residents were counted in the dozens, not in the thousands.

Ruidoso Country, from the 1500s to near the year 2000, is Frank Mangan's magnificent opus. Based on interviews, newspaper accounts, and government and county records, he has put together a never-before told story. This is the vibrant history of an empire that is still changing and still growing.

Leon C. Metz

Acknowledgments

For decades my thoughts of producing a history of Ruidoso and the surrounding area danced through my head like visions of sugarplums. I had been saving photographs of Ruidoso since the 1940s, just in case.

But, if it hadn't been for my wife, Judy Peterson Mangan, this book might not have progressed beyond a big fat wishful think. A few years ago Judy suggested that we should have a home away from home in Ruidoso. No sooner had we moved in than she said, "Now, why don't you get off your duff and go ahead and write that book?"

"Not a bad idea," said I, "Glad I thought of it."

It would be trite to describe Judy's total role which far transcended the usual wifely support of typing, proofreading and transcribing taped interviews. She participated in every phase of this four-year effort. She selected photographs with an unerring eye—most of the time. She slashed at my sparkling prose and we improved it with her journalism background. She drove over dirt roads with me, eyes glazed over, as I checked out ghost towns and dry riverbeds one after another. She looked over my shoulder at the drawing board, suggesting changes in page layouts—and all of this with the utmost enthusiasm.

I have also enjoyed the assistance of countless friendly and generous people in putting together this book. I am deeply grateful to Evelyn and Wayne Estes of Denver, Colorado, part of the Ruidoso Wingfield clan. They allowed me to sift through boxes of family pictures and letters. Tillie Jack of El Paso pointed the way to the Estes family.

In Ruidoso, Bill Hart guided me through the maze of early day electric plants and gambling dens. Emadair Jones recalled fascinating history including the story of Ruidoso real estate and its connection to the Three Rivers Ranch. My friend Bill Green introduced me to Tom Ryan in Mesilla, New Mexico. Ryan owned Three Rivers for many years and filled in a number of blank spots regarding that historic ranch. Bill McCarty furnished background on the original Cree Ranch and the resulting real estate sales of the Cree property.

Long-time Ruidosoan Marie Rooney accompanied me on several driving tours of old Ruidoso. Robert Keyes of Roswell spent days with me on the road and recounted everything that happened in Ruidoso and the Sacramento Mountains since the last Ice Age. When Robert got interested in this project, he couldn't do enough to help me.

John Meigs was my art guide through San Patricio, and Peggy and Dan Fenton provided information on the Ruidoso art scene. So did Dorothy and Tom Knapp, Ken Hosmer, and Gloria and Bill Rakocy, painters and museum owners.

Joetyne Wright, who has lived in Ruidoso all her life, furnished hours of information on Ruidoso Downs, as did Jerry Knott, Mark Doth, Margaret Varner Bloss, Margaret DuPont, Hazel and Bob Haynsworth, Ray Sanchez and Ray Reed.

On the Mescalero Reservation, Berle Kanseah came to our A-frame cabin and shared Apache history with me. Ellen Big Rope Lathan of the Culture Center at Mescalero, Jo Kazhe, Jonathan Adams, Wendell Chino and Mark Chino also shared Apache knowledge. Betsy Bryant Rose of Hobbs, New Mexico, pointed me in the right direction on the Reservation research. Roy Parker and Riker Davis helped me navigate my story across the snowy slopes of Ski Apache, owned by the Mescalero Tribe.

Carolyn Mayfield Driver and Eleanor Lorentzen had saved their mothers' early papers and snapshots and they let me browse. Peggy Snell Shaifer, my first high school date, who now lives in the Texas Hill Country, told me of earlier days in

Hollywood, New Mexico, and she proved to be a superb teller of whimsical tales.

Robert McCubbin opened his extensive historical collection and generously provided me with rare photographs, some never before published. Collector Bob McNellis literally unlocked his vault for me.

The late Bill Hostetter, until recently Ruidoso's resident meteorologist, helped me describe the mountain climate. My uncle, Charles B. Little, first told me about early Ruidoso long ago while driving to the mountains in a 1930 Chevy. He smoked unfiltered Chesterfield cigarettes all the way. I loved it. In Capitan, Toni and Herman Otero furnished documents on the area's original Hispanic settlers. Also in Capitan, historian Herb Traylor shared his memories.

As always, photographer and good friend José Andow added his talents by copying and enhancing old pictures. Charles Keesey helped immensely with his magical retouching abilities. Peggy Feinberg, Pancho Mangan, Cliff Trussell and Wally Sheid made special photo trips to Ruidoso. Herb Brunell provided a number of striking photographs for this book. Some of the 1940s Main Street pictures are from Herb's extensive collection. Bob Hart and Donna Crandall of the Lincoln County Heritage Trust practically gave me the key to the Museum in Lincoln. Bob Hart is a world-class authority on Billy the Kid.

Among those who read the manuscript are Pancho Mangan, Martha Patterson Peterson, Mandy Zabriskie and Patty Gilbert. I am deeply grateful also for the good will and assistance of Mary Sarber, Wayne Daniel and Marta Estrada at the El Paso Public Library. To Tim Blevens and Austin Hoover of the New Mexico State University Library, my thanks for digging out and making available historic photographs and information. Claudia Rivers at the University of Texas at El Paso Library furnished solid research on Old Spain. At the Ruidoso Public Library, Mary Lou Gooch deserves my gratitude.

Bill Cornell, geology professor at the University of Texas at El Paso, went far beyond the call of duty to locate information about the Sacramento Mountains. Louise Perkins, formerly from Alto, New Mexico, described her childhood days growing up in the mountains. Wayland Burk sold us the cabin and speculated about a bright future for Ruidoso. Joan Bailey of the Ruidoso Chamber of Commerce provided dozens of vital statistics.

I have also had the indispensable assistance of one kind or another from Anne and Tom Rone, Cara Mae Coe Marable Smith, Tom Starkweather, Sam Tobias of the Forest Service, Marilyn Poel, Donna Mangan, Millard McKinney, Jim Schwartzback, and Ernest and Robert McDaniel.

Vicki Trego Hill added her many talents for the production of this book. She is a fine illustrator, book publisher, commercial designer and typographer. Her computer graphics made each page of this volume.

I am deeply grateful to my good friend Leon Metz, one of America's leading western writers. Leon took a special interest in this book and broke into his busy schedule of television, radio and personal appearances to edit the manuscript. He gave of himself—several hundred hours of time—cutting and revising to help this all come about. He loaned me a five-foot section of his extensive western library for three years of research. Having these books at my fingertips saved countless hours and days of tracking down information. I couldn't have done without him.

Finally, my sincerest thanks to Chris Sicurella and his superb, creative and enthusiastic team at Tri Star Commercial Printing in Phoenix, Arizona.

1

Ruidoso Country

A trout fisherman tries his luck in the icy, boulder-laden Rio Ruidoso. The stream has its headwaters high on the slopes of Sierra Blanca Peak, then tumbles downward paralleling the Village of Ruidoso. (Frank Mangan)

RUIDOSO COUNTRY is the green spot on most maps of south central New Mexico. It is an island of pines rising high above the desert, a verdant display of grandeur stretching ninety miles in the southern Rocky Mountains. The hub is anchored by the Village of Ruidoso, but the region extends outward to include the Mescalero Apache Reservation, Cloudcroft, Lincoln, and a collection of other mountain communities each with its own charm and personality.

The most dominant landmark is Sierra Blanca Peak which towers above what I call Ruidoso Country. My first attachment to Sierra Blanca goes back to the time a group of boy scouts, myself included, wheezed up its slopes toward the summit. The Apaches had kindly permitted us to camp inside the Mescalero Reservation in a grassy glade on the banks of the Ruidoso River.

Early one June morning we followed the South Fork of the river to timberline. Fairly easy going. Above the tree line the slope became a boulder-strewn expanse of short grass.

As we struggled ever upward we were guided by what looked like the top of the peak. Yet upon reaching that point, the mountain still loomed skyward, seemingly forever.

Until—there it was, the rocky summit of Sierra Blanca. A small sign proclaimed: 12,003 feet above sea level. The year was 1933 and there was no such thing as pollution in New Mexico. The view was outstanding. As a twelve-year-old, I could almost see eternity.

After catching our breath in the thin atmosphere and consuming a large box of Fig Newtons, we began the long trek back down Baldy (as it was called then). Going down seemed tougher than climbing up, but we reached our tents before dark.

Of course, this wasn't my first trip to Ruidoso Country. Some years earlier, at about age six, I spent part of a summer in the tiny village of Ruidoso with my mother and my sister Mary Lou in a cabin belonging to Warren Barrett. He owned a small grocery store as well as some of the town's first summer rental places. Later, about 1930, I camped out along the river with my uncle, Charles Little, on a bed of soft, deep sawdust from a sawmill owned by a man named W. R. White.

In the thirties my family bought a cabin in Ruidoso's Upper Canyon, in a lovely meadow along the river a quarter mile below the Mescalero Apache Reservation fence. Later, when the Ruidoso River rampaged through during the massive flood of 1941, the place appeared ruined beyond repair. We walked sadly away forever from the twisted jumble of boulders and splintered wood. The property was sold while I was overseas during World War II.

Except for brief, occasional visits, I didn't return to Ruidoso until 1991 when my wife Judy and I bought an A-frame cabin with an unobstructed view of Sierra Blanca. Even today, we are only part-time residents but it's good to be back again in the pines where I can relax on the back deck feeling like a lawn-chair Tarzan watching thunderstorms gathering over that mountain.

Sierra Blanca Peak is part of a mountain chain called the Sacramentos. Fifteen to twenty million years ago they were uplifted seventy-five hundred to ten thousand feet along a still-active fault system. The result was a high country of beauty and serenity.

The west side of the forest drops almost vertically to the prickly deserts of the Tularosa Basin, which moved downward as the mountains soared upward. On the east slope of the Sacramentos, the ridges dip into the plains of the Pecos River Valley.

The Sacramentos have always been the source of water, and thus life, in this arid country. Ancient Indians considered the springs, lakes and peaks to be homes of the gods. To this day the Mescalero Apaches look to Sierra Blanca as a sacred ground. Visitors and Apaches alike share the beauty and solitude.

An outdoor lifestyle brings people to the Sacramentos. Some come to ski, climb mountains, hunt and fish, vacation and take care of businesses. Others are fortunate enough to live on nearby ranches and in small mountain towns.

But whatever the reason, and no matter how often travelers drive from the desert to the mountains and the village of Ruidoso, each journey becomes another gratifying experience. Every odyssey brings an awareness of nature's majesty. People feel a communion of spirit upon approaching the alpine mountains and abandoning the flatlands.

Roads penetrate the mountains from various directions, but one of the most captivating approaches is from U.S. 70, east of Las Cruces, New Mexico. Motorists challenge the rock escarpment of the Sacramentos that loom more than a mile above the desert.

From atop San Agustin Pass, fifteen minutes out of Las Cruces, White Sands Missile Range sprawls out before you on the desert. At this overlook, highway traffic is occasionally halted by MPs while a missile is fired.

Driving through the Range, motorists are occasionally startled by African oryx, massive elk with straight horns of nearly four feet. New Mexico state wildlife officials imported these exotic animals during the 1960s, relocating them on the three-thousand-square-mile missile range, the largest military installation in the United States. The herd now numbers eight hundred, and you may see thirty or forty of these inquisitive beasts standing by the roadside at night. A few roam to within fifteen miles of the El Paso, Texas city limits. Since there are no natural predators, the oryx thrive, sharing the remote Tularosa Basin with several thousand wild mustangs.

Highway 70 continues alongside the snow-white dunes of White Sands National Monument. A few miles beyond, while approaching Alamogordo, travelers often observe flights of surrealistic Stealth fighters taking off from Holloman Air Force Base. The planes slash in and out of sight in the twinkling of an eye.

From Alamogordo, this journey takes you through five distinct habitats—desert, grassland, chaparral, woodland and forest. Nine miles up the road from the little town of Tularosa, the red sandy desert changes abruptly. Here the famous landmark of Round Mountain, a former battlefield, stands with its large white cross outlined against an immense sky. In 1868, a hard-fought

engagement raged between Apaches and Mexican farmers from Tularosa. Both sides claimed victory.

At Round Mountain the land breaks into jagged stone outcroppings and the first stands of cedar and juniper appear. The country turns greener, lush by desert standards. You leave the yucca, cholla, greasewood and mesquite almost as though God had drawn a line to signify a change of scenery. The round-shouldered hills come alive with blue-green, shrub-like trees. Another mile upward and piñons assume authority over the hills. The real beginning of the Sacramentos stretches behind the crests of the rugged walls, shaggy with fir and pine. Tularosa Creek tumbles clear and fast down the desert-mountain canyon from the Mescalero Apache Reservation. Clusters of cottonwoods and willows line its banks. The stream provides water for shady, slumbering Tularosa.

The road between Tularosa and Ruidoso climbs three thousand feet. And since every thousand-foot rise in elevation is the equivalent of traveling roughly two hundred miles northward, this puts you (on paper at least) north of Cheyenne, Wyoming. Moreover, every thousand-foot increase in altitude causes a three-degree drop in temperature.

Three miles farther up the road, Tularosa Creek winds through a wide valley at the little town of Bent, a settlement named for George B. Bent who operated a mine and mill there about 1906. The temperature cools. A New Mexico state highway sign (placed three miles west of its proper location) mentions the crumbling ruins of Blazer's Mill, scene of a classic Old West gunfight during the

Lincoln County War in 1878. Here, Dick Brewer, Billy the Kid and a dozen deputized cowboys attempted to arrest a brave but foolhardy gent named Andrew "Buckshot" Roberts. Roberts and Brewer were killed and two others wounded in the violent but brief shootout. The ruins of Blazer's Mill melt away inside a fenced-in corner of the Mescalero Apache Reservation.

Mescalero is an attractive forest community with its Apache tribal offices, homes, stores, churches, museum, community center and elementary school. Nearby, horses graze in lush mountain meadows that reach from the highway to the foot of the mountains.

At Apache Summit, Highway 70 plummets into Dark Canyon, a stretch of road that before it was paved and widened, was literally quite murky and unforgiving. Fallen trees had to be dragged away so traffic could slither through. Huge pines and firs crowded its edges and blocked out the sun. You could sense the woodspirits that once roamed there.

When today's highway abruptly twists, your windshield fills with a startling view of Sierra Blanca, usually snow-powdered until summer. Minutes later a junction leads into the village of Ruidoso where the altitude varies between sixty-eight hundred to eight thousand feet. The air is cool, crisp, and clean with the faint pleasing aroma of pine needles.

Other approaches to the mountains, of course, have their own fascination—like the ascent from Roswell, New Mexico and the Pecos Valley. From the outskirts of Roswell, Highway 70 slopes gradually up to Ruidoso through a grassy prairie and some of the best ranch land in New Mexico.

Six miles west of Roswell is a small landmark called (what else) Six Mile Hill, the furthest extension of the mountains into the Pecos plains. This is the beginning of the foothills. Driving west, you pass two prominent features; the first is Border Hill, the highest spot on the plains until you reach Picacho. From here Highway 70 drops down into the Hondo Valley where cottonwoods and tall poplars line the banks of the Hondo

River. Dark shapes of cedars and junipers appear on the hillsides, your first indication of mountain forests ahead. Next is the tiny village of Tinnie, with its popular Silver Dollar restaurant and turn-of-the-century atmosphere created by Robert O. Anderson and John Meigs. Tinnie came to life in 1876 as Analla, went through several name changes, and in 1909 was bought by the Raymond family. They named the place Tinnie for their eldest daughter.

Eight miles farther up the road is San Patricio, a picturesque region of high rolling hills that some people refer to as Peter Hurd Country. Renowned artist Peter Hurd lived and painted here in the San Patricio Valley. Many people can remember a half century ago when the famous "Peter Hurd Hills" were practically barren. Now they're studded with piñon, juniper and cedar trees. The reason? Some environmentalists agree that a halt to overgrazing plus fifty years of plentiful rainfall, and forest fire prevention have been kind to these hills. In the twenty miles from San Patricio through Glencoe, to Ruidoso there is a marked change in the look of the land. The air becomes cooler and the ponderosa forest greets you as the highway reaches Ruidoso.

Travelers heading east into the mountains from Carrizozo, the county seat of Lincoln County, don't have far to go. In fact, some people commute to jobs in Ruidoso from this mile-high, semi-desert community thirty miles away.

Carrizozo is several miles east of Valley of Fires State Park, a moonscape of black badlands believed to be the youngest lava flow in the continental United States.

Highway 380 climbs rapidly from Carrizozo into beige velvet foothills backed by forested purple mountains. State Highway 37 and 48 lead into Ruidoso through the communities of Nogal and Alto.

Ruidoso's busy main street, Sudderth Drive, winds six miles through the village to the limits of the Mescalero Reservation in the Upper Canyon. Most businesses along the downtown strip are

Round Mountain, with its white cross, is a familiar sight to motorists heading east into the mountains from the desert on U. S. Highway 70. Nine miles from the community of Tularosa, Round Mountain marks the spot where the country abruptly turns greener. Forested hills in the background are the beginning of the Sacramento Mountains. (Frank Mangan)

These massive oryxes are African elk with straight horns nearly four feet long. Motorists driving through White Sands Missile Range are occasionally startled by the exotic animals which were imported to the range by New Mexico Wildlife officials in the 1960s. The oryx herd now numbers eight hundred, roaming freely on the missile range, the largest military installation in the United States. (Courtesy White Sands Missile Range)

Dark purple clouds threaten momentary rain at the tiny town of Bent near the western edge of the Mescalero Apache Reservation. The church is Our Lady of Guadalupe. (Cliff Trussell)

single-story affairs, a classic study in eclectic architecture. There are adobe art galleries, tin-roofed gift shops, Swiss chalet-styled eateries, A-frame ski shops, knotty pine western wear stores, wood-shingled boutiques and log cabin motels. The storefronts, paralleled by the Rio Ruidoso, say a lot about the community; many of them sport a generous sprinkle of bright colors—turquoise, lavender, and yellow. The road continues up the canyon through several more miles of rustic private and rental cabins.

At a busy intersection, Mechem Drive leaves the main street and heads north toward Ski Apache and the communities of Alto, Capitan, Nogal and Carrizozo. Along the way are more restaurants, motels, ski shops, other small businesses, and a four-story glass and steel office building.

There is little cohesiveness in the appearance of Ruidoso. Take the upside-down sign that proclaims the Wild Snail, a long-out-of-business French restaurant. For decades, the sign has perched atop one of the business district's more prominent two-story buildings. The Wild Snail invigorated Ruidoso's dining scene in the late 1960s and early 1970s. And yes, they did serve

St. Joseph's Mission is a familiar sight from U. S. 70 in the Mescalero Reservation. The church is the life's work of Franciscan friar, Albert W. Braun. Soon after the First World War he gathered a few faithful Indians and priests and began constructing the huge building by hand. Except for the stained glass windows the church was completed by the beginning of World War II. Father Braun served in the famous 200th Coast Artillery and was taken prisoner at the fall of Corregidor. He returned to Mescalero after the war in 1945, finished the construction, and the church stands today as a striking centerpiece in the green hills of Mescalero. (Frank Mangan)

Nearing the Village of Ruidoso, motorists' windshields fill with a startling view of Sierra Blanca, snowcapped much of the year. (Frank Mangan)

OFFICIAL SCENIC HISTORICAL MARKER

SIERRA BLANCA

Sierra Blanca, a complex ancient volcano, rises more than 7,300 feet above Tularosa Basin to peak at 12,003 feet. Vertical geologic movement between ranges and basin is about 2 miles. San Andres Mountains on west side of Tularosa Basin are uplifted on east side and tilted westward. Elevation 4,670 feet.

snails in elegant surroundings. Even during the laid-back sixties, diners needed reservations. Ask directions to the post office and people may say, "Go about a mile and you'll see the upside-down Wild Snail sign on your right. Then..."

Since Ruidoso's main street isn't lined with Old West Victorian bank buildings or courthouses, it's often described as a "new" town. But most residents scoff at that perhaps because an adobe building called the Old Mill, the town's most famous landmark, has been there since Civil War times.

Ruidoso is a locality not yet plundered and photographed into oblivion, nor is it marred by bulldozers, post-war housing and industrial zones. People are friendly and five thousand residents call it home. It's a haven for tourists, yet a real sense of community exists. It has a first rate school system as well as a branch of Eastern New Mexico University.

Many people have purchased second houses and retirement homes. Any number of residents have relinquished lucrative and prestigious employment elsewhere to remain in this enchanted place.

Not the least of what attracts people is the image of The Mountain. Some still call it "Baldy" but the Forest Service calls it Sierra Blanca (White Mountain). This ruggedly handsome peak in the Mescalero Apache Reservation is the highest mountain this far south in the United States. It looks down on Ruidoso like a benevolent god.

A collar of pine forests surrounds the mountain on three sides. To the west, sandy deserts of the Tularosa Basin shimmer in the sun. Since Sierra Blanca is snow-covered much of the year you can identify it easily from Roswell, New Mexico, seventy-five miles away. And on crisp winter days you can see it from El Paso, Texas, the white profile floating like a ghostly cloud on the horizon one hundred and thirty miles distant.

Still, Sierra Blanca is much more than a major landmark looming above southern New Mexico, it's a weather maker. People use it as a barometer to see what the weather's doing. If you're playing golf, it's not unusual to see a snowstorm atop Sierra Blanca. During summer months blue-black clouds build over the peak. The muttering of thunder usually starts by mid-afternoon and rain showers bring freshets cascading down the slopes. The water finds its way into several small mountain streams that run clear, fast and icy—the Rio Bonito (pretty river), Three Rivers, Eagle Creek, Cedar Creek, and the largest and best known of all, the Rio Ruidoso (noisy river). The North Fork of the Ruidoso begins as a cluster of springs on the north side of Sierra Blanca near Ski Apache. As it trickles downward it gathers rivulets from springs fed by melting snow and rain percolating down into the mountain. Several miles downhill, another creek, the Middle Fork, enters and a few miles farther it is joined by the South Fork tumbling down the south slope of Sierra Blanca. At this juncture the Ruidoso is complete, a real river—at least by New Mexico standards.

The boulder-laden stream plunges through forested canyons. Further along it parallels the village of Ruidoso and ripples past Ruidoso Downs, San Patricio and Hondo. Here it is joined by the Rio Bonito. At the confluence, the two mountain streams become the Rio Hondo which flows eastward across the plains to Roswell, emptying into the Pecos River for its lonesome journey to the Gulf of Mexico.

Nature produced a lively bounty here in Ruidoso Country. The abundance of water and the fertility of the soil in the Ruidoso, Bonito and Hondo valleys led to the settlement of Native Americans, then the Spaniards, Mexicans, and ultimately the Americans. This part of southern New Mexico was nirvana for settlers seeking new lives far from a hum-drum existence of plodding behind a plow out on the plains or suffering from years of drought in Texas. The climate was braced with pleasant summers and low humidity, brief, snappish winters and sparkling blue skies. And all of it was surrounded by pine forests patiently following the valleys eastward to the buffalo plains beyond.

The growth of Ruidoso Country is, of course, amazing. I have always been fascinated by the region and felt that it should be documented—all the way back to New Spain. For while the events around Ruidoso and Lincoln County were relatively local, they were influenced by occurences many miles distant. Much of what we see today is the result of circumstances in Mexico four hundred years ago.

The story of Ruidoso Country is one of Hispanic settlers along the Bonito and Ruidoso rivers, of million-acre ranches in the nineteenth century. It is the saga of Billy the Kid, the Lincoln County War, the American takeover of much of Mexico, and today's bustling Village of Ruidoso. These are all strongly connected to the thread of history weaving through the desert, mountains and plains; a chronicle and a dream which led Spaniards north from Mexico City.

2
The Rise and Fall of New Spain

Conquistador Juan de Oñate and an Indian guide on the way to northern New Mexico in 1598 are depicted by southwestern artist José Cisneros. Oñate crossed the Rio Grande at today's El Paso, Texas from central Mexico. He became New Mexico's first governor and was the first convincing evidence that the Spanish had come to stay.

BEFORE THE ARRIVAL of the Spaniards, Apaches roamed the empty Ruidoso Country at will. They didn't farm the land like Pueblo tribes along the upper Rio Grande. Apaches preferred instead their mountain hunting grounds. They also wandered to the plains of what is now eastern New Mexico and the Texas Panhandle, living off the buffalo. During freezing winters the Mescalero Apaches migrated from the high country to the warmth of the Rio Grande valley. Some went south in Texas to the Guadalupe and Davis Mountains, the Big Bend, and into Mexico where they traded buffalo hides to other Indians.

However, approaching events would have monumental effects on the Apaches and what is today's Ruidoso Country. The first Europeans seen by Native Americans in New Mexico were white men with beards and armor. They were Francisco Vásquez de Coronado and his army of conquistadors who passed through in 1540 after crossing Arizona and peering in wonderment over the rim of the mile-deep Grand Canyon.

The young, handsome Coronado presented a fine appearance with his sparkling blue eyes, dark blond beard and mustache. A plumed helmet set off a suit of armor overlaid with gold. The general led a great column of cavalry and infantry, a thousand Indians, a thousand horses and six hundred pack animals. To Indians along the Rio Grande Valley the expedition, led by this man in golden armor, was an awesome, intimidating sight. It would be even today.

Two decades after the Spanish conquest and plunder of Mexico, new stories surfaced with visions of gold and silver and precious stones to be found in the northern frontier of New Spain. These wondrous accounts described fabled golden cities—The Seven Cities of Cíbola, which the Spaniards under Coronado searched for to the point of exhaustion. They found seven Indian pueblos, villages built of mud.

Chagrined but undaunted, Coronado crossed eastward to the Pecos River and on to high, pancake-flat plains across eastern New Mexico and the Texas Panhandle. He named this hostile

23

Gaspar Pérez de Villagrá was a captain in Oñate's expedition to colonize New Mexico. He was a good soldier and a bad poet, but he wrote the first history of New Mexico as a colony of Spain. His book, *Historia de la Nueva Mexico,* was published in 1610, written entirely in verse. (Special Collections, University of Texas at El Paso Library)

GASPAR PÉREZ DE VILLAGRÁ

environment, inhabited by Apaches, the *Llano Estacado* (the Staked Plains). A popular story has it that the Spaniards drove wooden stakes into the ground every mile and a half, marking their trail and providing a way out.

Coronado led his army, some scholars say, to near present-day Wichita, Kansas before conceding that the fabled Seven Cities of Cíbola did not exist. He returned in defeat to the Rio Grande and retraced his trail to Mexico's interior.

Meanwhile, the Apaches thrived in the immense landscape that Coronado had encountered. They considered this country their domain. They didn't own it in the sense that Americans think of the word "ownership," but they did dominate it and they resented and detested the Spaniards. Fortunately, the Spanish continued to explore and move on, that is until the expedition of conquistador Juan de Oñate. He crossed the Rio Grande at El Paso, Texas on May 4, 1598, and he was the first convincing evidence that the Spanish had come to stay.

Oñate's wife was the granddaughter of Cortez and the great-granddaughter of Montezuma, and Oñate dreamed of becoming the first governor of remote New Mexico. He had the credentials for it, notably his wealth from the silver mines of Zacatecas in central Mexico.

Oñate marched north out of Mexico to colonize New Spain's sparsely populated frontier. With him were four hundred men, many with families. The expedition also included seven thousand head of livestock. Oñate's mission was to conquer and colonize, and he was determined not to allow anyone, particularly Apaches, to stand in the way.

After miserable, waterless days under a relentless sun, the expedition struggled to the green banks of the Rio Grande near present San Elizario, Texas where the Spaniards leaped into the river, gorged on water and gave thanks to God. On April 30, 1598, Oñate planted the staff of the red and gold silk banner of Spain firmly in the soil of New Mexico.

He proclaimed: "I take...possession...at this Rio del Norte, without excepting anything...including the mountains, rivers, valleys, meadows, pastures, and water...together with the native Indians...with civil and criminal jurisdiction, power of life and death...."

Oñate's pronouncement claiming the entire territory drained by the Rio Grande for his monarch Philip II led to the formal founding of the Spanish Province of New Mexico. This audacious proclamation made Spain's intentions quite clear, except to the local Indians who of course didn't understand Spanish.

On May 4, trumpets sounded a fanfare and Oñate's colonists and animals forded the river near today's downtown El Paso, Texas. Then the expedition trekked up the Rio Grande and, as governor, Oñate established his capital at San

What later became known as the Texas Longhorn breed was introduced into New Spain by Spanish conquistadors. Oñate brought seven thousand head of livestock with his expedition to colonize New Mexico in 1598. After the American Civil War, hundreds of thousands of longhorns from the mesquite thickets of South Texas were driven up the trails to New Mexico and beyond by John Chisum and other cattle barons. (Drawing by José Cisneros)

Juan, north of present-day Española. By 1610 Santa Fe was established.

The native Indians found themselves trespassers on their own land. And farther south, in Ruidoso Country, the Mescalero Apaches would soon discover the good old days were about to change.

For centuries the Apaches had taken what they wanted and done what they pleased. Now their nomadic life, their food and clothing supplied by buffalo, deer and other game was threatened. In self-defense, they swept south from Ruidoso Country raiding and plundering the villages and towns of the newcomers, initiating a bloody war of reprisal that continued for almost three hundred years. Spain had challenged a formidable foe.

Other expeditions, authorized by the Crown, kept a firm hold on the frontier of New Spain. Running battles continued for generations, the Spaniards attempting to retain a foothold in

territory the Apaches refused to relinquish. In one respect the Indians won a major victory; they came into the possession of horses for the first time. Spanish mustangs, brought to the New World by the first conquistadors, escaped onto the plains and multiplied by the thousands. Unwittingly, the Spaniards had provided Native Americans with the ideal form of transportation. Indians could now ride as well as walk. Some of them, especially the Comanches on the Great Plains, became perhaps the best horsemen in the world.

As the flag of Spain waved briskly over New Mexico, Spaniards took possession more often by decree than by colonization. They were not interested in the back-breaking tilling of soil. Instead they preferred gold and silver, which was easily obtained by capturing and enslaving Indians to labor in the mine shafts.

Fresh expeditions rode northward into New Mexico's wilderness. While the Crown offered

Spanish explorers crossed Ruidoso Country in the 1700s. This spur was found about fifty years ago by Ruidoso resident Emadair Jones' brother, Albert Fall Chase, on the Three Rivers Ranch west of Sierra Blanca Peak. Jones and her brother were grandchildren of A. B. Fall who owned the ranch. Speculation is that the spur had been lost, then buried by the elements for years before being washed to the surface in a flash flood. José Cisneros, authority on Spanish horsemen of the borderlands, has identified this spur as being from the Spanish period of the mid-1700s. (Courtesy Emadair Jones)

generous land grants to colonizers, there were relatively few takers because of their fear of the Indians. In 1680 the Pueblo Indian Revolt in northern New Mexico caused the slaughter of four hundred hated invaders and priests. Survivors escaped down the Rio Grande to the safe haven of El Paso.

Even after a successful reconquest by Diego de Vargas fifteen years later, the skirmishes continued. New Mexico towns and villages were so far apart, and the population so sparse, that the Spaniards didn't have the soldiers, arms or funds to defend their northern provinces. Some officials in Mexico were not even sure of New Mexico's location.

Meanwhile, the Apaches had been gradually driven out of their traditional buffalo hunting grounds by now-powerful horsemen, the Comanches. On the verge of starvation, Apaches stepped up their raids on Spanish settlements. They plundered ranches and pillaged the countryside. And each year settlers came closer to desperation since they received little protection from the government.

New Mexico remained a lonely outpost of a fading empire as the hand of Spain slipped from the Americas. In 1821 Mexico rebelled against the mother country and achieved independence. Mexico was under new management. Following

independence, Mexicans began to look over their shoulders, fearing inroads by the United States. The Santa Fe Trail from Missouri to Santa Fe carried a brisk trade as creaking wagons from Independence, Missouri rolled into Santa Fe.

And as if that intrusion weren't sufficient, hundreds of mountain men, burly fur trappers from the southern Rocky Mountains descended upon Taos in northern New Mexico to participate in an annual rendezvous. They sold thousands of fur pelts and drank staggering amounts of whiskey.

Be that as it may, Apache raids still decimated the northern provinces of Texas, New Mexico, Chihuahua and Sonora. Mexico's ability to defend its outlying possessions was as impractical and as feeble as that of Spain. The Louisiana Purchase brought the United States closer to New Mexico and formed a common border with the Mexican province of Texas. Realizing that it was impossible to retain a territory with so few people, the Mexicans instituted a desperate security plan in Texas. They invited Anglo-Americans to settle Texas in hopes these people would fill the empty lands and establish a presence for official Mexico.

Empresarios like Stephen F. Austin brought groups of colonists to Texas and they received land in return for accepting Mexican citizenship and shifting loyalties. The Americans also vowed to accept

Early Spanish explorers wore medieval helmets like this one as they rode north to colonize New Mexico in the sixteenth century. (Courtesy Skip Clark)

the Catholic faith. Each family received 177 acres for farming, and 4,428 acres if they planned to raise livestock. The aggressive Anglo settlers quickly became ranchers.

The stream of immigration continued until thousands of families had cast their lot with Mexico. They were heavily Scots-Irish from Tennessee, Georgia and Kentucky, the same breed that had moved westward from the English colonies on the Atlantic Coast years before.

But Mexico's dream was turning into a nightmare. The government felt like the Arab whose camel stuck his nose inside the tent flap. Soon the camel was completely inside. Mexican General Manuel Mier y Terán argued that the North Americans were taking over the country. The Anglo population grew to twenty-five thousand as Mexican authorities became more alarmed and befuddled. Consequently, in 1830 Mexico halted all American immigration to Texas. Relations between the Texans and their adopted country deteriorated and the sound of war drums rolled across the Rio Grande from Texas. In 1834 Antonio López de Santa Anna overthrew the Mexican government and declared himself dictator. The following year, Texas revolted against Mexico, a giant step that was to have profound effects on today's State of New Mexico—and Ruidoso Country.

The Texas Revolution began on October 2, 1835. Santa Anna moved swiftly to suppress it, overrunning the Alamo, then ordering three hundred Texan prisoners executed at Goliad two weeks later on March 27, 1836. At the Battle of the Alamo, all of its 187 defenders lost their lives. These were days when "take no prisoners" meant just that. There was no money-back guarantee in getting captured; usually neither side had enough to eat anyway, so what was the point?

General Sam Houston and his Texas army retreated to the coastal prairie at San Jacinto. Then on April 21, 1836, his vengeful Texans surprised the twelve-hundred-man force of Santa Anna, destroying it. With the Mexican army in tatters and its president in captivity, the San Jacinto victory ended the Texas Revolution.

A reluctant Santa Anna signed the Treaty of Velasco, effectively making Texas an independent country. It now had its own army and navy. Texas diplomatic envoys served in England and France until Texas entered the United States in 1845. In December 1846, General Zachary Taylor moved the American army into a still-disputed strip between the Nueces River and the Rio Grande, claiming the Mexicans were now illegally on U. S. soil. Mexican cavalry inflicted sixteen casualties. President Polk proclaimed that American blood had been shed on American soil and Congress promptly declared war.

By 1846, General Stephen Watts Kearney marched into Santa Fe and raised the Stars and Stripes in the plaza. He called for the end of the Mexican period and the beginning of American ownership. When the Mexican War ended with the Treaty of Guadalupe Hidalgo in 1848, Mexico relinquished all claims to Texas as well as to New Mexico, Arizona, California, Utah, Nevada, and parts of Colorado and Wyoming.

But another territorial dispute arose, an internal struggle within the United States. The American victory complicated the rights of Texas. Back in 1836, after winning its independence, Texas claimed a vast piece of western territory, reasoning that a sovereign people were entitled to a large share of the republic they had just defeated. The Texas map of 1836 included more than half of

This Mescalero Apache basket, probably two hundred years old, was used to trade with Mexicans and Americans in the Ruidoso area. (Courtesy Robert Keyes)

New Mexico—the Ruidoso and Hondo valleys, the homelands of the Mescalero Apaches, and all the eastern plains and mountains as well as Albuquerque and Santa Fe. Texas also claimed portions of Oklahoma and Kansas, a large chunk of Colorado, and part of Wyoming.

And the Texans were serious.

The struggle over who owned New Mexico now began between Texas and the United States. The American government refused to recognize Texas claims.

In Texas there were protest meetings, threats of secession, and cries for military intervention in New Mexico. The new state had no intention of forfeiting any of its territory and Texas Governor Peter Bell requested two regiments of mounted troops. U. S. President Millard Fillmore warned that he would send American troops against Texas militiamen if they attempted to occupy New Mexico. Fillmore also sent an additional 750 soldiers to New Mexico to make his position perfectly clear.

With the Compromise of 1850, Congress finally brought an end to the crisis. Texas renounced all claims to territory beyond what eventually became today's map of the state. Texas collected $10 million (strangely enough, a sum roughly equaling the Texas national debt as a republic), and New Mexico became a territory of the United States. In 1850 the town of El Paso voted to abandon New Mexico and join Texas.

The Treaty of Guadalupe Hidalgo called for a boundary survey by American and Mexican commissioners to mark the new border from the Gulf of Mexico to the Pacific Ocean. The survey hit a major snag in a disputed area called the Mesilla strip. At that time the southern border of New Mexico was slightly north of Mesilla, forty-two miles north of El Paso. Most of the region was considered worthless except a small part known as the Mesilla Valley along the Rio Grande.

Secretary of War Jefferson Davis wanted a transcontinental railroad built across the Mesilla Strip to avoid the Rocky Mountain barrier. James Gadsden was appointed minister to Mexico with instructions to purchase enough land to build the railroad. Gadsden implied to President Santa Anna that if a purchase couldn't be worked out, the necessary territory might have to be taken by force.

Santa Anna considered his options. He could see Mexico losing even more of its northern frontier and getting no payment at all. It would seem a better deal to sell part of the country.

In the end, Gadsden secured an area much larger than the original Mesilla Strip. The new territory began three miles north of El Paso, continued westward through what is now southern New Mexico and Arizona, ending at the Colorado River.

The Gadsden Purchase was proposed to cost the United States $15 million and include almost thirty thousand square miles. Amendments to the treaty by Congress reduced the purchase price to $10 million. This came to fifty-two cents an acre. Santa Anna was understandably furious, but he agreed to the transaction. Congress approved the funds and the Mexican minister to Washington called to

In 1830, Mexico had a land mass nearly the same as the United States. At the end of the Mexican War in 1848 the Americans obtained territory (if most of Texas counted) which today comprises all or parts of eight states. (Map by Vicki Trego Hill and Brad Ruminer)

MEXICO
1830

pick up his check. Instead of the total amount, he received a check for $7 million. The remaining $3 million would be paid, said the Americans, when boundary surveys were complete. Writing about the boundary surveys, historian Leon Metz said the blighted regime of Santa Anna blew the $7 million in three months.

Chihuahua's Governor Angel Trías was shocked and he first refused to hand Mesilla over to the Americans. But he could also see no easy way out and finally lowered the Mexican flag and abandoned Mesilla.

An American column of troops appeared as Trías departed. The Americans ran up the Stars and Stripes and welcomed unhappy Mexican residents to the United States while a military band played "Yankee Doodle."

Mexican farmers, many of whose families had lived in New Mexico for two hundred years, became citizens of the United States following the Treaty of Guadalupe Hidalgo. They yearned to be Mexicans, so a few of them had moved south across the international line and established Mesilla. Five years later when the Gadsden Purchase went into effect, these Mexican citizens of Mesilla, Chihuahua, now found themselves citizens of Mesilla, New Mexico. The Gadsden Purchase dashed their hopes of remaining Mexican. In this strange twist of fate they were Yankees once more as additional Mexican territory vanished forever into the consuming maw of the United States.

These cattlemen arrived in Lincoln County in the late 1860s bringing large herds from Texas. Most cowboys lived in unbelievably harsh conditions but were resourceful, fearless, fairly honest and competent gunmen. (R. G. McCubbin Collection)

3
They Rode to Lincoln

THE STAGE WAS SET for a wave of settlers. After the American Civil War, numerous families who had lived through four years of bloody turmoil began to revive the dream which had inspired them originally—settling down farther west in a spot still relatively untouched by civilization. They headed for New Mexico, specifically Lincoln County, with its vast expanse of mountains and plains. Lincoln had been created by the Territorial Legislature in 1869 as the largest county in the United States. It included one fourth of New Mexico, and was larger in area than the states of Connecticut, Massachusetts, Rhode Island, Vermont and Delaware combined. The county and its seat were named for Abraham Lincoln. Lincoln County included the present-day counties of Chaves, Curry, Eddy, Lea, Lincoln, Otero, Roosevelt and a part of De Baca.

Captain Saturnino Baca, who served with distinction in the Union Army, was known by some as the "father of Lincoln County." As a member of the Territorial Legislature in 1869, he sponsored the bill that created the county. To accomplish this, he made a trade-off with Thomas B. Catron from Mesilla, recently elected to the legislature from Doña Ana County. Catron had served with the Confederacy during the Civil War and had never taken the subsequent oath of allegiance to the United States. He feared opposition in being seated. Baca introduced a resolution

for Catron's membership in the legislature, and Catron introduced the Baca Bill creating Lincoln County. Both succeeded unanimously. A committee of prominent citizens backed Baca in forming the new county. They were Lawrence G. Murphy, post trader at Fort Stanton; William Brady, a retired Army major; Florencio Gonzalez, a rancher on the Rio Ruidoso; and Dr. J. H. Blazer who owned Blazer's Mill at Mescalero.

Millions of southeastern New Mexico acres sprawled vacant and wide, free for the taking. Much of the land, drained by mountain canyons, was ideal for small farms in the valleys. Ranches arose on grassy slopes and on plains below the timbered areas. The upper Ruidoso, however, with its deep forests and narrow canyons, attracted only a smattering of new settlers.

Starting about 1849 native Hispanics migrated to what is now Lincoln County. Many found their dream along the banks of the Bonito River and the lower Ruidoso. They arrived from the middle Rio Grande valley and small villages east of the Manzano Mountains near Albuquerque.

The Carbajals, Padillas, Chaveses, Oteros and other families led the way. Herman Otero and his wife Antonia live in Capitan today. "My ancestors were the Padilla family," says Antonia. "They first came to New Mexico in 1706. My mother's family, the Carbajals, were pioneers in the town of Lincoln, coming there from Manzano. They

John Chisum grazed eighty thousand head of cattle on a Lincoln County range that stretched one-hundred-fifty miles from north to south. (R. G. McCubbin Collection)

Mrs. Saturnino Baca at age sixty. Her husband served with distinction as a captain in the Union Army. Saturnino Baca was known by some as "the father of Lincoln County." (R. G. McCubbin Collection)

had a ranch on the Bonito, and my mother went to school in the old schoolhouse that's still there. My great-grandmother knew Billy the Kid in Lincoln and fed him supper any number of times."

Antonia spoke reverently of the Rio Ruidoso. "Most people will tell you it is merely Spanish for 'noisy river,'" she says, "but to me the Ruidoso River has a more subtle connotation. It implies a blissful happy sound."

Herman Otero's great-grandparents were also part of this early migration. "They settled in the little village of Patos," he says, "and claimed a spread where they raised sheep and cattle. The ranch house sat alongside a trail sixty miles northwest of Capitan. Merchants always stopped to trade. Later, when I was a kid we had a sheep and cattle ranch on the north side of the Capitan Mountains. It was a long three miles to school in Encinoso. The ranch was a big spread, no fences at that time and it was protected by six-shooters."

Otero remembered his family selling the ranch during the Depression of the 1930s for $11 an acre. "Those were awful hard times," he said.

A one-street adobe village was originally called Las Placitas, then Rio Bonito and later, Lincoln. It served the needs of nearby settlers. Other Lincoln families, also native New Mexicans, had survived in the Territory for generations. Their narrow strips of land fronted the Ruidoso, Hondo or Bonito rivers. They raised corn, wheat and beans and herded livestock. They weren't greedy about the free land, assuming only what they and their families could comfortably handle. Technically the land was in public domain and the Hispanics held the property by right of possession. Farms passed down from father to son, and the United States recognized their distinctive right to title. In time however, many of the early settlers lost their property to unscrupulous land grabbers. The original owners were frequently unaware of their rights and duties under U.S. laws.

The Coe family, soon to be prominent in Lincoln County and to remain a household word along the Ruidoso, began arriving from Missouri. They

headed southwest for land and opportunity.

Eighteen-year-old Lou Coe joined a wagon train in 1859 at Independence, Missouri, crossed the Santa Fe Trail and was the first Coe to reach New Mexico. He landed in the northeast part of the Territory. The nearby Maxwell Land Grant was the largest single tract of land owned by any one individual in the United States. The Missouri settler supposedly trespassed on the Maxwell property. Threats and litigations followed, so Lou Coe joined a wagon train headed south toward Lincoln. This time he settled at the junction of the Ruidoso and Bonito rivers.

His brothers Frank and Al hauled freight over the Santa Fe trail to New Mexico. Frank looked around Fort Union, couldn't find employment and went to work with a buffalo hide-hunting outfit. One season proved so distasteful that he moved to Lincoln County and began farming. The Ruidoso provided irrigation. By 1874 five Coes were in New Mexico; Lou, Frank, Al, Jasper (called Jap), and their cousin George.

Al claimed land in the heavily-forested wilderness of the Peñasco Valley, south across the mountains from the Ruidoso River. Here he met and married the pretty Molly Mahill, whose parents had settled in the approximate location of today's Mayhill, New Mexico—the name became misspelled sometime later.

Frank Coe married the daughter of another prominent pioneer family, Helena Anne Tully, and they purchased three hundred acres along the Ruidoso River. The property was formerly occupied by Jack Gilliam, a pioneer sheriff of Lincoln County who was slain in a gun battle. The five Horrell brothers from Lampasas, Texas had owned the land as had Dick Brewer.

The first of the Missouri Coes, Lou, was more interested in apple growing than ranching. He headed for Farmington in the northwestern part of the Territory where he planted the first apple trees in the San Juan Valley.

In his autobiography, *Frontier Fighter*, George Coe noted, "We had no mail delivery. It was necessary to go to Fort Stanton, twelve miles distant, to get our letters....As we progressed, we were given a community mail pouch, carried by any responsible individual who happened to be coming our way. A little later we petitioned the United States postal authorities for a post office and rural mail service....This being a Coe community, we sent in the name of Glencoe." The first post office in the area was established in Frank Coe's ranch house and Frank became the postmaster. The Glencoe post office still does a lively business.

The families prospered, grew rapidly, and the Coes were faced with educating their children since no public school laws had yet been enacted in the Territory. Schools had to be privately built and operated. Frank's son, Wilbur, later wrote that "only land and children were plentiful."

The three Coe brothers built a schoolhouse while Frank's wife Helena Anne advertised in St. Louis for a teacher and brought her to the Ruidoso. Each family boarded the teacher for a month and paid her twenty-five dollars. A three-month term was all they could afford. Eventually, the nineteen Coe children and a few others filled the one-room building.

The little schoolhouse built by the Coes later became part of the Bonnell Ranch. Two brothers, Bert and Nelson Bonnell came to Glencoe from the mining town of White Oaks and worked for the Coes. Later they married Frank's daugthers, Agnes and Sydney. Nelson and Agnes Bonnell

The establishment of Fort Stanton in 1855, nine miles north of Lincoln, encouraged permanent white settlement. The frontier post not only offered protection from the Apaches but was a lucrative market for beef raised by Lincoln County ranchers. (R. G. McCubbin Collection)

homesteaded a place of their own about a mile-and-a-half from the Coe place. Bert Bonnell and his wife Sydney bought the former Jasper Coe home.

Years later, the Bonnell Ranch became a popular roadhouse and meeting place. Wilbur Coe noted, "It was situated at the meeting of the Ruidoso River and Eagle Creek at a road junction that connected Tularosa, Lincoln, Fort Stanton and Capitan, at whose two extremes lay Roswell and El Paso." Its facilities were used for community picnics, parties, and livestock conferences; its final success had to wait only for the transition from horse and wagon to the auto—and graded roads.

Meanwhile, the arrival of Anglo settlers brought additional Apache depredations. In southern New Mexico the Mescalero Apaches could not comprehend or accept this newest invasion. They fought fiercely and the Americans reacted in kind. Both sides matched cruelty with cruelty. In *The Mescalero Apaches*, C. L. Sonnichsen explained that "it need not to have been that way….they [the Apaches] held no grudges at the start. They were not unfriendly toward the Spaniards until the Spaniards betrayed them. There is no evidence to show they were unfriendly toward the Americans until the Americans betrayed them in turn. Once the cycle of murder and revenge was started, the situation went from bad to worse….And time and again as the years went on, good men tried to help their Indian friends towards self-respect and independence, only to see them slip backward under the pressure of starvation, coercion, or outrages by white men more savage than they."

The Ruidoso Valley was splendid to look upon and it's easy to understand why the Apaches fought to retain it. As the Indians liberated cattle, horses and sheep from the settlers, Captain Henry Stanton left Fort Fillmore, south of Mesilla in January 1855 to recover livestock. With him were fifty infantrymen and dragoons (the latter rode horses into battle, then fought on foot). Captain Richard Ewell and eighty dragoons from Los Lunas south of Albuquerque joined him on the Ruidoso. The troopers trailed the Apaches to the Peñasco River in the Sacramento Mountains. The soldiers camped near present-day Mayhill.

The Apaches attacked during darkness and a running battle in snow and ice continued into the next day. Stanton with twelve men engaged Apaches in the mouth of a timbered canyon. Three troopers were killed. Captain Stanton died instantly with a bullet in his head. In 1855 Fort Stanton arose in his memory, at a site nine miles north of Lincoln town on the banks of the Bonito River.

The establishment of Fort Stanton encouraged permanent white settlement since the post not only offered protection from Indians but became a source of supply. A vital need of any cavalry post was hay, and the fort was a ready-made customer for farmers cutting the wild grama grass. Fort Stanton was also a lucrative market for beef and farm staples raised by the local settlers.

Although New Mexico Territory was partly isolated from the Civil War devastation, it did not completely escape. Confederate troopers marched up the Rio Grande from Fort Bliss, Texas at El Paso to occupy Mesilla in 1861. Union troops evacuated Fort Stanton, burning some of its stores and buildings as they retreated.

By the fall of 1862 Colonel Kit Carson's First

At left on white horse is Frank Chisum, horse wrangler at the Chisum ranch. Frank had been a Negro slave Chisum bought in Bolivar, Texas when the child was four years old. Chisum showed almost a fatherly interest in the boy. When the Negroes were freed, Frank became his own master and remained with Chisum working for wages.
(Rio Grande Historical Collection. New Mexico State University Library)

New Mexico Cavalry had reoccupied the fort. It remained in Union hands for the duration. After the Civil War, troops of the Ninth U.S. Cavalry Regiment arrived. These were the "Buffalo Soldiers," Black frontier cavalrymen so named by Indians because their curly black hair resembled buffalo hair. Their courage and ferocity in battle inspired respect. Though they were admired and feared by their enemies, probably their toughest opponents were the white civilians they fought to protect and the white cavalry officers they served under.

During the Civil War, Indian raids by Apaches and Navajos stunned New Mexico. General James H. Carleton, a man without weakness or apparent mercy, campaigned to round up or exterminate all warring Indians. With shocking savagery Carleton issued his order: "All Indian men of that [Mescalero] tribe are to be killed whenever and wherever you can find them…." Colonel Kit Carson was ordered to spearhead the attack. Carson was appalled; the thought of slaughtering Indians was repugnant to him as he desired a more humane solution. In 1862, General Carleton established the infamous Bosque Redondo (round grove), a forty-

square-mile Indian reservation north of Fort Sumner in the Pecos Valley. Its story evolved into one of the blackest pages in American history. By the spring of 1863 over four hundred Apaches had been captured and confined at the Bosque Redondo.

Along with U. S. troops, the New Mexico Volunteers in 1864 moved against the Navajos in the northwestern part of the Territory. Starved into submission, the Navajos surrendered in Canyon de Chelly, Arizona, and eight thousand were sent to Bosque Redondo. The Navajos still refer to this trip as the "Long Walk." They traveled over three hundred miles and many died from icy northers whistling off the Pecos plains.

The Reservation was plagued by drought, insects, bone-chilling winters. The country was flat, a treeless prairie suitable for stock raising but not for agriculture. Families traveled miles to dig mesquite roots for firewood. The Army had compounded the Bosque Redondo tragedy by placing historical enemies such as the Apaches and Navajos on the same reservation. The Mescalero Apaches had arrived first and they resented the Army's confiscation of their fields, land the government turned over to the Navajos.

Since nine thousand Indians and four hundred troops had to be fed, small ranchers couldn't furnish sufficient beef. So the Army beckoned toward South Texas where thousands of wild longhorns roamed the mesquite thickets. Texas steers were soon trailing north to New Mexico. Texas cattlemen Oliver Loving and Charles Goodnight drove cattle to Fort Sumner and the Bosque Redondo, arriving in 1866. Another Texan, John C. Chisum, and his bronzed, weather-beaten riders followed later that year with longhorns destined for the Reservation.

Meanwhile, dishonest officials used every known method of graft. Indian clothing was cheap and shoddy; tools were old and rusty. Indians consumed the meat of cattle dead of disease. They were also exposed to the white man's illnesses from which they had scant immunity. Sanitary arrangements were deplorable, and the Pecos River alkali caused more sickness.

Ruidoso's Eve Ball, one of few Anglos privileged to have had in-depth conversations with the Mescaleros, said that Big Mouth, a well-known Mescalero Apache, recalled "seeing the bodies of Navajos who had died of smallpox contracted from the soldiers, float by the camp. Their [the Apaches'] only drinking water was obtained from the river, and they knew that they, too, would contract the dread disease."

When inadequate rations for the Apaches were further reduced in 1865, the Indians had had enough. On the night of the third of November they quietly slipped away. To confuse their captors, some headed for their ancestral home in the Sacramentos, some went south into the Davis Mountains of Texas, others headed west to the Mimbres country of New Mexico. Another group crossed the Pecos and struck out onto the Texas plains. The Mescaleros literally vanished for seven years. The Navajos were sent home in June 1868, and the Bosque Redondo became a desolate monument to stupidity and greed.

Washington persuaded the Mescaleros to "come in" by promising them a reservation in Ruidoso Country near Fort Stanton. In 1873 the government officially made the Mescalero Reservation a reality. The Indians were issued supplies at Fort Stanton, and contracts for feeding and clothing them were to become a cause of the Lincoln County War five years later.

By the late 1860s hungry easterners looked toward the West for beef cattle. John Chisum (not to be confused with Jesse Chisholm of the Texas-Kansas Chisholm Trail) became known as the Cattle King of New Mexico less than ten years after trailing his first herd of longhorns to Fort Sumner. Chisum grazed eighty thousand head of cattle on a Lincoln County range stretching from near Fort Sumner down the Pecos almost to the Texas line, a distance of one-hundred-fifty miles. Rich grama grass stood three feet high in good years, and it extended as public domain from the Rio Grande to Canada without a fence.

Chisum headquartered near the fledgling hamlet of Roswell, the village taking shape around a store and post office. One hundred cowboys worked for Chisum and they all claimed it could be springtime at the south end of the ranch and winter in the north of this treeless wilderness. One year Chisum reportedly sold thirty thousand head to a single buyer in Kansas City, and lost ten thousand head to rustlers.

The Chisum herd was known as the "Jingle Bob" from a distinctive earmark on each cow. Cowboys cut a slit in both ears. One part of the ear stood up and the other half dangled, bobbing up and down. His first brand was the Long Rail, a bar burned down the side of a cow from shoulder to flank. It could be read a mile away. This brand lost popularity with Chisum as hides rose in value, and New Mexico's first cattle baron changed that brand to a large U high on the cow's left shoulder.

Cowboys who worked for Chisum and other big ranchers were a special breed. They had the same traits as the first American colonists who pioneered through the mountains from the Atlantic Coast in search of adventure in the West. For the most part they were unmarried young men who worked hard and blew their wages in saloons and dance halls. They were free-wheeling, independent outdoorsmen whose very existence depended upon each other in the hard and unbelievably harsh conditions of early Lincoln county. Most were resourceful, fearless, fairly honest, and competent gunmen.

Drifters and riffraff flocked into the Territory. Since Lincoln County bordered Texas on two sides (east and south) it opened a New Mexico escape hatch for desperadoes. Almost any unruly white man was a *Tejano*. In 1878 the State of Texas published a 226-page book containing the names and offenses of more than four thousand fugitives.

Lincoln County attracted these Tejanos since its immensity provided endless space for outlaws to lose themselves from Texas posses. Nearly all men went armed. They liked the distances between settlements, the shortage of roads and the lack of law enforcement. Many crossed the Texas line penniless and nipped at longhorn "strays" from the great herds of John Chisum, Heiskell Jones, Robert Casey, John Slaughter and Joseph C. Lea. Since the nearest law was often a hundred miles distant, many successful rustlers formed ranches of their own. They used John Chisum's herds as starter stock.

Rustling occurred on a grand scale. Robert Casey, on his first drive from Texas to New Mexico, traveled with another cattleman and his herd for mutual protection. Even so, he was hit by Indians who stole fifteen hundred head of livestock.

In 1866, before Lincoln became a county, there were three hundred Hispanics and only five Anglos living along the Rio Bonito. In the years immediately following the Civil War, expansion of the cattle industry brought numerous settlers to New Mexico. Darlis Miller in *Women of New Mexico* says that "You could not go ten miles on any road without seeing the covered wagons [of Texans] with from six to sixteen tow-headed children aboard."

Historian Robert Utley, in his *Billy the Kid: A Short and Violent Life*, says "…Lincoln and its environs excelled in habits of violence. The combination of whiskey and guns so prevalent throughout the West seemed particularly volatile in Lincoln County. Adding to the mix were ethnic tensions of Anglos and Hispanics, intensified by a racism that pitted Texans against 'Mexicans,' whites against the 'nigger soldiers' at Fort Stanton, and everyone against the Indians of the Apache Reservation."

Today's Lincoln County Heritage Museum sums it up succinctly in describing the old town of Lincoln: "It wasn't a town like most places. It was a town on the edge. The edge of civilization and the edge of danger….Some were drawn here for the lush river valleys. Others came here because it was a long way from the men who wore a star."

In explaining the motives of the early Texas settlers in Lincoln County, the Museum comments, "In the days when Texas was a nation…constantly under arms against the invading Mexicans making brief forays, farm boys drifted down into the country between the Nueces and the Rio Grande. Many of them had lost their fathers in the Texas Revolution or had actually fought against Santa Anna's troops in 1836. To many Texans, Mexicans meant trouble, and when the *Tejanos* arrived in New Mexico they already had a built-in prejudice…."

When new settlers began building farm houses in the Ruidoso and Hondo valleys they drove wagons upstream and loaded up with newly-sawed lumber from Dowlin's Mill. The mill, which became the hub of the village of Ruidoso, was built by Captain Paul Dowlin, a gray-eyed, ruddy-faced Pennsylvanian. He was a Civil War veteran of the New Mexico Volunteers who later became post trader at Fort Stanton.

Dowlin built the mill perhaps in 1868 at the junction of Carrizo Creek and the Ruidoso River, a point farther up the narrow Ruidoso canyon than any of the settlements. His timber came from the nearby stands of ponderosa pine. The combined waters of both the Carrizo and the Ruidoso powered the twenty-foot-high wheel, and the sawmill supplied lumber within a radius of a hundred miles. Grain raised on the Ruidoso, the Hondo and the Bonito was ground into flour and corn meal. Paul Dowlin was shot and killed in 1877 in

an argument with a former employee named Jerry Dillon. Paul Dowlin's brother Will assumed control of the property and sold it that same year to Frank Lesnett.

Lesnett was a prosperous Lincoln County entrepreneur who often flashed his bankroll after having too much to drink. Nevertheless, he avoided robbery and in 1882 established Ruidoso's first post office in a nearby building. The facility was named, appropriately, Ruidoso, for the noisy little stream that rippled down the canyon. Several years later Lesnett moved the post office to the sawmill.

Emadair Jones, a long-time Ruidoso resident and historian, says the Dowlin Mill site was once a substantial settlement. In addition to a gristmill and sawmill, there was a carpenter shop, corrals, bunk house, smoke house, and a string of cabins. When colorful characters such as Pat Garrett arrived, the Dowlins supplied trout from the willow-lined Carrizo Creek. The willows later washed away in a flood. The original water wheel collapsed, and was rebuilt from redwood taken from tanks at the old Parsons gold mine northwest of Ruidoso.

In his book *Robert Casey and the Ranch on the Rio Hondo*, James Shinkle said life on the frontier in

Drifters and riffraff flocked into the Territory in the 1870s. Since Lincoln County bordered Texas on two sides, it opened an escape hatch for such as these unidentified desperados. Almost any unruly white man was a *Tejano.* They nipped at the great herds of John Chisum and participated on both sides of the Lincoln County War. (Leon C. Metz Collection)

Lincoln County was one of the most dangerous in the world. Nowhere in the country was violence as prevalent and brutal as it was in West Texas and southeastern New Mexico in the early 1870s.

Justice on the cattle trails was quick and final. On two recorded occasions, Chisum cowboys witnessed cold-blooded murders. The culprits were arrested, tried, convicted and executed on the spot. One was hung, the other shot. And the cowboys went on with their work as though nothing had happened.

As hostility festered throughout Lincoln County, the first large scale confrontation arrived with the so-called invasion of the Horrell brothers in 1873. The five brothers, along with families and a few relatives and friends, rounded up their cattle in Lampasas County, Texas and cut out for Lincoln County, one jump ahead of the law. With their followers they numbered about twenty; natural troublemakers who had left a trail of blood and four dead Texas law officers.

They settled on the banks of the Ruidoso on land that would ultimately become the Frank Coe Ranch. They had a strong dislike for Mexicans (Spanish-speaking New Mexicans were universally called Mexicans). The Horrells were ruthless; dead cold mean, the kind who gave *Tejanos* a bad name for generations.

In December 1873, the Horrell men shot and killed Constable Juan Martinez who was attempting to disarm and arrest them for disorderly conduct — a tragic mistake on the constable's part. But three troublemakers were also killed. One of them, his body pierced by nine bullets, was picked up and thrown across the Rio Bonito by the infuriated Hispanics.

The Horrells returned to Lincoln, this time with reinforcements. They barged into a dance and shot four Hispanic participants. Afterward, sixty enraged citizens rode up the Ruidoso to the Horrell headquarters and engaged them in an all-day gun battle. Strangely, neither side received any casualties. Still, the Horrell shooting frays continued until residents appealed to the government—going as high as President Grant—but he refused to dispatch federal troops.

While armed groups of Hispanics and Horrells roamed the county taking pot shots at one another, the honest citizens had had enough. Sheriff "Ham" Mills obtained an arrest warrant for the desperados. Mills had married a New Mexican woman and was considered by the Horrells as part of the Mexican community. With a posse of sixty men, Mills drove off or shot all the Horrell horses—and shortly afterward burned the Horrell ranch house. The Horrells were literally run out of Ruidoso Country. They retreated back to Texas via Roswell. There was joy in the Ruidoso valley.

On their retreat, a Horrell brother-in-law was ambushed at Picacho for no other reason than "he probably deserved killing anyway."

During that same departure the Horrells committed a final outrage fifteen miles west of Roswell. They opened fire on five ox teams and all five drivers died.

All but one of the Horrells experienced violent death after returning to Texas.

Even though the Lincoln populace breathed a sigh of relief peace and quiet did not prevail after the Horrells left. The following year (1875) witnessed the first legal, and most bizarre, execution in Lincoln—one remembered as the "double hanging."

Robert Casey, a respected Texas rancher, purchased a ranch six miles below the junction of the Ruidoso and Bonito rivers. Casey's wife, Ellen, was the first Anglo woman to live permanently on the Rio Hondo. Casey denounced the political corruption and high-handed business practices of L. G. Murphy, Lincoln's largest mercantile owner, and Casey attended a Lincoln convention aimed at cleaning up the county.

Having no idea that he was being set up for assassination, Casey ate lunch at the Wortley Hotel with William Wilson. He even picked up the check. Shortly afterward, Wilson ambushed Casey on the dusty street with two rifle shots. Casey fell, mortally wounded, and Wilson was arrested before he could flee.

In her autobiography *My Girlhood Among Outlaws*, Casey's daughter, Lily Klasner, accused Murphy and his partner James Dolan of paying Wilson $500 to kill Casey. Murphy and Dolan promised Wilson a release if arrested.

Wilson was tried, convicted of murder and sentenced to be hanged by a jury of twelve Hispanics who rendered a verdict in fifteen minutes. Colonel Albert J. Fountain of Mesilla was prosecuting attorney.

On December 10, 1875, Wilson, who had been imprisoned at Fort Stanton, was brought to Lincoln under military guard and prepared for execution. Wilson mounted the gallows, which had been erected the same day, for a public event before a large crowd.

According to Lily Klasner, "Wilson turned to Major Murphy and said bitterly, 'Major, you know you are the cause of this. You promised to save me, but....' Murphy kicked the trigger that sprung the trap door and Wilson's body shot down through it until the rope was taut."

After swinging for nine minutes, Wilson was pronounced dead. Several men cut his body down and placed it in a coffin. As the crowd then went about gossiping, a Mexican woman noticed that the cover was not tightened, and her curiosity made her raise the lid enough to peek in. No sooner had she done so than she screamed, "For God's sake! The dead has come to life!" Wilson was still breathing.

Several of Casey's friends tied another rope around Wilson's neck while he was still in the coffin, and threw the free end over the gallows beam. While some lifted the limp body of Wilson, five men dragged him into the air until he was once more swinging by the neck. They suspended him for twenty minutes until entirely satisfied he was dead, then promptly buried him.

There was also some strong feeling expressed for lynching either Murphy or Dolan—or both. But it went no further than talk. In short, people had learned to view murder with a casual attitude.

As it turned out, these uncontrolled killings were merely a dress rehearsal for future mayhem. Lincoln County residents were about to come face to face with a decade of violence rarely matched on the western frontier.

Frank Coe in 1922. Coe was an unwilling participant in the Lincoln County War, riding and fighting beside Billy the Kid. Frank later became a prosperous apple grower in the Ruidoso Valley. He died in 1931. (R. G. McCubbin Collection)

4

War in Lincoln County

THE RAW FRONTIER TOWN of Lincoln in 1877 consisted of a few adobe homes and stores, all shaded by cottonwood trees, and strung out for nearly a mile on both sides of the dirt street. The new two-story mercantile store and saloon belonging to L. G. Murphy & Co. was the town's only imposing building. On the north side of the street behind the buildings, the Rio Bonito rippled through the canyon. To the south, the town was backed by rolling hills and mountains dotted with piñon and juniper.

If Billy the Kid rode into Lincoln today, things would look much the same—except for the paved main street and a few pickup trucks and old dogs languishing under the cottonwoods.

In the late 1870s this obscure village erupted with an ugly explosion of violence rarely rivaled in the American West—the Lincoln County War. It remains the most widely written about and romanticized series of frontier episodes. As a complicated tale with a cast of characters as mind-numbing as a Russian novel, it is also a very basic story of murder, greed, racial prejudices and politics inflamed by whiskey, power and firearms.

The big troubles in Lincoln, most of which took place in 1878 and 1879, were not merely a series of dry-gulching, raping, pillaging and personal vengeance episodes usually associated with long-standing feuds. The Lincoln County War was nearly a *war* in a real sense. Dozens of professional gunmen sold their skills, the government intervened with the U.S. Cavalry, and every kind of new weapon available in the post-Civil War era, including a mountain howitzer and a Gatling gun served a purpose and had a use.

The first player in the Lincoln County War was Lawrence G. Murphy, mustered out of the Union Army at Fort Stanton as a major after the Civil War. He liked what he saw in New Mexico, and he took over as post trader at the fort. Murphy had a wide streak of larceny and a yearning for power matched only by his capacity for consuming copious amounts of whiskey. In his enviable position on the post, he stocked merchandise and then sold it at inflated prices. Murphy also prospered from government contracts. In 1870 he was suspected of defrauding the government, so the commanding officer ejected Murphy from the military reservation.

Murphy simply moved his operation to nearby Lincoln where, with the small fortune he accumulated at Fort Stanton, he built the impressive adobe two-story mercantile store at the west end of the street. Lumber for the building came from Dowlin's Mill on the upper Ruidoso thirty miles south. His first partner was Emil Fritz, an ex-colonel and former commanding officer at Fort Stanton. Fritz, a native of Germany, became seriously ill and returned to Germany where he died in 1874.

After the death of Fritz, Murphy took his former clerk, James J. Dolan, into business with him. And as Murphy's own health deteriorated from excessive drinking, another partner shored up the firm, John H. Riley, also an ex-soldier. With the financing of Thomas B. Catron, leader of the Santa Fe Ring and the most powerful man in the Territory,

the so-called House of Murphy assumed a monopoly on beer, cattle and merchandise sold to Fort Stanton.

Since L. G. Murphy & Co. had the only large store in town, local farmers and ranchers paid outrageous prices for the necessities of life. While Murphy prospered through underhanded deals, the populace grumbled, yet remained passive. Lincoln's other merchants—Juan Patrón, Isaac Ellis and José Montaño offered little competition.

Partners in the House of Murphy were foreign-born, and some were Union veterans of the California Column who had occupied New Mexico during the Civil War. They mustered out at Fort Stanton and remained in the area. They saw opportunities for profits in land and business.

Major Lawrence G. Murphy was born in County Wexford, Ireland. Colonel Emil Fritz, who had been Murphy's partner was from the town of Eglosheim, near Stuttgart, Germany. James J. Dolan, another Murphy partner was born in County Galway, Ireland. John H. Riley, also a partner in the Murphy enterprises, was another Irishman—from County Tipperary. Major William Brady, an ex-commanding officer of Fort Stanton, was born in County Cavan, Ireland. He became sheriff of Lincoln County.

Brady's biographer, Donald R. Lavish, blamed the potato famine in Ireland for Brady's immigration to America in 1851. It is a fair assumption that the other Irishmen in Lincoln were also victims of this catastrophe which depleted Ireland of much of its population.

These immigrants were not middle-aged businessmen as their tintypes seem to depict but young entrepreneurs in their twenties and thirties, not many years removed from the old country. A stranger entering the Murphy store in Lincoln might have thought he was in Ireland after listening to the Irish dialects.

As Lawrence G. Murphy's drinking problem increased, his health degenerated to the point that he became a business liability. In 1877, the besotted Murphy sold out to his two partners, Dolan and Riley, and the firm became officially J. J. Dolan & Co. Murphy moved to Santa Fe and died

Lincoln County Courthouse, formerly the Murphy-Dolan store, the scene of Billy the Kid's spectacular breakout in 1881. This is the earliest known photo (probably taken about 1887) of the courthouse and it shows Sheriff James Brent (center) and his deputies. (R. G. McCubbin Collection)

the next year. The cause of death is unknown, but a good guess would be cirrhosis of the liver.

Meanwhile, the near monopoly on Lincoln business was about to undergo upheaval. Enter Alexander McSween, an ambitious thirty-three-year-old attorney, who would arrive and become a formidable rival of the Dolan operation. McSween, probably born in Canada, came to Lincoln in 1875 with his red-headed, strong-willed feisty wife, Susan. His bankroll established a law practice. He would be the town's only lawyer and the only attorney for a hundred and fifty miles in any direction.

Another major player whose arrival precipitated the Lincoln County War was London-born John Henry Tunstall, a tweedy speculator-adventurer whose father owned a successful mercantile

company in London. The starchy Tunstall was an elitist. He dressed in the latest London fashion and looked out of place on the American frontier. He had family money to invest and after evaluating business prospects in California and British Columbia, the twenty-three-year old Tunstall decided that New Mexico was the place to make his fortune. Letters to his father bubbled with optimism about this grand Territory and its possibilities for future wealth in the cattle business. Unfortunately he was out of step with the times and the Territory.

McSween and Tunstall opened a mercantile store and bank in Lincoln. Dolan and Riley stood by and watched with considerable apprehension as Tunstall's English money bought lumber to build the store, law office, bank and a home. As

merchandise he ordered from St. Louis rolled down from Las Vegas, New Mexico in heavy wagons, Tunstall purchased a cattle ranch on the Rio Feliz. He had grand ideas of exploitation, but he never fully understood his trigger-happy adversaries.

In August 1877 the Lincoln County Bank and the Tunstall store opened for business. The good times appeared over for J. J. Dolan & Co.

On cue, it seemed, Billy the Kid drifted into Lincoln just as Tunstall and McSween were setting up shop to break the political and economic stranglehold of Dolan and Riley. The Kid was seventeen. Two years earlier in Silver City, New Mexico, he was known as Henry Antrim, jailed for stealing a bundle of clothing from a Chinese laundry. He squeezed his slight frame up the jail

chimney and lit out for Arizona where he stayed two years and became Kid Antrim. Until his death, he also answered to the aliases of William F. Bonney, Billy Bonney and Kid.

On various Arizona ranches he learned the skills of handling cattle and horses. He dealt monte and became extremely adept with a rifle and pistol while becoming a smalltime cattle rustler and horse thief. Looking for better opportunities, he rode over to Camp Grant, Arizona, where on August 17, 1877, he killed his first man. A burly blacksmith named Frank Cahill had the bad judgment of slapping the lightweight Billy around and humiliating him more than once in front of other saloon hangers-on. The two had been playing cards and arguing. Cahill called Billy a pimp, and he lived only a few hours to

James J. Dolan, at left, and Lawrence G. Murphy headed up the Murphy-Dolan store in Lincoln. Together, they had a stranglehold on the economic and political life of Lincoln County. John H. Riley, below, became a junior partner in L. G. Murphy & Co. (R. G. McCubbin Collection)]

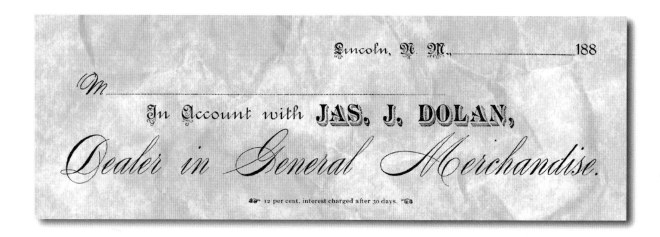

Alexander McSween, at left, Lincoln's only lawyer, challenged the monopoly of L. G. Murphy & Co. Susan McSween, center, came to Lincoln with her lawyer husband. She later became "Cattle Queen of New Mexico." (R. G. McCubbin Collection) At right, the Englishman John Tunstall. His murder triggered the Lincoln County War. (Leon C. Metz Collection)

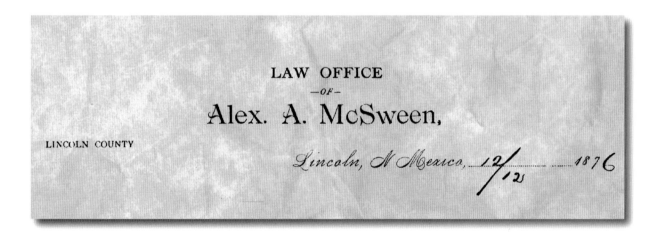

LAW OFFICE
—OF—
Alex. A. McSween,

LINCOLN COUNTY

Lincoln, N Mexico, 12/ _____ 1876
12

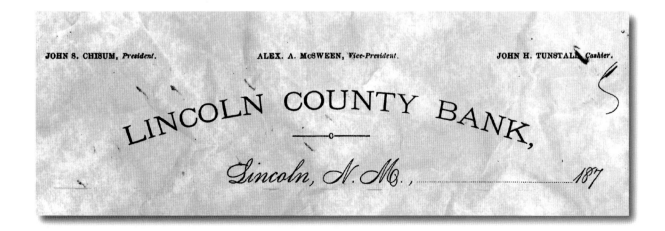

JOHN S. CHISUM, *President.*   ALEX. A. McSWEEN, *Vice-President.*   JOHN H. TUNSTALL *Cashier.*

LINCOLN COUNTY BANK,

Lincoln, N. M., _____ 187

regret it. The two wrestled to the floor, where the Kid rammed his pistol into Cahill's stomach and pulled the trigger. Billy fled immediately, now a wanted killer in Arizona.

The Kid next showed up in eastern New Mexico where he worked for John Tunstall on the Rio Feliz ranch. He dropped the name of Antrim and became William Bonney. People called him Billy the Kid or simply, the Kid—because of his boyish appearance. Still only a teenager at the time and always heavily armed, he quickly became a popular figure at *bailes* (dances) on the upper Ruidoso around the Coe ranches and in Lincoln. His careless gaiety set him apart from others of the border breed. He was very popular with the *señoritas* particularly since he was fluent in Spanish as well as English.

In his biography *Billy the Kid: A Short and Violent Life*, Robert Utley describes him as "slim, muscular, wiry and erect, weighing 135 pounds and standing five feet seven inches tall, he was lithe and vigorous in his movements. Wavy brown hair topped an oval face betraying the down of an incipient mustache and beard. Expressive blue eyes caught everyone's notice. So did two slightly protruding front teeth. They were especially visible when he smiled or laughed, which was nearly always, but people found them pleasing rather than disfiguring."

Almost by accident this cheerful if dangerous youth was about to loom large in the approaching Lincoln County War. He remains to this day an international legend of the American West.

Although the first volley of the Lincoln County War was fired on February 18, 1878, the spark that set it off was a $10,000 insurance policy on the life of Emil Fritz, the partner of Lawrence G. Murphy. The insurance company disputed payment, even two years after Fritz' death. The Fritz heirs, backed by L. G. Murphy, retained Alexander McSween as their attorney.

McSween went to New York, collected the long-overdue $10,000, deducted his fee plus expenses and offered the heirs $3,000. They were understandably furious, and brought suit against McSween for embezzlement. When McSween still refused to pay, the court issued a writ of attachment. Sheriff Brady, beholden for his job to Murphy and Dolan, attempted to attach McSween's property—not only the store jointly owned with Tunstall, but his personal livestock on Tunstall's Rio Feliz ranch. When it became obvious that McSween refused to make additional payments, he was indicted for embezzlement. Warrants were issued for the arrest of both McSween and Tunstall since they were business partners.

Tunstall defended himself against incarceration by hiring gunmen, one of whom was Billy the Kid. The Kid already had a reputation of being fast and deadly with firearms. No one ever doubted his personal courage.

John Chisum and other prominent cattlemen became Tunstall-McSween partisans. Many of the small livestock raisers sided with the Murphy-Dolan faction because the House of Murphy extended credit to them. Besides they didn't like Chisum preempting public grazing lands for his vast herds. So the lines were sharply drawn as the House also rapidly filled its ranks with well-known gunmen. The noted desperado, Jesse Evans, and his gang hired their guns to J. J. Dolan.

Sheriff Brady sent a posse to attach Tunstall's livestock. Meanwhile, Tunstall and four of his cowboys, with foreman Dick Brewer in charge, rounded up nine of the Englishman's fine horses and at dawn on February 18, 1878, rode toward Lincoln via a mountainous shortcut to the Ruidoso. They still hoped for a non-violent settlement. Along with Tunstall and Brewer the party consisted of Robert Widenmann, John Middleton and Billy the Kid. The sheriff's posse pulled up at the Rio Feliz ranch to find only one old cowboy remaining. He explained that Tunstall had left with the horses.

What happened next is controversial. Official testimony accused Billy Morton, a deputy of Brady's (as well as a Dolan hired gun) of selecting eighteen men to overtake Tunstall and confiscate the horses.

At dusk, posse members Morton, Frank Baker, Jesse Evans and Tom Hill spotted Tunstall riding alone with the horses. The Kid and Middleton

William Bonney drifted into Lincoln just in time to take sides in the Lincoln County War. He was still a teenager at the time, but always heavily armed. Because of his boyish appearance, people called him Billy the Kid or simply, the Kid. (Lincoln County Heritage Trust)

brought up the rear a quarter mile behind while Brewer and Widenmann rode into scrub timber near Ruidoso after a flock of wild turkeys.

Middleton screamed a warning to Tunstall as the posse galloped toward him. Tunstall seemed not to realize the danger and was shot down. They even killed his horse.

George Coe wrote many years later that "It is my impression that the boys knew nothing of Tunstall's predicament until they heard shooting. They immediately turned back to see what was happening and discovered a posse of men in the valley. They believed that Tunstall was dead. Knowing there was danger ahead, they hid in the brush until the posse, shouting and swearing, rode away. They rode down to where Tunstall's dead body lay, his face turned to the sky...."

The posse then entered Lincoln and sacked Tunstall's store. Billy the Kid and the others rode on into Lincoln that night. Tunstall's body, lashed to the back of a mule, arrived the next day. Probably feeling remorse because of his flight from the posse, Billy threatened those who had gunned down the Englishman.

George Coe recalled that "Billy was not given to outward demonstration....But after Tunstall's death there was a faraway, lonely look in his eye that I had never seen before. He would walk rapidly back and forth, then suddenly remark, 'George, I never expect to let up until I kill the last man who helped kill Tunstall, or die myself in the act."

The Rev. Taylor Ealy, a stiff-necked Presbyterian missionary and physician arrived just in time to handle the funeral. He had come to Lincoln from Pennsylvania at McSween's request—to shore up civilization in this raw town. Ealy and his family arrived in Lincoln in a buckboard after a five-day bone-jarring ride from the end of the railroad in the February cold. Their initiation was

startling. One of the town's leading citizens had just been murdered and his body brought in the day they arrived, on February 19. The entire community, with the exception of the Murphy-Dolan faction, was aroused. The Rev. Ealy handled the funeral arrangements and performed the last rites. Frank Coe, Dick Brewer, Billy the Kid and George Coe carried the coffin to a grave behind the House.

This was the first of thirty funeral services Rev. Ealy was to conduct during five months in Lincoln. Only one man died a natural death.

"Lincoln's slide into anarchy began before Tunstall was in the ground," wrote John P. Wilson in his *Merchants, Guns and Money*. By the day of the funeral, says Wilson, bands of armed men were roaming the town. Sheriff Brady told Captain Purington at Fort Stanton that a state of lawlessness beyond his control existed in Lincoln. Reports were sent to President Hayes in Washington requesting assistance. According to Wilson, "Captain Purington had seen thirty-five to fifty armed men gathering around McSween's house a day or so after Tunstall's death. Most of them were employed by McSween, some for as much as four dollars a day. They were the beginning of The Regulators, the group of men who fought on McSween's side...."

The Regulators, including Billy the Kid, received their authority as lawmen from Justice of the Peace John B. Wilson and Lincoln's constable, Atanacio Martinez. Dick Brewer was appointed as a special constable with a warrant to apprehend those responsible for Tunstall's murder.

Consequently, both factions considered themselves legitimate arms of the law. Lincoln became an armed camp. On one side the Murphy-Dolan faction attempted to hold together its political grip and financial power. The Regulators (the Kid's side), now headed by McSween since Tunstall's

47

Blazer's Mill, near the western edge of Mescalero was the site of one of the Old West's classic shootouts in April 1878. Here, Buckshot Roberts singlehandedly took on Billy the Kid, Dick Brewer and twelve others. Roberts and Brewer were killed and several, including George Coe, suffered gunshot wounds. In top photo (around the turn of the century) Tularosa Creek furnished power for the mill and ran full at right of the adobe building. (Herb Brunell Collection) Photo below shows the same building in the 1990s. The remaining adobe walls continue to crumble away slowly, but Tularosa Creek still tumbles through the canyon. (Frank Mangan)

DICK BREWER
(Leon C. Metz Collection)

A. N. BLAZER & CO.,
GENERAL MERCHANDISE
AND INDIAN CURIOS

BLAZER'S ROLLER MILLS
HAY, GRAIN, FLOUR AND FEED

Mescalero, N. M., _____ *190* ____

TO A. N. BLAZER, DR.
LICENSED TRADER

murder, was intent on dethroning Murphy-Dolan. As in most of the world's wars and feuds, both groups acted out of a sense of righteousness. Neither group murdered, burned and pillaged because they enjoyed the wickedness of being wrong, but because they fought for justice—as they understood it. Thus outlaws became lawmen and lawmen became outlaws.

On the morning of April 1, Sheriff William Brady and his deputies were walking from the Murphy store to the county courthouse. Six rifles blazed from behind the adobe wall in front of the Tunstall building. Brady and deputy George Hindman were killed as the Kid and other Regulators took vengeance. Whose shots actually dropped the two men is unknown, but Billy the Kid seemed a natural and a warrant was sworn out against him for murder. Be that as it may, the assassins had fled. The street turned quiet except for dogs loudly lapping up the blood.

What happened next—the Battle of Blazer's Mill—was a classic shootout. It took place on April 4, just three days after Sheriff Brady's assassination. Led by Dick Brewer, a group of fourteen Regulators including Frank and George Coe, Charlie Bowdre, John Middleton and Billy the Kid were roaming the countryside around the Mescalero Reservation some forty-five miles southwest of Lincoln. They stopped for lunch at Blazer's Mill, a sawmill, gristmill and road-house on Tularosa Creek. Blazer had provided lumber for Fort Bliss in El Paso as well as

Fort Stanton and other frontier posts.

In what had to be the most unfortunate decision he ever made, a gritty little scrapper named Andrew "Buckshot" Roberts blundered into the Blazer's Mill site while Brewer and his group were eating. Andrew was about five feet five inches tall, and a load of buckshot in his right shoulder prevented him from raising a rifle. He shot from the hip, and he was deadly with a Winchester. He had been with the posse that killed Tunstall in February.

Frank Coe went outside to persuade him to give up. Roberts knew he had only two options: surrender and most likely be killed, or face more than a dozen hardened shooters all alone. Not much of a choice but he chose the latter.

Buckshot told Coe to go to hell and take the rest of his murdering friends with him. Coming around the corner of the building Charlie Bowdre commanded Roberts to throw up his hands. "Not much, Mary Ann," answered Roberts. The tough little ex-soldier began firing from the hip with his Winchester as Bowdre blasted Roberts with a single round to the stomach. Roberts then got off a bullet that removed George Coe's trigger finger and mangled his hand; he also wounded Jack Middleton with a shot to the chest that lodged in a lung.

Now out of ammunition, Roberts stumbled backwards into Blazer's office where he picked up Blazer's single-shot Springfield rifle. Meanwhile, Brewer moved to a pile of logs near the sawmill for a better shot. Lying prone, Roberts

(Left to right) Juan Patrón, McSween supporter and storekeeper. William Brady, sheriff of Lincoln County. Emil Fritz, business partner of L. G. Murphy. (R. G. McCubbin Collection)

took careful aim and from a hundred yards, as Brewer raised up, he hit Brewer square in the middle of his forehead. A difficult shot even with today's modern weapons.

The Kid, now the leader of the Regulator posse, figured they'd had enough. They gathered their gear and rode off. Buckshot Roberts died the next day and he and Brewer were buried side by side behind Blazer's house. A couple of adobe corners are all that remain of Blazer's Mill and it can still be seen today by motorists on U. S. Highway 70 through the Mescalero Reservation.

For the next three months, confrontations and killings continued sporadically, each faction still claiming to be an authorized arm of the law. There were battles at San Patricio, up and down the Hondo, and all the way to the Pecos and John Chisum's ranch headquarters. Governor Samuel B. Axtel appointed George Peppin as the new sheriff. Peppin had been one of Brady's deputies and was an adherent of the Dolan faction.

By this time McSween had decided that a life of skirmishing was not for him. On the night of July 14, 1878, while most of the sheriff's possemen were out scouring the county, McSween swept into Lincoln with about sixty men, including Billy

the Kid. They barricaded themselves inside McSween's house, the Montaño store, the Ellis store and the home of Juan Patrón. The next day Sheriff Peppin's posse rode into town, spread out, and controlled the rest of the village. Meanwhile, the military had been neutralized with the War Department's announcement that the commander at Fort Stanton could not participate in civil disorders.

Sheriff Peppin's forces were now strengthened by cowboys and hired gunmen from Seven Rivers, a reinforcement bringing his group to about forty. Some of his men moved into the Wortley Hotel, just down the street from the McSween house. He scattered others around town, three of whom were posted on the mountainside above the McSween residence.

Why McSween holed up, taking a defensive position instead of attacking the smaller force, no one will ever know. But the strategy cost him his life.

Sporadic shooting occurred up and down the street as the Five Day Battle began. School was dismissed and women and children were kept indoors. For three days the factions remained barricaded, exchanging heavy sniper fire. Charlie Crawford, one of Peppin's men posted on the

James Dolan was a fifteen-year-old drummer boy in the Union Army during the Civil War. (R. G. McCubbin Collection)

mountainside, was killed by an incredible nine-hundred-yard shot (a little more than half a mile) from Fernando Herrera in the Montaño house.

At Fort Stanton, Commander Nathan A. Dudley believed military intervention was necessary since one of the fort's soldiers had allegedly been fired on by a McSween supporter. On the fourth day, Colonel Dudley swooped into Lincoln with a force of forty troopers, a Gatling gun and a mountain howitzer. The pompous Dudley announced he was there only to protect women and children. He took up a position whereby the McSween forces would have a difficult time shooting without hitting the soldiers, a risk that would certainly provoke cannon fire against them.

The McSween force, on the defensive and intimidated by the presence of the military, started evaporating. A number left their positions, crossed the Bonito and disappeared. By now, the end was in sight, with only McSween, his wife Susan, and about fourteen men bottled up in the family house. By some accounts Susan McSween played *The Star Spangled Banner* on Lincoln's only piano, accompanied on a violin by a black servant. She denied this almost to the end of her life.

Sheriff Peppin's men figured if they couldn't force the enemy out with guns, they could burn

them out. On July 19, five days after the initial siege, a deputy torched the twelve-room McSween home, one of the showplaces of the Territory. Flames spread from room to room and Susan McSween courageously went out into the street, pleading with Colonel Dudley to intervene. He rudely rebuffed her, but did give sanctuary to noncombatants in the house.

Billy the Kid devised a plan of escape: wait until dark then make a run for it. Not much of a plan, but under the circumstances, the only one. The Kid and several others dashed from the flaming building. One Regulator was shot down, but the Kid disappeared into the darkness. McSween stepped outside to surrender himself and three others. Gunfire broke out again and when it was over, McSween and the three men lay dead. Yginio Salazar was shot and left for dead and was even kicked by one of the shooters to make sure. He lay motionless all night, contemplating man's immortality while the Dolan men celebrated. But at dawn the wounded man rolled down the hill to the safety of the Bonito River and lived to tell the tale. The others in the flaming house escaped into the darkness.

Thus ended the Five Day Battle as well as the Lincoln County War. Posse members broke into the Tunstall store and looted it. While it would seem that Dolan and Riley had won, the conflict had cost them everything. Their business was bankrupt and the House in which they had been partners had lost its political and economic power. The climax of the Five Day War signaled the end of organized fighting. Many on both sides were dead and all that remained was a final body count.

Tunstall and McSween had died violently within five months of each other. Sheriff Brady was dead. Lawrence G. Murphy died before the war he helped start ever ended. John Chisum died of cancer in 1884.

Two years after her husband's death, Susan McSween married a lawyer named George Barber who organized the Three Rivers Land and Cattle Company. She later divorced Barber but continued to raise cattle, becoming the "cattle queen of New Mexico." She managed her ranch near White Oaks,

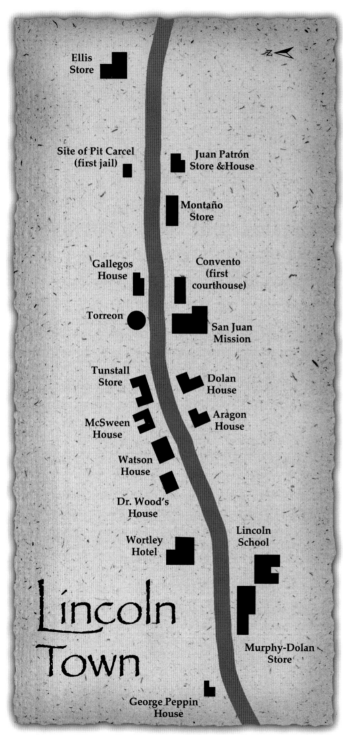

Map of Lincoln showing prominent locations of Lincoln County War. The town seems to be caught in a time warp and looks pretty much the same today as it did in the 1870s. (Map by Vicki Trego Hill and Brad Ruminer)

U. S. commemorative stamps honoring the buffalo soldiers were issued in 1994. After the Civil War, troops of the U. S. Ninth Cavalry Regiment arrived at Fort Stanton. Two black cavalry regiments, the Ninth and Tenth, fought courageously during the Indian Wars in New Mexico.

now a ghost town near Carrizozo. Susan lived until 1931 and is buried in the White Oaks cemetery.

James Dolan, his business in shambles, became a minor politician and rancher and lived another twenty years before dying at his Feliz ranch in 1898 of "stomach trouble." Dolan's partner, John Riley, moved to Las Cruces after the Lincoln County War and entered politics. He eventually went to Colorado and lived until 1916.

Tom Catron, who had financed the House of Murphy, became a U.S. senator. He died in Santa Fe in 1921.

Colonel Dudley, at a court of inquiry in 1879, stood accused of allowing the McSween home to

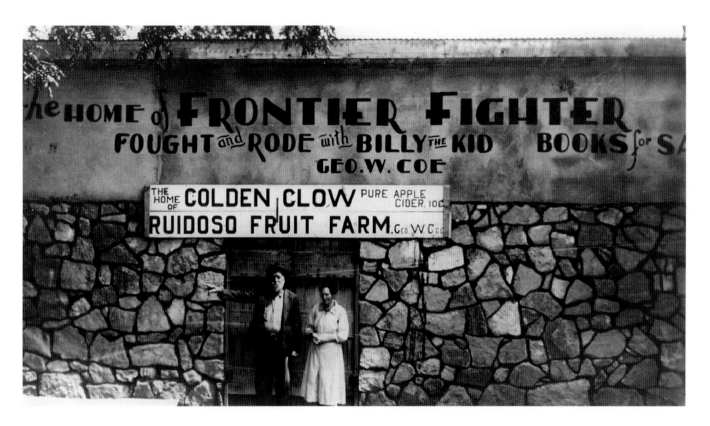

be burned, as well as using bad judgment in the whole affair. He was relieved of command at Fort Stanton.

Tired of the strife and peril that went with the Lincoln County sheriff's job, George Peppin accepted the comparatively dull occupation of post butcher at Fort Stanton. He lived until 1904 and died in Lincoln.

Yginio Salazar, who had played dead during the burning of McSween's house was one of the last survivors of the Lincoln County War. He lived until 1936 and his tombstone includes the inscription "Pal of Billy the Kid."

Reverend Ealy realized how fleeting life was in Lincoln County and began brooding excessively on mortality. He packed up his little family and headed for Zuñi Pueblo where he became a missionary.

Jesse Evans, who sold his fast guns to the House of Murphy, was wounded while plundering a sheep camp. He fled to the Texas Big Bend country only to be captured in 1880 by Texas

Rangers. A judge gave him ten years at the Huntsville Penitentiary, but he escaped in 1882 and vanished into history.

Frank and George Coe, unwilling participants in the Lincoln County War, struck out for northwest New Mexico. They rented several ranches near present-day Aztec and stayed until the situation in Ruidoso Country improved. Later they resettled on the Ruidoso River and became prosperous apple growers. Frank died in 1931. George Coe was the last survivor of the Lincoln County War, spending his golden years signing copies of his autobiography, *Frontier Fighter*, published in 1934. He sat under the shade trees in front of his store, selling apples and telling first-hand stories as the world wheeled madly by on Highway 70. He lived to the age of 85 and died in 1941, three weeks before the Japanese bombed Pearl Harbor.

As for Billy the Kid and his pals, most of them were loose and running, this time not as lawmen but as outlaws.

Billy the Kid was perceived as everything from a short-tempered and dangerous adolescent to the Robin Hood of the Ruidoso. The truth lies somewhere in between, neither hero nor villain. Even his killer, Pat Garrett described him as brave and resourceful.
(Dedrick-Upham tintype from Lincoln County Heritage Trust. Enhanced by Charles Keesey)

5.

Wanted: Billy the Kid

PEACE WAS NOT TO COME QUICKLY to Lincoln. Violence continued even though the two factions had practically shot themselves to death.

Western historian Leon Metz, in *The Shooters*, says Billy the Kid's legend began at the moment of his escape from the burning McSween home. "Until then," says Metz, "he had been simply another gunman, an obscure fugitive on the wanted list. Now he would come into his own with exploits and feats destined to make his name a household word for generations."

Meanwhile, another outlaw with a gang of about fifteen New Mexico and Texas desperados had ridden into the arena creating havoc. This was John Selman, a "border scum" Texan who had joined neither of the county's warring factions. He and his cutthroats raided George Coe's ranch and burned his house to the ground. Selman was not one who advertised his presence, yet he and his gang, The Rustlers (or Wrestlers), were responsible for some of the worst violence in these explosive times.

Strangely perhaps, history has tended to ignore Selman and his raiders in favor of Billy the Kid and more well-known hard cases. But for pure cussedness John Selman had few peers. Selman rustled Tunstall cattle and flexed his muscles on defenseless victims. In *John Selman: Texas Gunfighter*, Metz describes how Selman and his men attacked a party of laborers cutting hay near the home of José Chavez on the Bonito River. The outlaws were stealing the Chavez horses when his two boys objected. The objections were handled in the customary fashion; both lads, along with another youth, Lorenzo Lozano, were killed on the spot. The band headed south to the home of Martín Sánchez where they shot and killed his fourteen-year-old son and wounded a farmhand. The gang then drifted down to the junction of the Bonito and the Ruidoso and on September 17, 1878, two months after the Five Day Battle in Lincoln, they looted and demolished a store owned by Avery Clenny.

Selman 's Wrestlers intimidated the population until the outlaws were forced out of New Mexico in early 1879 and began blazing a path of fear in West Texas before disintegrating. Through the years, Selman maintained a lower-than-ever profile. He moved to El Paso and was elected constable. In his lawman's role he killed the infamous Baz Outlaw in a gun duel, and then, in 1895, in El Paso's Acme Saloon, put an end to the blood-stained career of John Wesley Hardin, probably the West's most notorious gunfighter. Selman himself was shot to death the following year by another El Paso peace officer, U.S. Deputy Marshal George Scarborough.

At the height of the Lincoln County War in mid-1878, President Rutherford B. Hayes had

Tom O'Folliard (above) was a favorite sidekick of Billy the Kid. O'Folliard was slain by Pat Garrett's posse at Fort Sumner in 1880. At right, three *Tejanos* who roamed Lincoln County in the 1870s. Standing in center is John Kinney, one of Dolan's men in the Five-Day Lincoln Battle. Here they indulge in a favorite pasttime, sitting for a studio portrait with weapons on display. (R. G. McCubbin Collection)

been getting bleak reports from Lincoln County—as well as political pressure stemming from the complete breakdown of law and order. Hayes wanted an end to the mayhem in Lincoln County, so he dismissed Territorial Governor Samuel Axtel and replaced him with General Lew Wallace. Since the powder keg in Lincoln had become impossible to defuse, the general issued a proclamation of amnesty to anyone involved in the Lincoln County War as the struggle had come to be known.

Although Governor Wallace was finishing the manuscript of his novel *Ben Hur* in Santa Fe, he traveled to Lincoln to personally interview those in the conflict. "The end result," wrote Francis and Roberta Fugate, in their *Roadside History of New Mexico*, "was to make William H. Antrim, alias William Bonney, alias Billy the Kid into a national celebrity….The governor's amnesty proclamation did not apply to Billy the Kid because he was under previous indictments in the territorial court for the murder of Sheriff Brady and in federal court for the murder of Buckshot Roberts."

The governor promised to protect the young outlaw if he would testify against the Murphy-Dolan-Riley faction. The Kid met with the governor and explained what he knew. However the plan soured when the men whom Billy was to accuse escaped from jail. Billy also testified at an army court of inquiry but it was too late to retreat to the side of law and order. Fearing he would be

Inscription on back of this Lincoln County Sheriff's badge reads, "Pat Garrett from A. J. Fountain." (Robert McNellis Collection)

killed, he ignored the governor's promise, rode out of Lincoln and reverted to his old ways. Governor Wallace responded with a $500 reward for the delivery of Billy to the sheriff of Lincoln County.

The new sheriff of Lincoln County was Pat Garrett, an ex-buffalo hunter who in 1878 arrived in Fort Sumner from the Texas plains at the height of the Lincoln County War. He had a tough and courageous reputation and was a deadly shot with a pistol or rifle. John Chisum persuaded him to move to Roswell and campaign for sheriff.

As we think of the Old West today, Pat Garrett even looked like a lawman. Standing six-foot-five in cowboy boots, his long frock coat and black drooping mustache gave him a commanding appearance.

Garrett won the election in 1880 on a long-overdue law and order platform to clean up the mess in Lincoln County. His first order of business was to incarcerate Billy the Kid. The long-legged Garrett enlisted a large posse and began tracking the Kid and his gang of outlaws. A shootout occurred at an old hospital building in Fort Sumner where Garrett killed Tom O'Folliard, one of the Kid's pals.

Billy and his gang headed north through the vast sea of grass along the Pecos, and holed up in an abandoned rock house at a remote spot east of Fort Sumner. Folks called it Stinking Springs because of its sulphurous odor. Garrett and his twelve-man posse trailed the gang through a December snowstorm and quietly surrounded the little one-room building before dawn. Unaware of the posse outside, Charlie Bowdre, one of the Kid's trusted friends, stepped through the open doorway carrying a feed bag for the horses. Garrett gave a signal and the possemen's guns blasted at the figure, thinking it was the Kid. The rifle bullets drove Bowdre back inside the doorway. The Kid looked at his friend and said, "They've killed you, Charlie, but you can get a

few of the sons of bitches before you die." With that, he put a pistol in Bowdre's hand and shoved him out the door. Bowdre reeled out into the snow with his hands lifted, staggering toward Garrett. "I wish—I wish—I wish," he whispered. Then he collapsed in Garrett's arms and died.

The standoff continued until late afternoon in bitter cold. Garrett and the posse built a fire, brewed some coffee and fried a pan of bacon. (Some historians say it was a tantalizing stew). But whatever, the delectable aroma wafted into the rock building and the hungry outlaws waved a neckerchief out the window. It seemed as good a time as any to surrender, as they were close to freezing anyway. Garrett promised them fair treatment and he accepted their surrender on December 23.

At Stinking Springs, even today, there are reminders of the frontier—in the form of cattle rustling. Rancher C.W. Grissom and his wife Janean, who played host to a group of historians near Taiban in 1991 told this writer that what is left of Stinking Springs is on their place. They keep it closed to the public because a few people drove across their ranch in covered pickups, located a calf miles from the ranchhouse, butchered it, placed it in their truck, and calmly drove it to market.

Meanwhile, despite numerous letters from Billy to Governor Lew Wallace belatedly asking the governor to keep his promise of clemency, none was forthcoming. The Kid's hopes melted away as he was sent to Mesilla, the seat of Doña Ana county, forty miles up the Rio Grande from El Paso to stand trial for the murder of Sheriff William Brady. Albert J. Fountain was counsel for Billy's defense.

Billy the Kid's trial took place in April 1881 in the adobe courtroom on the Mesilla Plaza (where the original building stands today). The trial lasted two days. A jury found the Kid guilty of

Lew Wallace (above) was appointed governor of New Mexico Territory in an effort to clean up Lincoln County. He enjoyed moderate success, but spent much of his time writing his famous novel Ben Hur.(Leon C. Metz Collection) Charles and Manuela Bowdre (left). Bowdre fought alongside Billy the Kid in the Lincoln County War and is the man who killed Buckshot Roberts at Blazer's Mill. He was later slain by Pat Garrett at Stinking Springs in 1880. This picture was taken off Charlie's body by Pat Garrett. (Note the blood stains at left center and top right.) (R. G. McCubbin Collection)

murder in the first degree. On April 13, the court ordered the Kid returned to Lincoln by Sheriff Pat Garrett and on Friday the 13th of May to be hanged by the neck until dead. Billy the Kid was the only person ever sentenced to death for crimes committed during the Lincoln County War.

On April 16, 1881, the Kid, handcuffed and shackled with leg irons, was shoved into a wagon and headed toward Lincoln for his date with the hangman—a date which he had no intention of keeping.

Heavily guarded by seven men, the wagon rolled out of Mesilla, eastward across rocky San Agustin Pass, through the Tularosa Basin skirting the White Sands, then up Tularosa Creek to Blazer's Mill. The party continued through the Mescalero Reservation to Ruidoso and then eventually to Lincoln—a trip of one hundred fifty miles and five days.

The county had recently acquired the Murphy-Dolan store for a courthouse. Taking no chances that the Kid might escape from the old Lincoln jail, Garrett ordered his prisoner confined on the second floor of the courthouse in the northeast corner room next to the sheriff's office. His hands *and* feet were shackled and the Kid was chained to a heavy steel ring anchored to the thick wooden floor, making an escape virtually impossible. He was guarded twenty-four hours a day by deputies Bob Ollinger and James Bell. Ollinger and the Kid despised each other, since they had fought on opposite sides in the Lincoln County War. From what we know, Ollinger was a brute of a man and a bully, with a mustache and long blondish hair. He tormented the Kid with grisly descriptions of the impending hanging. Bell, on the other hand, treated the Kid with a certain amount of respect under the circumstances.

By April 28, time was running out. Pat Garrett was in White Oaks collecting taxes (or as some

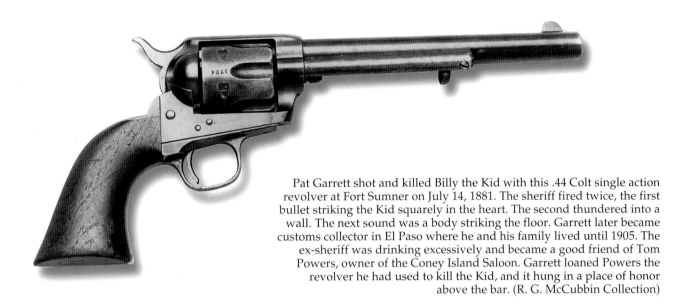

Pat Garrett shot and killed Billy the Kid with this .44 Colt single action revolver at Fort Sumner on July 14, 1881. The sheriff fired twice, the first bullet striking the Kid squarely in the heart. The second thundered into a wall. The next sound was a body striking the floor. Garrett later became customs collector in El Paso where he and his family lived until 1905. The ex-sheriff was drinking excessively and became a good friend of Tom Powers, owner of the Coney Island Saloon. Garrett loaned Powers the revolver he had used to kill the Kid, and it hung in a place of honor above the bar. (R. G. McCubbin Collection)

say, to buy lumber for the gallows). Ollinger, after loading his double barreled shotgun with eighteen buckshot in each barrel, leaned it against the wall in Garrett's office and left the Kid with Bell. Several other prisoners went with him across the street to the Wortley Hotel for lunch.

It was now-or-never-time for the Kid, and Billy made his move. He persuaded Bell to take him to the outhouse behind the building. On returning, the Kid sprinted to the top of the stairwell ahead of Bell. He turned the corner into the hall, out of sight for a moment. Billy had one advantage no one was aware of—his wrists were larger than his hands. He easily slipped one hand out of the cuffs, and as Bell reached the head of the stairs, the Kid swung the steel cuff—which had become a lethal weapon—striking Bell on the head. The two men scuffled in the hall as the Kid grabbed Bell's pistol from his holster. Billy fired, Bell tumbled down the stairs, fell out the door and died at the feet of Godfrey Gauss, the courthouse custodian.

The Kid slipped out of the other handcuff, entered Garrett's office where he picked up Ollinger's double-barreled shotgun, and moved to the east window overlooking the street below. Hearing the shots, Ollinger rushed from the hotel, crossed the street and looked up in disbelief to see the Kid, armed with the deputy's own shotgun, leaning on the window sill and smiling down. Billy said, "Hello Bob."

These were the last words Ollinger ever heard, and the last things he ever saw were two gun barrels pointed at him. The explosion from both barrels sounded like a cannon, shredding

Ollinger's face and upper body with thirty-six pea-size pellets—about a quarter of a pound of lead—killing him instantly.

Billy shouted to Gauss to throw him a pickaxe so he could break the leg irons holding his feet together. Gauss didn't argue. The Kid was able to free only one ankle, and encumbered by trailing chains and shackles, he ordered Gauss to saddle up a pony. (Some of the terrified citizens later said that before coming down the stairwell, Billy smashed Ollinger's shotgun on the porch railing and threw the pieces at the victim's body.) With some difficulty he swung into the saddle, carrying a Winchester, at least two pistols and a belt of ammunition. To the stunned townspeople he expressed regret in killing Bell, then Billy the Kid rode out of Lincoln and into immortality.

After riding west toward Fort Stanton, he turned north to the Capitan Mountains where he had Hispanic friends. José Cordova and Scipio Salazar filed off the leg irons. Billy remained out of sight for the next couple of months, moving around the countryside, crossing the Ruidoso into the Sacramentos, and finally riding back into Fort Sumner, which had survived as a cattle town on the Goodnight-Loving trail after the Army abandoned it in 1868.

When Garrett learned the news of the Kid's escape and the killing of his two deputies, he was more shocked than the townspeople. Yet the tall lawman recovered and began quietly and methodically to pick up the trail.

In early July Garrett received a report from Fort Sumner that the Kid was being sheltered and fed

Estate of Robert Ollinger, Deceased

May 22, 1881

In Probate Court Lincoln County
Estate of Robert Olinger Decd,

Inventory of property found in Estate

One - Wallett, papers, no value
one Shotgun - Whitney's Patent (903)
(Broken) no value,
One Watch, Elgin. (979197) value, one Dollar,
One set clothes. no value,

Pat. F, Garrett
Administrator of Estate of
Robert Olinger Deceased,

Deputy Sheriff Robert Ollinger (left) slain by Billy the Kid in his spectacular escape from the Lincoln County Courthouse in 1881. The Kid pumped a quarter pound of lead into Ollinger from the deputy's own 10-gauge shotgun. Reportedly, the Kid smashed the gun on the porch railing and threw it at Ollinger's body from the second story of the courthouse. The weapon was later wired together and is owned by Jim Earle of College Station, Texas. Pat Garrett's rather pitiful inventory of Ollinger's property includes one wallet, no value; one broken shotgun, no value; one Elgin watch, value one dollar; one set of clothes, no value. (Photos of Ollinger and shotgun courtesy R. G. McCubbin. Inventory of Ollinger's belongings courtesy Lincoln County Records, Carrizozo, New Mexico.)

Lincoln County Sheriff Pat Garrett looms tall in the history of the Southwest, both physically and in legend. His major claim to fame was killing Billy the Kid. Garrett was an ex-buffalo hunter who arrived in Fort Sumner from the Texas plains at the height of the Lincoln County War. He had a tough and courageous reputation and was a deadly shot with a pistol or rifle. John Chisum persuaded him to move to Roswell and campaign for sheriff. Garrett won the election in 1880 on a platform to clean up Lincoln County, and his first order of business was to track down Billy the Kid. As we think of the Old West today, Pat Garrett even looked like a lawman. Standing six-foot-five in cowboy boots, his long frock coat and black drooping mustache gave him a commanding appearance. (Doña Ana County Sheriff's Collection, University of Texas at El Paso Library)

by the local people—mostly the women. It seemed incredible that the Kid would hang around that part of the territory but he felt safer with local friends, rather than heading south for the Rio Grande and Mexico.

Garrett handpicked two outstanding lawmen to back him up, John Poe and Thomas "Kip" McKinney. They rode out of Roswell, heading for Fort Sumner, eighty miles away. John Poe had been town marshal in Fort Griffin, Texas and had brought law to his part of the Texas Panhandle. The other deputy, six-foot-six Tip McKinney, came from a famous Texas family and was the grandson of Collin McKinney, a signer of the

Texas Declaration of Independence in 1836. A relative, Robert McKinney, died defending the Alamo. Kip, who lived in Roswell, had shot and killed a notorious horse thief two months earlier in southern Lincoln County.

So Garrett was well-prepared. He believed his tough two-man posse would be more effective than riding in force to Fort Sumner with a dozen or more.

On July 14, 1881, Garrett and his two deputies rode quietly into Fort Sumner. Around midnight, Garrett called on his old friend Pete Maxwell to determine the Kid's whereabouts. He went to Maxwell's house, posting Poe and McKinney on

Hundreds of books, magazine articles, comic books, TV shows and more than forty motion pictures have featured the Kid's life and the violence of the Lincoln County War. (R. G. McCubbin Collection)

the porch as he slipped into Pete Maxwell's darkened bedroom and sat down on the edge of the bed.

Meanwhile the Kid had been visiting with girlfriends where he relaxed, removed his boots and mentioned he was hungry. A fresh quarter of beef hung from a rafter on Pete Maxwell's porch. Carrying a butcher knife in one hand and armed with a .41 caliber revolver, Billy strolled in his stocking feet across the yard intending to carve off a steak for a midnight snack.

Outside the house, Poe and McKinney noticed a dark figure approaching but assumed it was a friend of Maxwell's. The Kid practically bumped into them on the porch. He covered them with his pistol, moved toward Maxwell's open door asking *"Quien es?"* (Who is it?). He vanished into the dark bedroom and asked, "Pete, who are those men outside?" Suddenly he was aware of another person in the room. He backed across the floor, his pistol leveled. Twice more he hoarsely whispered, *"Quien es? Quien es?"*

The sheriff jerked his gun and fired twice. The first bullet struck the Kid squarely in the heart. The second thundered into a wall. The next sound was a body striking the floor.

Billy the Kid had died with a gun in his hand. Some said disparagingly that Garrett never gave him a fair chance. But like a sensible man, Garrett fired first, thus ending the saga of Billy the Kid—and beginning the legend of Billy the Kid.

He was buried the next day in the Fort Sumner graveyard allegedly between his two outlaw pals Charlie Bowdre and Tom O'Folliard. Today the grave site is covered with a concrete slab and surrounded with a wrought iron fence. After his death the *London Times* ran his obituary and tales of Billy the Kid started to multiply.

Hundreds of books, magazine articles, comic books, TV shows and more than forty motion pictures have featured the Kid's life and the violence of the Lincoln County War. Among the film stars depicting the Kid were Johnny Mack Brown (1930), Roy Rogers (1938), Robert Taylor

(1941), Audie Murphy (1950), Paul Newman (1958), Marlon Brando (1961) and Kris Kristofferson (1973).

Howard Hughes produced the controversial movie "The Outlaw" with Jane Russell and Jack Beutel in 1943. In 1949 Lash Larue played the Kid in an epic called *The Son of Billy the Kid*, and in an even more bizarre movie, Chuck Courtney played the Kid in a 1966 movie *Billy the Kid Versus Dracula*. Billy the Kid is better known than most American presidents and his hold on the public's imagination remains firm. The Billy the Kid Outlaw Gang, Inc. of Taiban, New Mexico counts more than a thousand members in its non-profit organization.

By the turn of the nineteenth century, legends surrounding Billy the Kid were spreading and providing romantic grist for the mill of the pulp writers. Tradition credited the Kid with killing twenty-one men, one for each year of his short twenty-one-year life. However, most experts today agree that Billy the Kid did not kill twenty-one men, but more likely eight or ten. He was involved with other killings but those happened while the kid was with groups firing volleys.

After the deaths of many national figures, conspiracy theories tend to surface. And the slaying of Billy the Kid was no exception. Some said he was not killed in Fort Sumner by Pat Garrett's gun, but escaped, retired from stealing cattle and lived to a ripe and quiet old age.

In the late 1940s an old fellow called Brushy Bill Roberts surfaced in Hico, Texas to tell the world that he was, in fact, Billy the Kid and that Pat Garrett's story was a hoax. Roberts even appeared before Governor Thomas Mabry of New Mexico and requested a pardon. It was not granted. His story inspired *Alias Billy the Kid*, a book by C. L. Sonnichsen.

In the years following his daring escape from the Lincoln County jail, people perceived Billy the Kid as everything from a short-tempered and dangerous adolescent to the Robin Hood of the Ruidoso. The truth lies somewhere in between, neither hero nor villain. Records indicate he didn't use tobacco, didn't care much for alcohol

although he earned his living by gambling in the saloons. He loved to dance, spoke fluent Spanish and squired adoring Hispanic girls. People liked him because of his openness and generosity. Even his killer, Pat Garrett described him as brave and resourceful.

George Coe, in his *Frontier Fighter* said "…Billy was the center of interest everywhere he went, and although heavily armed, he was as gentlemanly as a college-bred youth. He quickly became acquainted with everybody, and with his humorous and pleasing personality grew to be a community favorite. In fact, Billy was so popular there wasn't enough of him to go around. He had a beautiful voice and sang like a bird."

While the Kid never robbed a bank, held up a stagecoach or took part in a high-noon-type gunfighter duel, he was a deadly avenger. Trouble seemed to seek him; and he wasn't known for side-stepping it. The murder of his benefactor and employer John Tunstall affected the Kid. To the Englishman, Billy represented a different and interesting type. To the Kid, the well-bred gentlemanly Tunstall represented a role model, something he had never experienced.

Two posse members who killed Tunstall, Frank Baker and William Morton, were hunted down in March 1878 by a posse that included the Kid. After a running fight the posse captured Baker and Morton. As soon as he surrendered, Morton suspected they were dead men. And he figured right. According to historian Leon Metz, Baker and Morton were "subsequently slain during what some scholars describe as an execution. Many authorities believe Billy not only instigated their deaths, he may have shot both men." Billy had no regrets about these killings.

One killing that the Kid alone can be positively credited with occurred in a Fort Sumner barroom in 1880. The Kid's biographer, Robert Utley, said that a Texas bully named Joe Grant challenged Billy with a twenty-five dollar bet that he would kill a man that day before Billy could. In the ensuing fiasco the Kid said he admired Grant's revolver and asked to see it. Then, unnoticed by Grant, Billy spun the cylinder until the hammer

The Tintype

More than a century after his death, Billy the Kid remains an enigma. The controversy continues regarding who he was and what he did. Still, the most enduring legend of the American West will never be complete without delving into the mass of information and misinformation that frequently surfaces, like the now famous tintype.

"It is the only authenticated picture of Billy the Kid," states Jerry Weddle, one of the renowned authorities on the photo. The picture was very likely taken in Lincoln, the Kid's town, in 1879. He would have been less than twenty years old, and he likely posed for one of the itinerant photographers who

The only surviving tintype of Billy the Kid. Since tintypes are reversed images, this photo, used in thousands of reproductions, led to the myth that the Kid was left handed because it showed a holstered revolver on his left hip. (Lincoln County Heritage Trust)

roamed the dusty New Mexico trails.

In the tintype, the Kid doesn't look much like Pat Garrett's description. Garrett is said to have described his attire as usually of black—a black frock coat, dark pants and a Mexican sombrero. One contemporary stated "he had a face fine and fair." The *Las Vegas* (New Mexico) *Gazette* in 1880 said that he "…had clear blue eyes with a roguish snap about them…all in all quite a handsome looking fellow."

The tintype shows the Kid wearing baggy clothing including a scruffy sweater, open vest, knotted bandana and trousers tucked into cowboy boots, all topped off with a silly looking oddly-shaped slouch hat. Certainly not a heroic image.

Forensic experts say this tintype was from a plate of four pictures. There were no negatives. The photo remaining today came from the upper left hand corner of the plate. No one knows where the other three are—or if they still exist.

Lou Sadler of the University of Chicago made the determination that the commonly seen image before 1986 came from the plate's lower right hand corner. It got copied early. Pat Garrett used an artist's reproduction of it in his 1882 book *An Authentic Life of Billy the Kid*. That same image appeared in newspapers and magazines and was obviously taken from one of the original tintypes. The one Garrett used was probably liberated from the Kid's personal belongings after his death. Other pictures from the same plate have appeared in print, modified and heavily altered.

Today's surviving tintype fell into the hands of Dan Dedrick, a crony of the Kid's who sold stolen cattle. After Billy's death, Dedrick headed for Trinity, California where he struck it rich in the gold fields. He changed his errant ways, started life anew and became a pillar of the community. There's even a little town named for him near Mt. Shasta. Speculation is that he exhibited his tintype of Billy the Kid by nailing it to a post in a northern California saloon. Even though tintypes are fairly indestructible, the picture suffered abuse.

Dedrick died at the age of ninety-two. The original tintype was passed on through his family to Frank P. Upham, a grandnephew of Dan Dedrick. Frank and his wife Elizabeth had seen postcards and reproductions of Billy the Kid for years, but they knew what they had—an original. Believing it should return to New Mexico, they made some inquiries to Bob Hart of the Lincoln County Heritage Trust.

In 1986 the Uphams journeyed to Lincoln and presented it to the museum, where it is now on periodic display. Bob Hart says, "The interesting thing about our image is that we can tell from the moment the varnish was drying it was different from the others. It's not that Billy moved. But there's a blot on the varnish, obviously made by the photographer who blotted the varnish to help it dry fast. And in so doing left an imprint of the cloth he used. This is absent from any other published image of the Kid that we have ever seen." This shot would explain why the crotch of the Kid's trousers seem to extend halfway down to his knees.

Closer examination of the tintype reveals the knuckles of a photographer's assistant holding a light reflector mounted on two poles at the side of the picture.

For years, most viewers assumed the Kid was left-handed because the picture showed a holstered revolver on his left hip. The reason was that in the tintype process the image was reversed in the camera giving the mistaken notion that he was left-handed. Paul Newman even starred in a movie about Billy the Kid called *The Left-Handed Gun*. When the mirror-image is reversed, the Kid holds the muzzle of a Winchester '73 carbine in his left hand and his pistol is properly on the right hip.

Forensic anthropologists working in conjunction with the Heritage Trust compared the original tintype with photos of people purported to be Billy the Kid. The known tintype became the standard, and a computer-mapped comparison is almost as accurate as fingerprint identification. The method is based on skeletal structure, not on cartilage, in nose or ears. Cartilage changes as a person ages. Bone structure is unchanging. Scientists measured points on a face that reflected the underlying skeletal structure. The computer operator manually placed a cursor on the picture to take measurements between fifteen points. The same procedure was done for comparisons. At this point there was either a physical similarity or there was not.

Bob Hart said the experts looked at a dozen photos of Billy the Kid claimants and not one was even close. Brushy Bill was out of the picture, so to speak. But other images continue to surface and are being scrutinized by scientists.

Computer comparisons can also be used by law enforcement agencies to identify people. Says Bob Hart, "I find it ironic that Billy the Kid may eventually end up helping cops catch the bad guys."

When the mirror-like image of the tintype is reversed as it should be, the Kid holds the muzzle of a Winchester '73 carbine in his left hand and his pistol is properly on the right hip. (Lincoln County Heritage Trust)

would next fall on an empty chamber rather than on a loaded round. He returned the pistol to Grant who was drunk and growing more menacing. Billy turned his back and upon hearing Grant's pistol click on an empty chamber, turned and put three bullets in the Texan's face. And as one witness commented, the three holes could be covered with a half dollar. Jake Page, writing in the *Smithsonian*, pondered whether this could be called self-defense or entrapment.

Partly as an effort to get the record straight, some eighty historians, scientists and researchers, including Tunstall's biographer Frederick Nolan of London, gathered in Ruidoso in 1991 to attend a five-day Billy the Kid symposium. Sponsored by the Lincoln County Heritage Trust and Recursos de Santa Fe, Bob Hart, director of the Trust, set up speakers panels and arranged tours and field trips led by Leon Metz and Robert Utley. Large screens displayed a photo analysis project identifying and studying a number of old photographs purporting to be Billy the Kid. After intense evaluation, the Brushy Bill claim went down in flames as did additional images claiming to be the Kid.

A common thread running through the discussion at Ruidoso was the concept of honor and how it shaped masculine behavior in the American West. It was the "Code of the West," based on the right to stand your ground and kill in self-defense. It was the "I'll Die Before I'll Run" syndrome, the title of a book by historian C. L. Sonnichsen. It was Owen Wister's classic challenge in *The Virginian*, "Smile when you call me that." It was Clint Eastwood saying to a criminal about to draw, "Go ahead, make my day!" And it was John Wayne's famous line, "Go ahead and draw. I'll wait for yuh." Since nearly every man carried at least one gun, generally drank too much whiskey and was a long way removed from the law, tempers flared easily and violence usually followed. These men weren't afraid to die—as long as they had something to die for.

The Code of the West originated in Texas during Reconstruction and was contrary to English common law which called for backing away from confrontation, thereby avoiding serious trouble. Even the Bible says turn the other cheek. The Englishman John Tunstall, according to his biographer Frederick Nolan, never really understood that his enemies would kill him. He died believing it was his duty to retreat from violence. Tunstall's partner McSween was adverse to carrying a weapon and was shot to pieces as he walked out of his burning house carrying only a Bible that bloody night in Lincoln.

Today's popular country singer Kenny Rogers reinforces the "back-off" theory of behavior in "Coward of the County." "Promise me son—you won't do the things I done....Walk away from trouble—if you can." Here the son follows daddy's advice until several bullies in a bar sexually harass his sweetheart. Going against the promise to his imprisoned father, the outraged boy proceeds to kick the living hell out of the aggressors. (Code of the West). In "The Gambler" Rogers sings, "You gotta know when to hold 'em, know when to fold 'em, know when to walk away, know when to run." More good advice.

C. L. Sonnichsen wrote that "It was right to shoot a man who insulted you, or for other reasons 'needed killing.' Even if it was against the law? Yes, even if it was against the law. Your friends stood by you if you did it, and protected you from the sheriff as long and as well as they could. It was justifiable also to kill an enemy who had been warned. Once an undesirable neighbor had been notified to leave the country, he stayed around at his own peril. If he absorbed a bullet any time thereafter, he was considered to have committed suicide."

The Ruidoso symposium separated facts from fiction, but the mystique of Billy the Kid and the fascination of the Lincoln County war will probably always be debated. Even eyewitnesses to the drama that played out in Lincoln near the end of the last century have recorded different versions of what they saw and heard. The fact is, however, that the War remains America's primary case study in western violence.

The Odyssey of Billy the Kid's Peacemaker

A centerpiece display at the Heritage Trust Museum in Lincoln is a revolver, almost certainly the one carried by Billy the Kid a few days before he was slain by Pat Garrett on July 14, 1881. The pistol has a long and interesting background. It is a model 1873 Colt .45 caliber Peacemaker, made by Colt's Patent Fire Arm Manufacturing Company.

The Peacemaker became the most famous gun in the West. Colt produced more than 300,000 copies of this classic model with a 7½ inch barrel. It sold for $17 by mail order.

Shooters bought a variety of versions, some modified for fast draw and some engraved and fitted with ivory or pearl handles. The Peacemaker in Lincoln does not have the original pistol grips. These were replaced with ivory. The gun was chrome plated. Speculation is that after Colt shipped it, the 7½-inch barrel was altered to 5½ inches. The sight disappeared in the two inches that were removed. The shorter length was preferred by gunfighters for ease of handling, although it reduced the power and accuracy. Its effective range in the confusion of a gunfight was only twenty yards.

The most recurring story about the Lincoln pistol's history is that it belonged to a Black camp cook named Cherokee Davis who worked on the Chisum Ranch. The story goes that Davis was given the pistol by some of the hands who appreciated his breaking horses for them. Early in July 1881 Davis was serving a meal when Billy the Kid rode into camp. And in July 1881 Billy didn't have long to live. It was not an easy meeting because everyone knew he had been stealing Chisum cows, but old trail law dictated that you fed somebody even if you didn't like him.

So Davis served Billy a meal, while the Kid expressed interest in a Colt .41 Thunderer lying on the chuck wagon tailgate. It was a brand new weapon belonging to Davis. Billy reportedly had a fondness for that type of pistol because it was small and fit his hands. He expressed admiration for the weapon and offered to swap his .45 for the cook's .41. Using extreme good judgment, Davis said that would be fine. And Billy rode off with the cook's new pistol.

Since Billy had shown up between the Fourth of July and the fourteenth (the day he met his fate and his maker), he never returned the pistol.

So Davis was out one revolver, but he now owned Billy the Kid's pistol. Theory has it that the .41 was eventually auctioned off with Billy's belongings after his death. Davis then carried the Peacemaker for most of his life.

Years later and short of cash, Davis settled legal fees with Maury Kemp, a lawyer in El Paso. For payment, Kemp accepted the pistol. Later the pistol turned up with Kemp's friend, Ross Rissler, an El Paso doctor and his daughter, Mrs. Priscilla Steelman. The Steelman's now live in California and are the ones who loaned Billy the Kid's pistol to the Lincoln Trust.

So the gun shuttled from New Mexico to Texas to California and back to New Mexico. The Steelmans felt it didn't belong in California. They wanted it placed with its history.

Twisting steel rails reached Cloudcroft, New Mexico in 1900 and the Old West would never be the same. Here, an excursion train puffs its way onto the S curve trestle before arriving at Cloudcroft. (Aultman Collection, El Paso Public Library)

6

How the Old West Became the New West

GOVERNOR LEW WALLACE'S AMNESTY offer was accepted by most Lincoln County War participants, leaving them free to move on to other—and for some—healthier and more legitimate lifestyles. This, as well as Pat Garrett's six-gun justice and the death of Billy the Kid, produced sighs of relief from a population weary of lawlessness.

Two great transcontinental railroads, the Southern Pacific and the Atcheson Topeka & Santa Fe arrived in New Mexico along with telegraph lines that lessened the isolation of Lincoln County. Most outlaws left the Territory since they couldn't compete on horseback with lawmen riding railroad cars and communicating by telegraph.

Even the scenery changed as the telegraph spun its web of copper wire on tall poles stretching from horizon to horizon. In addition, barbed wire fences intruded into the open range and the land never again looked quite the same. The Old West was becoming the New West.

Lew Wallace had arrived in Santa Fe in a horse-drawn stagecoach and departed three years later in 1881 in a shiny new Pullman car. Wallace experienced the Territory at its rawest and most dangerous and he left at a time of comparative calm. The hostile frontier was gone, and Lincoln County was becoming downright civilized. Wallace resigned as governor of the Territory and President James Garfield promptly appointed him minister to Turkey.

Pat Garrett, a hero for his killing of Billy the Kid, received criticism about the way he gunned down the outlaw. People muttered that the sheriff hadn't followed the accepted code of the West which was based on honor and the right to stand your ground and kill in self-defense.

However, most people today would argue that Garrett acted properly. The Kid was a convicted killer with a price on his head. He had been Garrett's nemesis for months. The sheriff was on a final search-and-destroy mission and had no intention of taking chances with his dangerous and elusive quarry. Accusations and poor pay went with the job but Garrett decided to tell his side of the story to correct the false statements appearing in cheap novels. He teamed up with an imaginative and hard-drinking ghost writer named Ash Upson. In 1882, one year after the Kid's death, he published a book, *An Authentic Life of Billy the Kid*. In the florid prose of the day, the title page read, "The Noted Desperado of the Southwest, Whose deeds of Daring and Blood have Made His Name a Terror in New Mexico, Arizona & Northern Mexico."

Garrett's book wasn't a financial success but it fed a continuing appetite for bloody news of the rawboned West. The book was as careless with the truth as the dime novels which sprouted by the hundreds. The romantic frontier was waning and artists, writers and actors surfaced to capture the dying Wild West as quickly as possible. Artists Frederick Remington and Charles Russell depicted for posterity the last of the great buffalo hunts as well as the Plains Indians and the U.S. Cavalry.

Larry McMurtry, author of *Lonesome Dove*, a modern Pulitzer Prize winner, noted that, "I have recently…attempted to convey how the West became show business almost immediately…. Buffalo Bill had his Wild West Show going, and only a decade later he was racing eight European kings around Earl's Court in a stagecoach at Queen Victoria's Jubilee, while Indians, resting between mock battles, played ping-pong behind the tents."

As the frontier disappeared, an idealistic dreamer named Charles Bishop Eddy pushed Lincoln County into the twentieth century. Eddy was a tireless promoter, a teetotaler with piercing black eyes who would later become a multi-millionaire. He was a native New Yorker, arriving in the Southwest in the early 1880s, and acquiring a sizable cattle ranch in southeastern New Mexico.

The visionary Eddy saw bright prospects for irrigation along the Pecos River. He and former sheriff Pat Garrett—and later with James J. Hagerman—put together irrigation and railroad projects and founded a town named Eddy (now Carlsbad) in 1888 on part of Eddy's ranchland.

Massive problems soon confronted the partners; a disastrous flood on the Pecos River, towering financial reverses, then drought, and personal

differences between the suave Eddy and the stiff and often grumpy Hagerman. Garrett became unhappy with the arrangement as Hagerman didn't consider him an equal, and eventually dismissed him. In 1891 Pat Garrett packed up his family and left New Mexico for Uvalde, Texas to raise horses. Then Eddy and Hagerman reached a parting of the ways. Hagerman dug deep into his own pocket to salvage the venture, but he eventually lost millions in New Mexico. He did, however, acquire the John S. Chisum ranch and spent the remaining years of his life in comparative quiet under the cottonwood trees of the old Chisum place in Roswell.

Eddy reluctantly left the Pecos Valley in 1895. The undaunted promoter headed for El Paso, Texas where railroad tracks had been laid ten miles north of the city to a spot near the infantry post of Fort Bliss. The tracks were owned by the El Paso and White Oaks Railroad which intended to transport coal and gold ore from White Oaks, New Mexico, and coal from the Salado coal fields in Capitan to El Paso.

White Oaks, in western Lincoln County, had experienced a gold rush ten years previously when prospectors and miners swarmed in, turning it into a prosperous mining camp. It was named for white oak trees surrounding two large springs near the settlement. The camp was an off-and-on home for Billy the Kid, and nearly $3 million in gold was taken from its shafts within the first twenty-five years. In the nineties, White Oaks had become a substantial town of twenty-five hundred people with a newspaper, schools, literary societies, dramatic clubs, two hotels, three churches, a bank and countless gambling houses and saloons. The citizens didn't allow White Oaks to linger as a hangout for murderers, cattle and horse thieves and holdover badmen from the Old West. In 1903, White Oaks became the setting for a novel by Emerson Hough entitled *Heart's Desire*.

The El Paso and White Oaks Railroad, with only ten miles of track laid, fell on hard times and was sold to financier Jay Gould who quickly realized that its potential was doubtful. In 1896 with eastern financing, and the help of a brilliant

Charles B. Eddy built the El Paso and Northeastern Railroad, first to Alamogordo and later to Carrizozo and a junction with the Rock Island at Santa Rosa, New Mexico. (R. G. McCubbin Collection)

railroad town within a hundred miles north of El Paso. Fortune smiled on the unflappable Eddy in the form of a large spring-fed pool of cool clear water, owned by rancher Oliver Lee, at the foot of the Sacramento Mountains. Eddy purchased the spring and solved one of his major obstacles.

Historian Dorothy Jensen Neal in *The Cloud-Climbing Railroad*, wrote that three cottonwood trees, each more than five feet in diameter, formed a triangle around the pool. Nailed to one tree was a pine board lettered with the Spanish words, "ojo de Alamo Gordo" (spring of the large cottonwood). Neal says Eddy was elated with the sight and exclaimed, "Alamo Gordo! Alamo Gordo! That will be the name of my town."

A new town of Alamogordo, several miles west of Alamo Spring was surveyed, and the first lots went on sale June 9, 1898. Since the village was touted as a railroad center with good job potentials, the lots sold briskly. A tent village emerged overnight. Even the Alamogordo depot was a tent. Within a week the first locomotive whistle signaled a new sound in this previously quiet land. The train puffed into town from El Paso, eighty-six miles south, on June 15, 1898.

Sprawling Lincoln County still occupied most of the southeastern quarter of New Mexico Territory but with the railroad and the new town of Alamogordo, and people settling on both sides of the Sacramento Mountains, it was time for major reorganization. The Pecos Valley, and the growing village of Roswell, argued the inconveniences in traveling such a long distance to their county seat in Lincoln.

Lincoln County was too big and unwieldy to efficiently handle law and order and business. In 1889 the Territorial Legislature sliced off the Pecos Valley from Lincoln and formed two new counties. The northern one included Roswell and was named Chaves in honor of José Francisco Chaves, a prominent legislator. The southern county became Eddy for Charles B. Eddy.

lawyer named William Ashton Hawkins, Charles Eddy purchased the failed railroad from Gould and laid track northward through the Tularosa Basin toward Orogrande (which was then called Jarilla) and on to Lincoln County. The railroad changed its name to the El Paso and Northeastern.

Big time problems arose immediately after construction began. There's a lot of desert in the Tularosa Basin, and Eddy seemed to have ignored the lack of water and timber in this tough country. Ties had to be shipped from East Texas, and water for steam locomotives was hauled fifty miles from El Paso. Water drilled along the right-of-way contained so much alkali and gypsum that the mineral corroded the steam engine boilers.

Track laying continued. Steam locomotives needed an engine shop about every ninety to a hundred miles and required water about every twenty miles. Eddy's plan included building a

Meanwhile, before the El Paso and Northeastern could continue northward, lumber had to be found for crossties and bridges. Fortunately for

Excursion trains (above) brought dressy desert dwellers to Cloudcroft in bright yellow, open air cars on the Alamogordo and Sacramento Mountain Railroad. Canvas side curtains were rolled down when mountain thunderstorms hit unexpectedly. (Aultman Collection, El Paso Public Library) Below, passengers await the next train back to Alamogordo. (McGaw Collection, El Paso Public Library)

Horse drawn station wagons stand by to pick up new arrivals on the "cloud climbing railroad." Elevation at the depot: 8,650 feet. (McGaw Collection, El Paso Public Library)

Eddy, thousands of acres of prime timber existed within a few miles of Alamogordo, but it was inaccessible atop the town's nine-thousand-foot backdrop in the Sacramento Mountains.

Since the mountains walled in the east side of the Tularosa Basin, Eddy decided to build a branch line into the high country and tap its resources. He would construct a standard-gauge railroad into the mountains so that logs in the great timber belt could be cut and hauled to a sawmill at Alamogordo. Eddy then organized the Alamogordo & Sacramento Mountain Railroad.

Surveyors charted a winding and twisting route into the mountains from the leafy village of La Luz, ten miles north of Alamogordo. Men with mules and dynamite followed the trail, blasting a path for track layers. Scores of heavy timber trestles and bridges had to be built. By conquering the mountains' steep grades, yawning canyons and sharp curves, the Alamogordo and

Sacramento Mountain Railroad became one of the most spectacular and legendary railroads in the West. By November 1898 the line was completed from Alamogordo to within a mile-and-a-half of what was soon to become the village of Cloudcroft, three miles south of the Mescalero Reservation.

To make the ascent from Alamogordo the railroad climbed over four thousand feet in little more than twenty miles. The steepness of the mountain, combined with an imposing canyon at a spot called Toboggan, became the most formidable obstacle. The problem was solved by building a switchback which, according to Dorothy Jensen Neal, was "one of the most famous feats of engineering on the railroad." The twisting steel rails reached Cloudcroft on January 25, 1900.

Charles B. Eddy and his Sacramento Mountain Railroad began bringing visitors to the new village of Cloudcroft. In addition to the logging of the Sacramentos, he accomplished the first step toward a summer migration from El Paso and Alamogordo to the cool pines, now only hours, instead of days away.

Cloudcroft was the first mountain retreat in Ruidoso Country to attract city dwellers, since a trip to Ruidoso still awaited the automobile and a road. The *El Paso Times* said in 1898 that "El Paso businessmen will have what they never had yet, a place [Cloudcroft] where they can go up Saturday afternoons in summer, spend Sunday amid cool refreshing picturesque surroundings, and go back to the city Monday mornings."

Before the rails were completed to Cloudcroft, with the aid of the switchback, excursion trains carried passengers from Alamogordo into the mountains. Beth Gilbert in *Alamogordo: The Territorial Years* writes about the activity and side benefits that were to turn Cloudcroft and later, Ruidoso, into summer resorts. "While timber was going out of the mountains, visitors were coming into the mountains on excursion trains from El Paso. At Alamogordo excursionists changed trains from the El Paso & Northeastern to the Alamogordo and Sacramento Mountain Railroad, which took them to the depot at Toboggan, a distance of twenty miles. The round trip from Alamogordo to Toboggan was $1.50, which offered many times the amount of genuine pleasure. From Toboggan, the passengers were taken a mile and a half by stage to Cloudcroft where the EP & NE officials were building a summer resort. One of the first excursions was on May 25, 1899."

Passengers rode in bright yellow open-sided cars protected from occasional rain by canvas curtains. The switchback at Toboggan allowed trains to go all the way to Cloudcroft, the switching maneuver providing a heart-stopping experience. It was a special thrill for youngsters, whose joyful shouts soon mixed with trepidation, as the open cars moved backward over swaying and creaking timber trestles.

Passengers were decked out in their summer finery which would seem strangely out of place today. Ladies wore pinched-at-the-waist skirts long enough to drag the ground. The men sported dark suits with ties, starched collars and straw boaters or derby hats.

The Sacramento Mountain Railroad furnished the comforts of genteel living in the new century by building a handsome structure called the Pavilion at the nine-thousand foot mountain resort. It was close to the depot where visitors could eat, sleep and admire the scenery while summer cottages, costing about $200, were being built for them. Short-time visitors rented tents for fifty cents a night.

In 1901 Eddy's company built the Cloudcroft Lodge. It was over two hundred feet long, two stories high, and covered with slab logs. A disastrous fire destroyed the Lodge in 1909. It was rebuilt in 1911 of fireproof masonry but its rustic, log cabin look was gone forever.

On its winding pull up the mountains, the little cloud-climbing railroad passed the fruit growing villages of High Rolls and Mountain Park, five miles from Cloudcroft. Residents of Mountain Park claim famous native son, cartoonist-author Bill Mauldin. In his book *A Sort of a Saga*, Mauldin describes the farm of his boyhood. "The country is really very handsome," says Mauldin. "There are two worlds very near each other, and Mountain Park is on the dividing line between them. In fact, our pasture, consisting of two skinny hills running parallel to the rest of the place, was covered on the lower end by scrub oak and piñon; the upper end was studded with tall pines. Even the rattlesnake line ends at Mountain Park. About a half mile below is the head of Box Canyon, a spectacular gorge which winds down to the plains. Rattlers are fairly common right up to our end of it, but not one has ever been found on our place."

Mauldin, a Pulitzer Prize winner and creator of the World War II cartoon heroes, Willie and Joe, took some of his first drawing lessons from a Ruidoso character named Larry Smith. Larry drew and colored thousands of cartoons and signs advertising Ruidoso businesses during the thirties. He literally painted for his supper and always signed his work "Hillbilly Larry."

The Cloudcroft railroad lasted almost a half century. Its demise began when the automobile

Visitors to Cloudcroft decked out in their summer finery (circa 1905). The Cloudcroft Lodge
was a rustic, deluxe hotel, over two hundred feet long and covered with slab logs.
(Rio Grande Historical Collections, New Mexico State University Library)

Muddy Main Street in Cloudcroft, circa 1905. (Aultman Collection, El Paso Public Library)

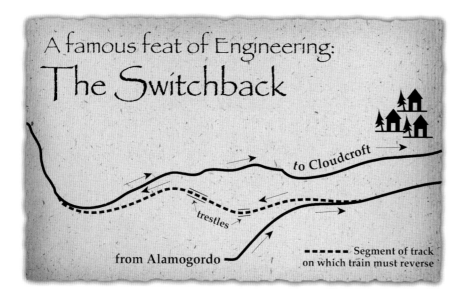

A famous feat of Engineering: The Switchback

to Cloudcroft

trestles

from Alamogordo

- - - - - Segment of track
on which train must reverse

Switchbacks solved the awesome engineering problem of climbing through the mountains. From Alamogordo, the trains traveled northeast to the top end of the track. A switch let it travel *backward* over trestles to the northwest top end of the track. Another switch allowed the train to travel forward on to Cloudcroft.

became the more accessible mode of transportation. But the narrow dirt road built from Alamogordo to the summit of the Sacramentos could be frightening. There were, of course, no guard rails to protect an unwary motorist from sliding hundreds of feet into the bottom of steep canyons. For some, this road evoked stark terror since two cars going in opposite directions would meet head on. So it was often necessary for one to back up to the nearest wide spot and wait for the other to pass.

El Paso author Martha Peterson remembered one unforgettable visit to Cloudcroft on the newly opened road. It was to be a one-day outing for the family. "Nearing Cloudcroft," she says, "on the scarey, winding rollercoaster road, we experienced a downpour. The rain came down, the road was so slick we were sliding all over, and here comes a car right at us. My husband John yelled, 'Everybody out!' I guess he figured that if anybody had to go over the cliff, it would be him and not us. Well, anyway, the cars passed each other in the slippery mud, and wet and soggy we all piled back in the car. I can't remember the rest of the day, but I sure remember that adventure."

In the meantime, regular excursion trains continued until the 1930s. After February 13, 1938, the railroad abandoned all passenger service and hauled only freight. From Cloudcroft to Alamogordo, railroad logging finally gave way to trucks during World War II, and the last scheduled train came down from the mountains in 1947.

In addition to timber for railroad building, Eddy discovered a ready market in the copper mines of Arizona, particularly at Bisbee and Morenci. In 1903, crews completed a spur line for log trains to Russia Canyon where they built the logging camp

of Russia, the end of the line. A number of other switchbacks got trains up and down through the rugged country. At Russia, the company constructed about a hundred wooden cabins, a commissary, railroad shop, post office, school house and two cook shacks and mess halls for the loggers and railroad employees. Later that same year the Arizona mines began buying timber in million board-feet lots, and Charles Eddy was becoming wealthy.

Today, Russia Canyon is a tiny dot on a few maps of New Mexico, five miles south of Cloudcroft.

Charles Eddy cut all the timber he needed for railroad construction, and since he had water from Alamogordo, he lost no time in pushing north with the El Paso and Northeastern Railroad. Originally aimed at White Oaks, the line bypassed the town, much to the resentment of White Oaks citizens who had waited twenty years.

There was no end of speculation about Eddy's change of route. Critics claimed White Oaks property owners demanded too much money for the railroad right-of-way, so Eddy swung the proposed route to the west. The real reason was that Eddy received dismal engineering reports on the mines at White Oaks and he by-passed the village for a new town twelve miles southwest, to be known as Carrizozo. It would be a railroad division terminal with repair shops and a roundhouse.

Carrizozo townsite lots began selling in 1907. Two years later the town boomed, becoming larger than old Lincoln town. In a 1909 election, voters cast their ballots in favor of moving the county seat from Lincoln to Carrizozo. Lincoln advocates appealed, but the decision was affirmed

Millions of board feet of timber were cut in the Sacramentos near Cloudcroft for markets in Arizona and throughout the Southwest. Railroad logging finally gave way to trucks during World War II, and the last scheduled train came down from the mountains in 1947. (McGaw Collection, El Paso Public Library) Below, troopers from the 82nd Field Artillery at Fort Bliss, Texas on maneuvers near Cloudcroft in the 1930s. (McGaw Collection, El Paso Public Library)

This disastrous fire destroyed the Cloudcroft Lodge on June 13, 1909. It was rebuilt in 1911 of fireproof masonry but its rustic log cabin look was gone forever. Photograph was taken by Jim Alexander. (McGaw Collection, El Paso Public Library)

by the territorial Supreme Court in 1910. Carrizozo was now officially the county seat. Lincoln county records were grudgingly hauled to Carrizozo, leaving Lincoln with not much to do but remember its history.

The town of White Oaks was also marooned. It remains today a ghost town crumbling into the piñon-dotted hills.

The railroad built a twenty-one-mile branch line eastward through the mountains to the Salado coal fields where Eddy bought property on S. T. Gray's ranch. He platted a townsite and named it Capitan. Production began immediately, but the original glowing reports of huge coal beds were overrated. The project would never be a commercial success. Eddy shut down the coal fields, and crews pulled the machinery out of the mines. Traffic over the Carrizozo to Capitan line dried up and the rusting tracks were removed.

With new vitality and additional capital pumping in from the East, Eddy extended his mainline north from Carrizozo to a junction with the Chicago, Rock Island and Pacific Railroad at Santa Rosa, New Mexico. The line was completed

on February 1, 1902. This link-up with the Rock Island give the Territory its third major railroad. Eddy then sold his railroad to the Phelps-Dodge Corporation which used the rails for transporting its Arizona copper. Phelps-Dodge bought the line in 1905 and renamed it the El Paso & Southwestern. In 1924 it was acquired by the Southern Pacific.

As for Eddy, he continued promoting other significant enterprises until his death in New York City in 1931.

After the turn of the century, New Mexico began a strong pitch for statehood. For fifty years the subject had created political controversy in the Territory. Those against statehood were generally the large landowners, railroaders, lumbermen and miners who used the public domain with little restraint. They figured statehood meant raising their taxes to pay for local government, a process presently being financed in Washington.

The opposing side, arguing in favor of statehood, believed it would be beneficial to everybody and would eventually raise land values.

Except for pickup trucks and telephone poles, Cloudcroft's main street still retains a frontier look. (Frank Mangan)

Statehood was nearly achieved by a plan to link Arizona and New Mexico as a single state—to be called Arizona. New Mexico was so anxious for statehood, it passed the measure even though it meant losing its historic name in the process. Arizona fortunately rejected the proposal. There was even a movement to change New Mexico's name to Ácoma (after the Indian pueblo west of Albuquerque) in an effort to rid itself of an identity problem with Mexico. Others suggested calling the state Lincoln; and a few proposed Montezuma. Neither received much popular backing.

Southern New Mexico rancher and politician A. B. Fall helped persuade President William Howard Taft to support New Mexico statehood. Taft signed an enabling bill in 1910 subject to an approved constitution.

Delegates to a constitutional convention met in Santa Fe that year. Most were Republicans, including the Hispanic delegates led by Solomon Luna, the largest sheep rancher in the Territory, a man for whom Luna County was named. For two years Democrats and Republicans bitterly opposed each other on statehood provisions of the document.

But in the end the Republicans were victorious in spite of a party power struggle between Luna and Octaviano Larrazolo for control of the Hispanic vote. According to Jerry L. Williams and Paul E. McAllister in *New Mexico in Maps*, the power struggle for control of the Hispanic vote ended when Luna drowned in a vat of sheep dip. On January 6, 1912, New Mexico entered the Union as the forty-seventh state. Arizona became the forty-eighth state on February 14, 1912.

In the years preceding the turn of the century, frontier violence in southern New Mexico had all but disappeared. Well, almost.

The area was torn between two powerful leaders, Colonel Albert Jennings Fountain and Albert Bacon Fall. In addition to Fountain and Fall, a relative newcomer to the scene was Oliver Milton Lee, who would become a legend of the dying Old West. And added to this power mix was the former sheriff of Lincoln County, Patrick Floyd Garrett.

One of the final chapters of territorial violence was about to be written.

The Great Gold Bonanza

The boom town of White Oaks was marooned when the El Paso and Northeastern Railroad by-passed it at the turn of the century and built the new town of Carrizozo as a railroad terminal. White Oaks remains today a ghost town crumbling into the piñon-dotted hills. (Frank Mangan)

Tall tales and myths are legion about the gold mining town of White Oaks and how it came into being. Almost certain, though, is that the first rich gold strike was made in 1879 near a place called White Oaks Springs, fifty miles northwest of Ruidoso. By some accounts, a character named George Wilson had escaped from a Texas jail. He stopped off at a mining camp at White Oaks Springs and was invited to share supper with three prospectors, Charles Baxter, John E. Wilson and Jack Winters.

The next day, George Wilson (the fugitive) climbed up a nearby ridge to plot his way west. While resting, he noticed a different outcrop of rock which he thought was pretty. He broke off a piece and shoved it in his pocket, then went back to camp where he showed it to the prospectors. Gleefully, they identified it as rich wire gold ore and insisted he show them where he found it. George nervously led them to the outcropping and the prospectors dug only four feet before exposing the gleaming vein of gold that would become the famous Homestake Mine.

The overjoyed prospectors staked their claims, but George Wilson's only aim was to put more miles between himself and the law back in Texas. His new pals then offered him two ounces of gold dust, nine silver dollars, a bottle of whiskey and a pistol for his share. He happily accepted his new-found wealth and headed west.

The Homestake Mine discovery led to numerous other mines with names like Lady Godiva, Comstock, and Old Abe. The Old Abe was to give up more than $3 million in gold. Winters and Baxter eventually sold their claims for $300,000 each.

The thriving mining town of White Oaks sprang into existence, first with tents dotting the hillsides, then with large brick Victorian buildings, some of which are still standing.

Several large old Victorian houses are still standing. This one, the Gumm mansion, recently restored, is an artist's studio and stands in stark contrast to the remains of once elegant homes and stores in White Oaks. (Frank Mangan)

The bonanza lasted twenty years. No more than thirty people live there today.

Most early miners and prospectors reached the area from California, being frustrated 49ers who arrived too late on the West Coast. There is evidence that the Spaniards and the Mexicans were the first miners in Lincoln County, but the first big gold strikes were made shortly after the Civil War in the Nogal District. (The mining districts were usually named for trees or rivers). In the area there are the Ruidoso, Eagle Creek, Bonito, Nogal, White Oaks and Jicarilla districts. Ruidoso and Eagle Creek never helped line the gold seekers' pockets, but the others have been extremely productive. During the Depression of the 1930s, more than two thousand families lived off placer gold panned in the Jicarilla District alone.

Gene Turner, Ruidoso's resident gold mining authority, says there's still gold in them thar hills. The glitter of gold has drawn prospectors and adventurers to Lincoln County for over a century. "Right now," says Gene, "the hottest mining district in southern New Mexico is right here around Nogal. Most people don't know it, but there are at least five large mining projects underway. One company is on the New York Stock Exchange. In addition there are about sixty people up

there operating dredges and trying to produce a half-ounce of gold a day. In the wintertime they wear wet suits and rubber gloves."

Over the divide from Nogal is the Bonito Mining District where the remains of the famous old Parsons Mine and Mill are quietly disintegrating into the forest.

The town of Parsons grew up near the mine. It was a bustling community around the turn of the century when promising gold mines attracted eastern investors. A building contractor from Chicago, John M. Rice, built a three story hotel high in Bonito Canyon called the Parsons Inn. Rice became postmaster, and the post office was located in one corner of the inn's long dining room. By the early 1920s, high operating costs closed most of the mines, effectively shutting down Parsons and its post office. The inn remained for many years, then finally burned.

Today, Gene Turner and his wife Ruby own two working claims. One, up Nogal Canyon, is producing small nuggets and flakes along a small mountain stream. For a fee, Gene will put you in a vehicle, take you twenty miles to their patented claim, teach you how to pan, let you get the gold, and bring you back. He comments, "Just remember, they say that only ten percent of the world's gold has been found."

The Great White Sands, center of the Tularosa Basin. These two-hundred-seventy-five square miles of brilliant gypsum comprise White Sands National Monument, the world's largest gypsum dune field. U. S. Highway 70 cuts through a white outcropping named Chalk Hill, the scene of one of New Mexico's oldest unsolved mysteries. (Courtesy White Sands National Monument)

7

The Mystery of
the White Sands

ACOLD BRITTLE WIND blew from snow-capped Sierra Blanca down Lincoln's single street. It was the last day of January in 1896, and Colonel Albert J. Fountain along with his nine-year-old son Henry bundled up and climbed into their buggy, preparing to head home to Las Cruces, one hundred and fifty miles west on the Rio Grande.

Fountain was a powerful political figure and successful lawyer representing the newly-formed Southeastern New Mexico Livestock Association. His mission was to chase down cattle rustlers, have them arrested and prosecute them in court. After spending two weeks attending court in Lincoln, Fountain felt victorious with a large number of indictments handed down.

As he left the courtroom, Fountain reportedly received a written threat telling him to drop his accusations or he would never reach home alive. Friends warned him of danger while returning to Las Cruces across the empty expanse of sand dunes and greasewood of the Tularosa Basin. They urged him not to make the trip without protection. But the aggressive Fountain, a product of the frontier West, placed his Winchester across his knees, waved farewell to anxious friends, and rode off in the direction of the Rio Grande.

He reached the Ruidoso settlement at Dowlin's Mill, then turned up Carrizo Creek and rode

through the Mescalero Apache Reservation past what is now the Inn of the Mountain Gods. He and Henry spent the first night at Blazer's Mill on the western edge of the Reservation. Dr. J. H. Blazer cautioned him about the danger of ambush, and several Apache friends offered to ride along for protection.

Fountain wouldn't hear of it. But the next day, as he moved out of the forest and into the desert, he became apprehensive and instinctively looked back over his shoulder. He noticed three horsemen following, too far away to be recognized. He knew he was a tempting target in that lonely, windswept country.

At the southern point of the White Sands, Fountain conferred with a mail carrier from Tularosa headed for Las Cruces. The colonel mentioned the three riders, but again declined additional protection. The buggy jolted along the ruts leaving a trail of white dust. He headed toward Chalk Hill, a limestone landmark protruding from the desert near the edge of the White Sands. The three horsemen followed, now closing in. Within an hour, Colonel Fountain and his little boy Henry vanished.

The Tularosa mail carrier rode to Las Cruces the next day and inquired about the Fountains, mentioning he had seen them on the trail. Fountain's frantic family knew something was

Oliver M. Lee established the Circle Cross Ranch in the Tularosa Basin and Sacramento Mountains. He was a prime suspect in the disappearance of A. J. Fountain. This picture was taken when Lee was in the New Mexico Legislature. (Leon C. Metz Collection)

terribly wrong, and within hours search parties were combing the Tularosa Basin about forty-five miles east of Las Cruces. The search continued day and night. Trackers found where the buggy had swerved off the trail, and twelve miles farther away they found the abandoned vehicle and a pool of blood. Today's U. S. Highway 70 crosses the Otero-Doña Ana county line just west of the scene of the Fountains' disappearance.

The sensational news shocked the entire Territory. Expert Apache trackers and scouts entered the search but only pieced together a few clues.

Albert Jennings Fountain was a power to be reckoned with. He was a man of many talents;

prominent in Republican Party politics, Union Army veteran, pugnacious newspaper publisher, playwright and actor, and ex-Indian fighter. He was also a handsome, stocky individual with a droopy mustache in the style of the day. After the Civil War he was seriously wounded in a skirmish with Apaches in Arizona and sent to El Paso to recuperate from two arrow and bullet wounds.

When his wounds healed he moved into the El Paso political arena and in 1868 was elected to the Texas State Senate where he represented thirty-two West Texas counties. His flamboyant style propelled him to president of the Senate.

Fountain's life took an abrupt turn in El Paso when the emotions of political factions within the Republican Party exploded into gunfire. An enraged lawyer named B. F. Williams abused Fountain, then shot and wounded him with a derringer. In the resulting shootout, a state policeman's pistol and a shot from Fountain's rifle killed Williams. Tempers on both sides boiled over and for the next several years Fountain was the target of threats. Though never accustomed to backing down from a fight, Fountain became convinced that his longevity was in direct proportion to the time it took him to get out of Texas.

So in 1875 he moved his family forty miles up the Rio Grande to the adobe village of Mesilla to start a new career in New Mexico. Mesilla was the county seat of Doña Ana County, and the ambitious and controversial Fountain began a substantial law practice. In 1881 he unsuccessfully defended Billy the Kid at Mesilla for the murder of Lincoln County Sheriff William Brady.

By the 1890s Fountain personified the new era just beginning in the West. He was a strong advocate of law and order, yet he continued wearing a gun since his memories of lawlessness in the Territory were vivid. Cattle rustling was still a big business.

With his intellectual and man-of-action background, a rare combination on the New Mexico frontier, Fountain became an investigator and lawyer for the Southeastern New Mexico Livestock Association. Its members were losing hundreds of cattle by brand altering and stealing. In

1894, he sent twenty rustlers to the state penitentiary—much to the satisfaction of the Association. Modesty was not one of the Colonel's virtues, however, and he made his legal and dangerous exploits known to anybody who would listen. Along the way he accumulated numerous friends and just as many enemies, becoming the best-loved and most-hated man in southern New Mexico.

A young Texas cowboy named Oliver Milton Lee placed himself in the latter camp. Lee established the Circle Cross ranch in the Tularosa Basin and Sacramento Mountains.

Lee arrived in New Mexico in the fall of 1884 from central Texas with a string of horses and a few cows. Like so many others, he had heard about New Mexico's free grazing land, open range and good markets. He was only nineteen, but his Texas upbringing made him into a superb horseman and an expert shot. The young cowboy pastured his livestock in Dog Canyon at the foot of the Sacramentos about ten miles south of present-day Alamogordo. Lee was a quiet, soft-spoken man. His erect and dignified posture made him appear taller than just under six feet. Most people liked Oliver Lee.

When he turned twenty-one, Oliver Lee filed a homestead claim on the flats near the mouth of Dog Canyon where plentiful water gushed down from springs near the summit. The rocky walls of the canyon, hung with cool green moss, extended almost a mile straight up to the pine forests. Indians had used the canyon trail for centuries as a direct line from the desert to the mountains.

Lee extended his holdings up and down the Tularosa Basin to include the Wildy Well Ranch, eight miles east of Orogrande. He enlarged his herds, built water tanks and erected windmills.

Five years after Oliver Lee settled on the grassy plains at the foot of the Sacramentos, a three-year drought hit the country, devastating homesteaders who had assumed there would always be rain. This part of the Territory literally shriveled. Cattle died by the hundreds. Many were grabbed from major cattlemen by farmers and small operators reduced to breaking the law and eating other men's beef.

Albert J. Fountain was a towering political figure in southern New Mexico when he and his nine-year-old son Henry were murdered at the edge of the White Sands in 1895. The trail is still as cold as it was a hundred years ago. (R. G. McCubbin Collection)

The big cattle companies, with the politicians, lawyers and lawmen on their side, took a keener look at some of the recent arrivals—Oliver Lee in particular.

Lee hired two Texans, Bill McNew and Jim Gililland, to keep the opposition at bay and protect his herd. Tall, lanky Jim Gililland rode up from the cattle ranges of central Texas. He wasn't afraid of anybody, a trait that can make a man dangerous. Bill McNew was a steely-eyed cowboy who had arrived earlier in New Mexico and lived atop the Sacramentos. Grandpa McNew's potato patch later became the Cloudcroft golf course.

Oliver Lee's superb marksmanship served him well in the 1890s when struggles over water and

(Left to right) Bill McNew was a steely-eyed cowboy hired by
Oliver Lee to protect his range. (R. G. McCubbin Collection)
Jim Gililland wasn't afraid of anybody, a trait that can make a man
dangerous. (Rio Grande Historical Collection, NMSU Library)
Miguel Otero, New Mexico Territorial Governor, was delighted
when Otero County was named for him. (Leon C. Metz Collection)

grazing rights tormented the region. Without
water rights, grazing land was worth practically
nothing. The man who controlled the waterhole
controlled the public range, and Lee was prepared
to defend his property with rifle and six-shooter.

No new evidence surfaced in the disappearance
of the Fountains, and the mystery deepened. But
conspiracy rumors were everywhere, and one
finger pointed toward Oliver Lee and his cowboys,
Bill McNew and Jim Gililland. One indictment
handed down by Fountain and the grand jury in
Lincoln accused Oliver Lee and Bill McNew of
changing the brand on a steer stolen from an El
Paso rancher. This, some people reasoned, gave
Lee and McNew motive for murdering the
Fountains. They became prime suspects.

Meanwhile, Pat Garrett, the tall slayer of Billy
the Kid, raised horses in the South Texas town of
Uvalde. Fifteen years had passed since Garrett
held the New Mexico limelight and he was restless. His fame was fading.

With the Fountain trail ice cold, New Mexico
needed Garrett, this time to solve the Fountain
mystery. His friends urged him to accept the
sheriff's office in Doña Ana county. Garrett agreed
after the current sheriff was bribed to resign.
County commissioners appointed Garrett to

the job in 1897; the next year he was more properly elected.

Garrett had little evidence and no bodies, so he
moved methodically—some said too slowly—on
the case. It wasn't until the spring of 1898 that he
swore out warrants for the arrest of Oliver Lee,
Jim Gililland and Bill McNew. Lee got word that
Garrett planned to kill him while attempting an
arrest. Given Oliver Lee's reputation with firearms
and not backing away from trouble, some people
believed Garrett was afraid to arrest Lee, that Lee
would shoot it out with him in broad daylight.

On a strangely peaceful note, in January 1898
the El Paso & Northeastern Railroad laid track
within three miles of Oliver Lee's Wildy Well
ranch house, the rails pointing north to what
would soon become the town of Alamogordo.

Two scenarios seemed incompatible. On the
one hand, here was Charles B. Eddy, always
dapper in his three-piece suits, bringing the mar-
vel of a railroad and the blessings of new capital
to the soon-to-be twentieth century. Simulta-
neously, in the same arena, Pat Garrett was playing out his last hand, a frontier lawman searching
for the heavily armed and extremely dangerous
Oliver Lee and his cowboys.

Garrett knew he didn't have enough evidence

to convict anybody, but he arrested McNew and let him sit glumly in jail for a year before being released. Lee and Gililland went into hiding to escape the same fate, and the next move was up to the sheriff. Big trouble lay just ahead.

Garrett received a tip that Lee and Gililland were holed up at Wildy Well, east of Orogrande. Before daybreak on the morning of July 12, 1898, the sheriff and a posse of four deputies reined up short of the flat-roofed adobe line shack. Nobody was in sight as the windmill groaned gently in the breeze. Garrett and his deputies slipped quietly up in the darkness, kicked open the door and found only the Madison family who worked on the ranch. Lee and Gililland had wisely curled up in their bedrolls and were asleep on the flat roof.

One of the deputies, Kent Kearney, noticed the Madisons glancing nervously toward the roof. Kearney climbed up a ladder to the roof just in time to look down the barrels of Lee's and Gililland's Winchesters. And all hell broke loose.

Garrett testified later that both he and Kearney called, "Surrender!" but he admitted that Kearney fired immediately. Kearney tumbled in agony from the ladder with two bullets in him. Lee looked down and shot at Garrett who twisted away and missed the bullet. Oliver Lee later told historian William Keleher, "I had no idea I hadn't killed Garrett because everything was quiet after we shot Kearney and I thought I had shot Garrett."

When the shooting started, Ben Williams, one of the posse members took refuge under the water tower and suffered a deluge of cold water as Lee and Gililland pumped bullets into it. At the same time the ranchers pinned the other deputies under a wagon shed.

Garrett was humiliated. Lee and Gililland had the drop on everybody, and Kearney lay dying. At Garrett's request, Lee permitted the posse to leave without their guns, one of them without his boots. It was not Garrett's finest hour as he and the remaining posse members meekly headed back to Las Cruces while Kearney lay bleeding in the sand. Garrett sent a section crew from the railroad to pick him up. The sheriff took him to Alamogordo later that afternoon, but Kearney died the next day.

A few days later Lee and Gililland were indicted by Doña Ana County on a new charge, the murder of Deputy Kearney. They reasoned their best move was to disappear, which they did. They were not seen officially for eight months. They had no intention of surrendering to the law unless they were assured of an even break. According to C. L. Sonnichsen in his book *Tularosa*, the two wanted men were welcome almost anywhere. Sonnichsen speculates that they spent most of their time in the San Andres Mountains with author Gene Rhodes, who had a ranch in one of the most picturesque and inaccessible spots in that whole country.

Albert Bacon Fall, one of the great political powers in southern New Mexico and former attorney general of the Territory, returned home to Las Cruces from the Spanish American War to handle the defense of his close friend Oliver Lee.

Fall was a tall handsome man with wavy hair. He wore a black Stetson cowboy hat, puffed at cigars and usually carried a cane. He predicted that sooner or later Garrett would either bring Oliver Lee to trial or attempt to kill him. He knew Lee had little chance of acquittal if the trial was held in Doña Ana County. A. B. Fall and attorney William Ashton Hawkins devised an ingenious plan whereby a new county would be carved from parts of Lincoln, Doña Ana and Sierra counties. The spot where the Fountains disappeared would be placed in the new county. This way, they reasoned, any action against Lee would be outside the jurisdiction of Pat Garrett and Doña Ana County. Territorial Governor Miguel A. Otero first yawned at the idea proposed by Fall and Hawkins. They offered to name the new county Otero. The governor reversed his position and suspected he might have been wrong in questioning the motives of the two attorneys. Anyone could see that New Mexico needed one more county. The deal was made and Otero became an official county on January 30, 1899. The railroad town of Alamogordo became the county seat.

Ruidoso remained in Lincoln County, but just barely. The Otero County line began about two

Wayne Brazel (center) admitted killing Pat Garrett. Brazel was not a bad looking young man, he just had a bad barber. Jim Lee is at left. At right is Will Craven. (Special Collections, UTEP Library)

Pat Garrett and his second wife, Apolinaria. This photograph was taken on their wedding day in 1880. Garrett was a good family man—with nine children. (Leon C. Metz Collection)

miles south of Ruidoso and stretched through the Mescalero Reservation all the way to the Texas line at El Paso.

Lee and Gililland decided to surrender and place everything in Fall's hands. Anxious to put the Fountain murder charges behind him, Lee wrote a letter to Governor Otero saying that he would come in and surrender to any sheriff but Pat Garrett. And he wanted assurance for his own safety that he would not be placed in the Las Cruces jail. The governor agreed. In the company of the popular author Eugene Manlove Rhodes (best known for his story *Pasò Por Aquì*, which was set near the spot of Fountain's murder), Lee and Gililland handed over their guns and surrendered to Judge Frank Parker, by-passing Pat Garrett.

Fall was concerned about animosity in Las Cruces toward Oliver Lee and the attorney forced a change of venue to the little gold mining town of Hillsboro, seventy miles north in Sierra County.

Hundreds of people swarmed to Hillsboro to witness the sensational trial that attracted

nationwide attention. Press correspondents packed the town, and many had no place to sleep except in tents. Western Union installed a special telegraph line for newspaper reporters to file their daily stories across the country. In this carnival atmosphere the trial unfolded in breathless excitement on May 25, 1899. It lasted eighteen days, hearing seventy-five witnesses, with A. B. Fall doing a masterful job of defending his clients. Fall delivered an impassioned plea for the defense, and finally it was all over. The jury retired, then rendered its verdict in fifteen minutes. Oliver Lee and Jim Gililland were acquitted. The judge ruled they should also stand trial for the killing of Deputy Kearney but the indictments were later dismissed.

Pat Garrett quietly served out the remainder of his term as sheriff, then applied for the vacant post of customs collector in El Paso. President Theodore Roosevelt had a weakness for lawmen and rugged western characters and Pat Garrett's name was well known to him. With the president's backing, Garrett landed the job, then moved his family to

El Paso where they lived in comparative elegance until 1905. He was not reappointed for another term, ostensibly for being away from his office a large part of the time and for "bad habits." These habits included excessive drinking and gambling in the Coney Island Saloon. Tom Powers, a one-eyed Irishman, who owned the Coney Island became a good friend of Garrett's. The ex-sheriff even loaned Powers the revolver that he had used to kill Billy the Kid, and it hung in a place of honor above the bar.

After losing probably the best job he ever had, Garrett left El Paso. He settled down with his family on a ranch he owned near Las Cruces on the eastern slopes of the San Andres Mountains.

Pat Garrett's life continued sliding downhill. He was gambling and drinking, and he was dead broke. The county took most of his cattle for back taxes. All he had left were memories, a ramshackle ranch house and his land. In desperation he leased part of his property to two local cowboys, Wayne Brazel and Print Rhode, who proceeded to drive a huge herd of goats onto the leased ranchland. Garrett was infuriated. He, as did most cattlemen, despised goats as they chewed range grass down much further than cattle. Garrett tried to break the lease, but failed.

Into this standoff rode a man whom Garrett believed might still save his dwindling fortunes. He was James B. Miller, known in many circles as "Killin' Jim" Miller and who was later lynched by a mob in an Ada, Oklahoma livery stable. Miller needed grazing land for Mexican cattle he was bringing across the border. He told Garrett that he and a partner and a brother-in-law, Carl Adamson, would buy the ranch if the ex-sheriff would get rid of the goats. He even offered to buy the goats, until he discovered there were eighteen hundred animals—more than he could afford.

Wayne Brazel agreed to cancel the lease if Garrett could find a buyer for his goats. In a final effort to solve the problem, everyone agreed that Brazel, Garrett and Adamson would travel to Las Cruces for a meeting with Miller, hoping to make a deal. It was to be Pat Garrett's last ride.

On February 29, 1908, Garrett and Adamson

left early in the morning in Garrett's buggy. Wayne Brazel overtook the pair several miles past the mining settlement of Organ and the three headed across the desert toward Las Cruces and the Rio Grande valley. Garrett and Brazel argued and cursed each other most of the way.

About five miles out of Las Cruces, Adamson stopped the buggy and he and Garrett got out to relieve themselves. Garrett stepped to the rear of the buggy and unbuttoned his trousers. A bullet slammed into the back of his head. Another bullet struck him in the body as he fell, groaned, stretched out and died. Adamson covered the body with a lap robe, then he and Brazel rode to Las Cruces where Wayne Brazel surrendered to Deputy Sheriff Felipe Lucero. "Lock me up," said Brazel, "I've just killed Pat Garrett. He pointed to Adamson. "He saw the whole thing and knows that I shot in self-defense."

Southern New Mexico erupted with accusations and arguments about several conspiracies in Garrett's death. And through the years different theories cropped up as to who may have really killed Garrett. Many eyes turned toward Jim Miller. About a year after the slaying, Brazel went on trial for murder and was defended by A. B. Fall, pleading self defense. The jury bought it and Brazel was acquitted. Historian Leon Metz says that to his knowledge, this is the only case of a man being shot in the back while urinating, and the accused pleading self-defense and getting away with it.

Much of the Old West died with Pat Garrett that cold February day on the trail to Las Cruces. By coincidence, 1908 was the same year that Butch Cassidy and the Sundance Kid were shot to rags in Bolivia. Perhaps there is no good way to die, but Pat Garrett deserved better than such an inglorious death. He is still a legend in southern New Mexico. He hunted buffalo on the Texas plains as the last great herds were slaughtered. He was the lawman who brought down Billy the Kid. He was a rancher, Texas Ranger, and played a part in the early Pecos Valley irrigation projects. Garrett was a good family man—with nine children. His eldest daughter, Elizabeth, blind

Albert Bacon Fall when he was a captain in the 1st Territorial Regiment of New Mexico in 1898. (Leon C. Metz Collection)

from birth, wrote the official New Mexico state song, "Oh Fair New Mexico." His youngest son, Jarvis Garrett lived until 1991. Pat Garrett carved a niche in history, but there is no other monument to him than the modest granite stone in the Masonic Cemetery in Las Cruces.

The other two main characters in the Fountain drama, A. B. Fall and Oliver Lee, survived those turbulent years at the turn of the century and went on to lead long and full lives. Fall became widely known in West Texas, establishing a law office in El Paso. In 1907 he built a hilltop home at 1725 Arizona Street, a two-story Greek Revival mansion set off by six white ionic columns. The Fall home is there today, overlooking El Paso and Juarez. A. B. Fall never relinquished his legal residence in New Mexico, however.

In 1921 Fall had become secretary of the interior under Warren G. Harding. After two years in the Cabinet, he resigned to return to private life and his Three Rivers Ranch at the foot of Sierra Blanca Peak west of Ruidoso. While still in office

he borrowed $100,000 from his old friend, oil man Edward L. Doheny, and used the money to buy the Harris ranch which adjoined Fall's Three Rivers property. The Harris place controlled valuable water sources, a necessity of life in New Mexico. To secure the loan, he gave Doheny a promissory note and a mortgage on Three Rivers.

Meanwhile, rumors circulated around Washington that the loan from Doheny was actually a bribe to A. B. Fall for the granting of leases on oil reserves set aside for the U.S. Navy. One of the oil fields was near Casper, Wyoming, close to a rock formation shaped like a teapot, thus the name of the scandal. Many people believe that Fall resigned as interior secretary because of the Teapot Dome Scandal, but that tempest did not erupt until months after his resignation. After years of trials and appeals, the leases were cancelled, Fall was found guilty, fined $100,000 and sentenced to a year and a day in the State Penitentiary in Santa Fe.

George Curry, a former Territorial governor of New Mexico wrote extensively about Teapot Dome in his autobiography: "I found it difficult to believe Fall guilty of accepting a bribe in connection with his official duties....Fall was guilty of bad judgement rather than the acceptance of a bribe....A grave error was Fall's acceptance of the Doheny loan in cash, lending an air of furtiveness to the transaction."

Then, to make matters worse, Fall, under heavy pressure, wrote a letter falsely stating he borrowed the money from E. B. McLean, wealthy owner of the *Washington Post*. (This was at McLean's suggestion.) McLean was then called to testify under oath, and to avoid perjuring himself, denied Fall's allegation.

In one of the strangest twists of fate in the American judicial system, Doheny was tried and found not guilty of bribing Fall—who was imprisoned for accepting the bribe. The decision became reminiscent of H. L. Mencken's comment, "There is an easy solution to every human problem—neat, plausible and wrong."
The years of litigation left Fall broken in health and finances, since he was unable to do

anything to make a living during that time.

Historian Nora Henn of Lincoln says that as long as Doheny was alive, Fall could rely on his friend's generosity in postponing payment of the loan, but in 1935 Doheny died. When Fall could not repay the money, he lost everything to the Doheny interests who foreclosed and that same year notified the Falls they would have to vacate.

Long after his meteoric rise to the top and long bitter court fights, A. B. Fall died peacefully in Hotel Dieu Hospital in El Paso in 1944. He was eighty-three.

During Fall's difficulties, there was always one man he could count on and that was Oliver Lee. Lee continued as boss of the Circle Cross Ranch while his standing in the area rose. He was twice elected to the New Mexico Legislature, and he was an officer and director in numerous business organizations. But the Circle Cross was his main interest in life, and it made him prosperous. In the early years of World War I he negotiated with a group of El Paso businessmen to build the ranch into a gigantic enterprise. The group was headed by James G. McNary of the First National Bank in El Paso. Buying up a number of ranches, they eventually controlled a million acres of rangeland stretching from Tularosa south one hundred miles into El Paso, Texas. In the timberland of the Sacramentos, Circle Cross cattle grazed from near Cloudcroft to present-day Timberon at the southern tip of the mountains. The range stretched eastward to the Cornudas mountains in West Texas.

Blaine McNutt of El Paso remembered Oliver Lee during deer hunting trips on the Circle Cross Ranch in the mid-1930s. Lee's headquarters then were in the forest near Timberon. "Lee was getting up in years when I knew him," said McNutt, "but he could still hit a playing card dead center with a pistol at fifty feet. He was the greatest natural shot I ever saw, and I've seen a good many. I never saw the old man smile, but he was fair and square and most people liked him. I don't think he would hesitate to kill you, though, if you crossed him."

Oliver Lee died in 1941, his life bridging the era from raw frontier days in New Mexico Territory until World War II. The State of New Mexico developed Oliver Lee State Memorial Park ten miles south of Alamogordo at the mouth of Dog Canyon. Along with Lee's restored ranch house, a museum and other facilities, the park commemorates the life and times of one of New Mexico's most colorful characters.

A century after the disappearance of Colonel Fountain and little Henry, New Mexico still hears rumors and speculation about the White Sands mystery. For years people who may have known the real facts whispered them in confidence. The old-timers, as well as the principal players in the Fountain drama are now all dead. The Fountain case was closed. The bodies were never found and the trail is still as cold as the winter of 1896.

8
Cabin Fever

New Mexico artist Peter Hurd painted landscapes and several summer cabins along the upper Ruidoso. Hurd painted this scene, a cabin owned by the author's family in the 1930s and early '40s. (Frank Mangan Collection)

THE DESERT SOUTHWEST is not renowned for its balmy summer days. All too frequently the desert is furnace-hot. The old saying in parts of the country that "It's not the heat, it's the humidity" has a hollow ring when thermometers register a hundred degrees plus in the shade and a hundred and twenty in the sun. Even with only ten percent humidity, it's downright hot.

Fifty years before houses were air-conditioned, folks in towns like El Paso, Roswell, Artesia, Alamogordo, Lubbock and Las Cruces slept in their backyards on cots placed next to wet-down shrubbery. City people sat on their front porches on summer evenings contemplating a trip to the cool New Mexico mountains. But contemplating was all they could do since the mountains, though not far away, were practically inaccessible. To get to Ruidoso, two important ingredients were missing: the automobile and a decent road. At the turn of the century there were precious few automobiles in El Paso and no real road northward through the sand dunes and mesquite.

But progress lay directly ahead. On the east side of the Sacramento Mountains people in Roswell looked longingly at the silhouette of Sierra Blanca only seventy-five miles away. Before the Model T left wagons and buggies rusting in backyards, the buckboard was still the old transportation standby. Hardy souls from the Pecos Valley headed for Ruidoso Country which was becoming a favorite spot for camping, hunting, and trout fishing in the Ruidoso River. Ruidoso was a three-day journey in horse-drawn buckboards over the same trail used by Pat Garrett, John Chisum and his drovers, Billy the Kid, and those involved in the Lincoln County War which had ended little more than two decades earlier. But folks felt the long jolting trip was worth it to escape the onslaught of the sun and to cool off for a few days.

For people in the Pecos River country it was a wonderful, peaceful time. They were searching for recreation instead of circling the wagons and barricading homesteads against the shooters and horse thieves of just a few years earlier.

Roswell's first automobile arrived in 1902 and it frightened horses and about half the population.

93

The very first summer cabin built along the Ruidoso River was constructed in 1915 by Judge Edward Medler and his wife Lillian of Las Cruces. (Courtesy Eleanor Lorentzen)

Within five years an auto stage and mail line was running between Roswell and Alamogordo through the Sacramento Mountains of Lincoln National Forest. Grading the old trails to Ruidoso with primitive equipment was a nightmare for the new auto stage company. Road crews fastened heavy timbers together, and these contraptions dragged by four horses, smoothed out the original ruts made by frontier wagon wheels. It was a bone-jarring ride, either by auto or wagon, but this little road, which would later become U.S. Highway 70, opened the Ruidoso canyons to thousands of people. The automobile had finally made the mountains readily available to desert dwellers.

Shortly, tents and the first summer cabins along the Ruidoso appeared. Usually the cabins were covered with pine bark slabs, the refuse from sawmills. Owners built on the banks of the river so they could sit on their porches and fish for trout. The very first cabin was constructed by Judge Edward Medler and his wife Lillian of Las Cruces. Medler was elected judge of the Third Judicial District of New Mexico after the territory became a state in 1912. He traveled over much of

the southern part of New Mexico and took his wife along on many of his trips.

Mrs. Medler's daughter, Eleanor Lorentzen of El Paso, retains her mother's memoirs, some published in the *El Paso Herald-Post* in 1974 by columnist Ann Carroll. Mrs. Medler recalls the trip that eventually led to the first cabin building in Ruidoso:

In 1914, with Dr. and Mrs. T. W. Watson (who was county treasurer of Lincoln County), we decided to take a trip. Especially we wanted to get up into the mountains somewhere. My husband wrote to the White Mountain Inn [an early roadhouse with rental accomodations located on the Roswell road about five miles east of today's Ruidoso Downs] to see if we could get reservations. But they were full.

There were considerable mining operations at Bent then. The mines were closed temporarily and Mr. and Mrs. Bent had left everything in charge of a Chinese who rented us rooms with three good meals a day. Each day we took trips around the vicinity of Bent, visiting little canyons and side roads.

We decided to go up into the Ruidoso country. We turned off the highway and took the road that led into Ruidoso. The first thing we saw was an old mill standing by itself. It was vacant and probably had been for years. We drove up and up, then came to the

Wingfield homestead. They had a nice big home and a large red barn. These three buildings were the only ones in Ruidoso.

The Wingfields were glad to see us and wanted to know if we had a camera. They had two little girls, Della and Opal, whose pictures had never been taken. We took a picture of the girls sitting side by side at the edge of the road. To this day I wonder if they still have this picture as it was a good one of these children.

Mr. Wingfield told us we could go on farther. We had gone about three miles when we came to a river crossing a short distance from the Mescalero Reservation fence. We didn't cross the river but had our picnic lunch right there. I went into raptures about the beauty of that spot. I thought I had never seen anything so beautiful. I raved on and on, and before we started home, I said, "Oh, can't we come back next year and camp in this lovely spot?"

Dr. Watson, being treasurer of Lincoln County, knew a lot about the acreage of the county. He corresponded with a Mr. Cree who owned vast amounts of acreage in Lincoln County but his home was in Scotland. Dr. Watson found that Mr. Cree was willing to lease us some acreage and that we could build summer cabins on it.

In 1915, three cabins were built on the very spot I had fallen in love with and where we'd had our picnic the year before. The third cabin was built by Benson Newell who was court stenographer.

Frank English of Carrizozo was the builder of the main part of all three cabins, but our three men did all the finishing work. The cabins were built on the same plan; large living room, four bedrooms, a big front porch, a small porch and a kitchen. We also built a garage with a cover to hold our automobiles. A Mr. Creley who had a farm on the highway built a fireplace of native stone in each cabin. He told my husband, "If this one ever smokes you won't have to pay me a cent." And it never did smoke. We had a fire night and morning all the days we lived there.

Our home was the closest to the Reservation fence. Next came the Watson cabin and then the Newell cabin. These three are almost the same today, with little change. Dr. Watson sold his cabin to Mr. and Mrs. Sylvester Johnson of Roswell. Benson Newell sold his to Mr. and Mrs. C. C. Martin of Roswell.

We lived in Las Cruces then and offered our friends the privilege of building on this large acreage we had leased. It extended from the Reservation down to within a few feet of where Noisy Water Lodge was later built. Friends in Roswell were offered land.

People from Roswell and Artesia began to build homes. The fourth cabin was built by Colonel and Mrs. Pistole of Artesia. The next cabin was built by the Jewetts of Roswell a short distance across from the Martins. Later came the Keyes, Grays, Nortons and Nixons from Roswell. Mrs. Gray's sister, Miss Olds, bought Mrs. Pistole's cabin.

We moved to California in 1928 and sold the cabin to Ernest McDaniel several years later. That part of Ruidoso has remained almost the same as in the early days.

Earlier, when Lillian Medler mentioned that "a Mr. Cree who lived in Scotland" owned vast amounts of acreage in Lincoln County, she was referring to James Cree who did, indeed, live in Scotland—Edinburgh to be precise—and who was a wealthy distiller of Scotch whiskey.

In the 1880s, James Cree, like many others in the British Isles, was intrigued by stories of empty land in the American West. For centuries most land in England, Scotland and Ireland was tightly held by relatively few landowners, members of the aristocracy, and the royal family. There was little property available even to wealthy merchants and well-to-do industrialists. England was literally a tight little island.

The fascinating idea of coming to America and acquiring vast amounts of land for a small fee was mind-boggling. Cree listened with more than casual interest to stories about far-off New Mexico. Keeping his business in Scotland intact, he sailed to America, journeyed to Lincoln County, and at bargain-basement prices purchased large tracts of land in the area and up and down the Ruidoso canyons, becoming the earliest big landowner.

James Cree and Brandon Kirby, a retired British army officer, became partners in the immense Angus VV Ranch with water-rights along the Rio Bonito, Eagle Creek and Little Creek north of today's Alto. They hired ex-sheriff Pat Garrett as ranch manager and imported registered bulls and Angus cattle in an attempt to improve the Texas longhorn breed. The settlement of Angus, near Alto, was named for the cattle breed. At its peak the VV Ranch carried a reported six thousand head of cattle; some say as many as fifteen thousand head. But by either count the partners met with little success.

Dowlin's Mill about 1886. The hill in the right background is barren, stark and bleak looking. One hundred years later, it is covered with dense timber. (R. G. McCubbin Collection)

Cree's partner Brandon Kirby referred to the cowboys as "cow servants"—much to the chagrin of the hands. As with a number of other large ranch operations run by English capitalists, Cree and Kirby did not understand raising livestock in New Mexico and making it pay. Pat Garrett resigned in disgust. The VV ranch lost money from the beginning, and in time James Cree finally bought out Kirby and sold off the herd. But he wisely held on to the ranch which became valuable real estate in later years. He willed all of his property in Lincoln County to his two sons, Charles and Gerald Cree.

The ongoing religious struggles between the Scots and the Irish were prevalent even then. Cree's last will and testament reads "I direct… that if at my death either of my sons shall have come to profess the Roman Catholic faith he shall forfeit his share of the bequest…or shall have married a person who professes the Roman Catholic faith…the estate will be dealt with by my

Trustees accordingly." The same determination would apply to his daughter.

A hundred years later the Scotsman's memory is alive in the Ruidoso area with familiar names like Cree Meadows, Cree Meadows Golf Course, Cree Manor, Cree Meadows Drive and Cree Meadows Heights.

During the years James Cree was acquiring large tracts of Lincoln County land, another name appeared on the Ruidoso scene. This was Charles Wingfield. The Wingfields left Texas for New Mexico in 1884 and arrived at what is now Ruidoso in a covered wagon with all their worldly goods. The wagon creaked to a stop at Dowlin's Mill.

What brought Wingfield all the way up this narrow, secluded canyon? Speculation is that he succumbed to gold fever as the news from mining camps in White Oaks, Bonito and Nogal spread quickly outside the territory. Fortunes were

Rare photograph of James Cree checking cattle on his VV Ranch near Alto. Cree was unsuccessful as a rancher; perhaps he should have worn chaps instead of a three-piece suit and gold watch chain. (R. G. McCubbin Collection)

tantalizingly within grasp, with a good chance of getting rich in the mine shafts or by panning gold in the New Mexico mountains.

But the story Wingfield heard at Dowlin's Mill was a bit sobering and certainly more realistic. Yes, there was gold in the mountains to the north, but it was tough, dirty work getting it out of the ground.

Wingfield looked up and down the river. It was spring runoff time and the Rio Ruidoso was running cool and clear, making a happy gurgling sound over smooth river stones. The pine forest was fragrant, the New Mexico sky was the clearest and bluest the Wingfields had ever seen, and the big white mountain loomed over everything. Pretty impressive.

Wingfield may have had second thoughts about this time. Did he really like the idea of wading around with a gold pan in pools of icy mountain water? Perhaps there was a better way to start a new life in New Mexico without traveling

additional miles through the wilderness.

There at Dowlin's Mill he saw a sizable settlement. Hispanic employees sawed pine logs and ground corn and wheat into flour for people downstream. The mill straddled the Chisum cattle trail which extended from the Pecos River to Arizona. A good location for a man with business instincts.

Wingfield was entranced with the place, especially when the mill's then owner Frank Lesnett offered him a job, which he happily accepted. After this good fortune the lure of the gold fields vanished. The Wingfields settled in and Charles was soon busily carving himself a place in Ruidoso's history. He saw the frontier changing even though it had been only three years since Lincoln County Sheriff Pat Garrett gunned down Billy the Kid in Fort Sumner.

Herb Seckler wrote in *Ruidoso Countryside: The Early Days*, that Cree bought the old Dowlin Mill in 1888 from Frank Lesnett. The original owner,

Pat Garrett.

P. O.: Roswell, Lincoln county, N. M.
Range, White mountains.
Also all cattle with a ▬ butt brand.
Horses branded same as cattle.

Advertisement for Pat Garrett's brand (right). Kirby and Cree's VV brand (below). These appeared in 1887 in *Stock Grower,* a Las Vegas, New Mexico newspaper. (R. G. McCubbin Collection)

THE ANGUS V V RANCH.

KIRBY & CREE.

Postoffice, Fort Stanton, Lincoln county, New Mexico.

Range, Rio Salado, Rio Bonito, Little creek, Eagle creek, and Rio Ruidosa.

Ear marks, underbit in each ear.

Horse brand, V on the left shoulder.

Additional Brands:

ʇ on right side, underbit both ears. WHS on left side, or either side.

V on either hip. 2W on the left side.

VVV on left shoulder, side and hip. Marked, crop right and underslope left.

Dinnertime for two dozen hungry cowboys on the Cree Ranch in the mid-1880s. Note the VV brand on side of the chuck wagon. (R. G. McCubbin Collection)

Paul Dowlin, had been shot and killed by a former employee named Jerry Dillon. Seckler said Dillon lit out for Texas and was never again heard from in New Mexico. Lesnett himself disappeared in 1892. He left for Santa Fe on a business trip and vanished on the way. Some think he was robbed and killed for the substantial amount of money he usually carried. Possibly his habit of flashing large rolls of bills attracted the wrong kind of attention. At any rate, Lesnett's disappearance remains one of the unsolved mysteries of Lincoln County.

Wingfield managed the mill property while the Crees lived on the VV ranch. In 1891, Charles Wingfield became Ruidoso's third postmaster at the mill. Four Wingfield children were born at the mill. One of them was Isaac "Ike" Wingfield who would later become a legend as a builder of the Ruidoso community.

In 1890, Charles Wingfield was elected Lincoln County tax assessor. He homesteaded on land up-river from the mill and about 1893 built a residence near today's intersection of Mechem and Sudderth. Although there were settlements on Eagle Creek and in Bonito and Nogal canyons, Wingfield owned the only building on the Ruidoso west of the mill.

In 1904 the post office moved from the Old Mill and opened for business across the highway from what became Clayton Bennett's Indian Store. In 1915 George Friedenbloom became postmaster, and he later developed Hollywood, New Mexico.

Charles Wingfield remained a Lincoln County commissioner until his death in 1910. Four years later the original Wingfield home burned. It was rebuilt, but the present building, called the Wingfield House, was not built until 1929. The house has since been occupied by families, gift shops and restaurants, and it sits today close to the traffic on Sudderth Drive across the street from the Pine Tree Square shopping center. Ike Wingfield's granddaughter Evelyn and her husband Wayne Estes lived in the family home until they moved to Denver, Colorado. They still remain in close touch with Ruidoso.

Della Louise was one of two daughters of Ike and Lula Robinson Wingfield. She was born in

1912 and most people called her Tootsie, because she grew up in Ruidoso during the Roaring Twenties and her vibrant personality epitomized the era. In 1972 Mrs. Lloyd Bloodworth, whose husband had been publisher of *The Ruidoso News* asked Della to speak at an Old Timer's meeting about her remembrances of early Ruidoso. Fortunately she wrote down her remarks and they were preserved by her daughter Evelyn Estes. Della Wingfield described beef being sold to the Mescalero Reservation when she was a girl. The cattle were butchered in a little slaughter house built of logs that stood near the present-day intersection of Sudderth and Mechem. Her memories were also very clear on many early business ventures and happenings:

The W. R. White sawmill was built in 1918 and operated by White and his wife Chloe just east of the first bridge on the Ruidoso, past today's traffic circle on the road that leads into the Upper Canyon. People from El Paso and Roswell and other towns were coming to Ruidoso to camp in the early 1900s [and to build cabins which used lumber from White's sawmill].

Many of the early visitors to the village had babies with what in those days was called "Summer Complaint." At first they came by our house and bought a quart of milk for a dime. This was the inspiration for Mama to go into the dairy business. She had two Holstein cows and saved this milk separately for those sick babies. As people came up the road through our place there were three gates to open. The first one was at our orchard, the second one at our barn, now Sudderth and Mechem, and the other one at the circle. My sister Opal and I would rush out and open the gates at the barn for nickels. All the area west of the house was in pasture.

A series of tiny one-room schoolhouses came and went but when the Wingfield sisters were growing up, there were not enough children to attract teachers and acquire permanent buildings. Part of Della's schooling was at the old town of Parsons and at Alto where she stayed with relatives. After the first early grades, Della began to grow up and had this to say:

In the fall of 1924, Opal and I were sent to Tularosa where I finished high school. A short time later there was a demand for a school here in Ruidoso. By 1930 two teachers were needed. Having graduated from high school the previous year I was granted a temporary teachers certificate and became Miss Della to several who still live in Ruidoso. My school room was the little building across the street from the Fire Hall, called the Pine Cone Cottage.

The post office was moved from down on U. S. 70 to our place in 1921 and things sprung to life in Ruidoso. Ike Wingfield became postmaster that year, served until 1937 when Jack Hull took over the job. [Wingfield rode horseback to and from Fort Stanton to get the mail. He used two horses and the trip took all day. Mail delivery was two or three times a week, depending on the weather]. Our grocery store was built across the street from the Wingfield home. [This was a general mercantile called the Ruidoso Store built and run by Ike Wingfield] It became a popular gathering place for campers, ranchers and people for miles around. The store handled everything from horseshoes, nails, bulk sugar, flour, and fresh meat. Much of the merchandise was hauled in from Roswell, some came from Champion and Hanau, Bonnell Hardware in Tularosa, Titsworth in Capitan, and from several firms in El Paso.

Gasoline was sold from a single yellow gas pump in front of the store, with coal oil or kerosene from a barrel with a hand pump. Eggs were gathered from the hen house just back of the store. And the restroom was the little house that sat down across the ditch near where the wash pots were.

In 1922 a barber shop was added to the east side of the store. We had no churches here but there were camp meetings at Angus, Alto and Bonito and we always attended when we could. Later the Baptists built a church about where the circle now is, and Reverend Barcus, Reverend Singleton and Mrs. Nora Pistole were responsible for a little church. The Catholic Church in Skyland was built in the early thirties.

In 1923 a cold drink stand was added on [to the store] and at eleven years old, it was my first partnership business. The first electric lights were powered by Delco plants. Ours was installed in 1922 at the Wingfield residence to serve the new business operations. As records show, Joe Mogel constructed the first little light plant in 1926 under the hill in what was our potato patch. About this time, people from El Paso and Roswell were building more and more cabins. Mrs. Amelia Church and her sister built the first rental cabins. Warren Barrett opened a small grocery store on the road leading to the Upper Canyon and put in a few summer rental cabins.

Ruidoso was becoming a popular place as cabins and little businesses moved up the river from Wingfield's home, store, dairy and post office. J. C. Duffo from Roswell put in a bakery in the Upper Canyon, a treat for summer visitors. Real estate, as inexpensive as it was, began to be a factor in Ruidoso's growth. Della Wingfield recalled:

In 1923, Horace E. Carter purchased eighty acres of land from Mary Purrington [another Ruidoso pioneer family]. I have a check showing Daddy had leased this eighty acres of land in 1921 for the huge sum of $8.80. Carter had a big free barbecue and began to sell lots. Ruidoso was off to a good start. My folks also built a roller rink which was used as a dance hall on Wednesday and Saturday nights.

H. A. Borcherding established an Odd Fellows camp on Cedar Creek and brought children up from the Southwestern Children's Home in El Paso. This was a project begun by the Odd Fellows so children could spend a cool vacation there. In 1926 my folks gave ten acres of land to the Southwestern Children's Home and since that time many of the children have spent a few weeks here in Ruidoso. One of the boys lived with the folks and has called Opal and me "sister" these many years.

The first riding stables were owned by Alfred Hale who also sold firewood from a horse-drawn wagon.

In the mid-twenties the turnoff from Highway 70 into Ruidoso from El Paso or Roswell was at a little grocery store and one-pump filling station called Ruidoso Junction. An automobile dealership occupies that spot today.

The Junction store was built and operated by Ed Gililland in 1925. Ike Wingfield and John Mims purchased the store from Gililland in 1927. About this time, fortune smiled on some of these people, particularly Clayton Bennett who had recently come to New Mexico for his health. The climate was obviously beneficial, since Bennett and his wife Helen still operate their neatly trimmed Indian store on U.S. 70. Wingfield hired Bennett to clerk in the Junction store. Bennett was always the entrepreneur while Wingfield was a born cowboy and rancher.

Long-time Ruidosoan Bill Hart has fond memories about both Wingfield and Bennett. Bill Hart says that, "Ol' Clayton got on his feet to where he could get around a little and Wingfield had that

In 1904 the Ruidoso Post Office was moved from Dowlin's Mill to a new location across Highway 70 from today's Bennett's Indian Store. (Herb Brunell Collection)

Ruidoso Store and post office circa 1925 after it moved from Highway 70. This location is now the site of Pine Tree Square on Sudderth Drive. (Evelyn Estes Collection)

Main Street (now Sudderth) in the 1920s. At left is the Wingfield home. Across the dirt street is the post office and Wingfield general store. The old Alto road (now Mechem Drive) intersected about where the auto is in center of picture. (Herb Brunell Collection)

store [the one in the downtown area] filled with old, old merchandise. Canned goods and stuff. And Clayton propositioned him one day with, 'Mr. Wingfield, why don't we sell this stuff?'

"Wingfield said, 'Well, hell, we cain't sell it. It's been there years and nobody wants it.' Clayton says, 'Well, I could sell it.' Wingfield says, 'Go ahead and do it.' So Clayton gets the dust off those canned goods and makes pyramids and displays and puts up signs like Two for a Dollar, 25 cents and all that. In a week's time they sold the whole stock of merchandise."

Most of the early cabin builders seem to have had the same feelings of elation after driving up from the desert; they fell in love with the place and the cheerful little river. Carolyn Mayfield Driver of El Paso still enjoys going up to the family property by the river more than seventy years after their first cabin was built. Her mother, Mrs. Davis Mayfield, at age ninety, jotted down her reminiscences of early Ruidoso and fortunately, they were saved by her daughter. Mrs. Mayfield recalls how it all began for them:

During the summer of 1922, when I was pregnant with Carolyn, we went camping in Ruidoso. The whole family, including the dog, drove up in an old Haynes car. It was to be the beginning of the most important and happy part of our life.

We drove up the road past the old Wingfield house, the post office and general store. The road stopped there. The boys opened the gate to the cow lot and we drove on up the river about one half mile from the second bridge across the river. Here we pitched camp. Two cabins had been completed, built by the Sweeneys and the Dixons of El Paso.

I told my husband I was going to have a cabin there and would stay there the rest of the summer. We moved to a tiny empty shack down the river and Davis immediately began to make arrangements to build us a cabin on the Ruidoso!

We leased a lot next door to the Sweeney family and Davis went to get carpenters and materials for our cabin from the sawmill. Mr. White, the owner of the sawmill, refused to sell Davis some siding from a small stack. When asked why he wouldn't sell it he replied, "Well, if I sell it to you, what would I do when the next customer came and wanted some?"

Business people in early Ruidoso were a rather laid-back lot, the word greed didn't seem to be in their vocabulary. Ike Wingfield with his amusing

This photo was taken before businesses lined the street in midtown Ruidoso. The area was called Ruidoso Springs (circa 1920). Building at right was later the location of the Wild Snail. Note the two tents in center. The little log cabin remained until the 1940s. Coke Hedgecoke had a shooting gallery about where the tent and cars are. (Evelyn Estes Collection)

approach to merchandising furnished another tale for Mrs. Mayfield:

I had an experience somewhat like the sawmill incident when, after a few days I went to the country store for supplies. I asked for chocolate Hershey bars and Mr. Wingfield said, "I haven't got any more. They just sold so fast that I quit bothering with them." I asked for tuna and he looked around the walls and the ceiling where horse collars, bridles, kerosene lamps, etc. were hanging and he shook his head and said, "Nary a tuna!"

Later, Carolyn and the boys hunted for coins underneath Wingfield's store. The floorboards were wide and there was about one half inch of space between them so that coins would sometimes fall through. Carolyn remembers the same kind of flooring in our cabin and that she enjoyed sweeping the floor because the dirt fell through and you could "see the difference immediately."

Well, Davis got the house built in five days! There was no provision for water in the house and every drop we used was hauled up from the river in tin buckets. There was no ice, so we kept the milk in jars standing in water in a little screened window cupboard, the "cooler." We had no bathroom, of course, but a well-beaten path led to a sturdy Chick Sales up the hill behind the house.

The big event of the week was the arrival of the men from El Paso, the daddies, bearing mail, gifts and sometimes guests. The men were tired when they arrived because they usually had to fix a flat or two. Or else in rainy weather maybe they had been stuck in the mud in Dark Canyon and hauled out by the Indians who were waiting there with their horses. In those days it took many hours to come from El Paso as the road was little more than a trail winding in and out among the sandhills. Driving was so slow, our dog, Dick, could run as fast as the cars.

Ruidoso was a very quiet little place. There were no bowling alleys, picture shows, cafes, shops, motels, supermarkets, ski runs and golf courses. Horseback riding was the only amusement that cost any money. The horse stable was run by Mr. Hale near where the river turns to go under the first bridge. Later, a very special treat for Carolyn was to take an all-day ride with a group from the stable. It was costly: $1.50.

But all this was to change forever as the twenties gave way to the thirties. Within a decade, Ruidoso took on an all-new look.

Alfred Hale (standing) was a favorite with kids in 1926. In wagon, left to right are Ellis Moore, Carolyn Mayfield and Bill Mayfield. (Courtesy Carolyn Driver)

The road through Dark Canyon, now Highway 70, was a nightmare of mud for pilgrims heading to Ruidoso. (Courtesy Carolyn Driver)

Ike Wingfield in 1947. He and his family helped build Ruidoso. (Photo by Carmon Phillips; Evelyn Estes Collection)

Alto

Louise Perkins, now of Sun City, Arizona was born on the VV Ranch, where her father, the late Barney Luck worked after World War I. In 1921, he became postmaster at Alto, five miles north of Ruidoso. Alto, with its picturesque setting high in the mountains, had been a thriving settlement since before the turn of the century. In 1901, nearby farms and ranches furnished enough population to establish a post office. Louise Perkins grew up in Alto and remembers that "the original Alto post office was in a log cabin and our house was in back of it. As Alto grew, Daddy built a larger building and an addition to the post office. He had a general store and a gasoline and oil pump, the first filling station in the community. He also provided water for the public from a faucet in front of the store.

"The summer tourist trade boosted our business, mostly people from up at Eagle Creek Lodge, four miles west on Eagle Creek. People from El Paso and Carrizozo had a cabin association on property they leased from the forest service. The post office was the hub of what happened around here. Our country schoolhouse used to be here, and it had all grades in one room."

In 1953, Barney Luck developed heart problems and was advised to move from Alto's high altitude. Louise Perkins remembers that her father owned the property now occupied by today's High Country Lodge and sold it for $2,000 in '53 or '54. It sold later for $50,000.

One of the largest ponderosa pines remaining along the Ruidoso. Cabin in right background (circa 1920s) still has canvas awning to keep rain off the porch. Before electricity, milk, butter and eggs were kept in screened window coolers. (Frank Mangan)

On the Coe Ranch this old barn defies the ravages of time along the lower Ruidoso. The Coe family began arriving in Lincoln County in 1859. (Frank Mangan)

9
The Lure of the Ruidoso

IN 1929 the American economic system broke down. "Back East somewhere," they said. The effect of the stock market crash hadn't reached southern New Mexico in 1929, but across the nation the gloom of the Great Depression spread like a great, gray blanket.

The president of Union Cigar watched his stock plummet from $113 to $4 in one day and promptly jumped to his death from the ledge of a New York building. Seventy-five thousand men lost their jobs in 1931 after Henry Ford closed his Detroit plant. The Depression sounded its depths in 1932 when one-third of the population of Pennsylvania was on relief. Families all over the country managed to live on stale bread, thin soup and garbage.

In spite of all this the little village of Ruidoso fared pretty well. Since there were no bankers or stockbrokers, few people were hurt to any degree. Besides, if a despondent loser had leaped off the roof of the Navajo Lodge, he probably would have suffered nothing more severe than a bad sprain.

Small area farmers who couldn't make it, pulled up stakes and headed for El Paso and other cities for what they hoped would be greener pastures. Most people hung on tightly to what they had, and although money was scarce, prices dropped accordingly. In *The Ruidoso News* of June 24, 1932, Warren Barrett advertised summer cabins for a rental fee of two dollars a day. Barrett also advertised four loaves of bread for 25 cents, six candy bars for 25 cents, Swift's Premium Bacon for 29 cents a pound, and butter for 23 cents a pound. But then a lot of people didn't have 23 cents. In spite of hard times, new businesses appeared in 1932: Holloman Bros. Lumber yard, Brook's Grocery, P.P. Doughty's Alta Vista Store, and a meat market. Barrett's Grocery was remodeled and enlarged.

In its July 10 edition that year, *The Ruidoso News* headlined a story that read, "RUIDOSO HAS REAL MOVIES. If you haven't seen and heard the talking pictures at Skyland in the Tent Theatre, a surprise awaits you. It is the first time that Ruidoso has had such splendid entertainment. The talking equipment is the best, and an effort

Ye Olde Pyne Tavern, one of Ruidoso's earliest restaurants, was built by Jack Hull who later became postmaster and a leader in the village. Water for the dining room came from the river; all cooking was done on a wood stove. (Courtesy Marie Rooney)

has been made to book only strictly first class pictures that are suitable for the whole family. *The Ruidoso News* recommends the Tent Theatre to the community."

Oddly enough, Ruidoso actually came of age during the Depression. Some families in El Paso, for example, who had been accustomed to heading for Long Beach or Santa Monica to cool off in the Pacific surf, were not able to afford this luxury in the thirties. But they could afford to go to Ruidoso and rent a cabin—or even build one. The *El Paso Herald* came up with a promotion that brought many new people to Ruidoso: For a six-month subscription to the *Herald* you could buy a building lot in the Skyland area for $59.50. The lots were small, but the promotion caught on and a number of new cabins were built.

One of the best bargains during the Depression was the purchase of the Medler cabin, the first summer place in Ruidoso. It snuggled in a se-

cluded spot near the Mescalero Reservation fence and was owned by Edward and Lillian Medler. They had moved to California and were interested in getting some good renters. Ernest McDaniel recalls, "My father with my mother and sister rented this cabin from Judge Medler in the early thirties. They enjoyed it so much that when they left they told Judge Medler that if he ever wanted to sell it, they wanted first choice. So during the Roosevelt Bank Holiday in the Depression, he wired my father that if he had $250 cash, he'd send him the deed to the place by return mail. My father sent him travelers checks which he always had on hand. An acre and seven-tenths. Right on the river, too."

Originally from Austin, Texas, Ernest and his brother Robert now live in a historic adobe house on the lower Ruidoso River near Glencoe where they raise horses and cattle. For many years Ernest held the record for catching the largest fish

Main Street in Ruidoso about 1930. Traffic was not a major problem except when the dirt street turned into a sea of mud during the rainy season. (Herb Brunell Collection)

in the river. It was a twenty-four inch brown trout caught in a large deep pool in front of the McDaniel cabin in 1934. The trophy fish was proudly mounted and it still hangs on the wall.

The McDaniel cabin was on a forty-acre plot owned by the Cree family, and the property was shared by some seven other families. According to one of the original owners, Dr. Earl Malone of Roswell, Cree wouldn't sell the property. "We were all leasing from the Crees who only charged some silly amount like fifty cents or a dollar a year. My dad kept after him and ran into one of the Cree boys one day in Santa Fe. He talked to him again about buying the land. And sure enough Cree offered to sell it."

The group bought the whole forty acres and in 1934 formed an association called the Ruidoso Cabin Owners. The corporation members were E.M. Nicholas, Ernest McDaniel, S.P. Johnson, G.W. Nickson, Meldrum Gray, G.E. French and

R.L. Malone. Each family owned twenty-five shares, and the stock could only be sold to somebody in the bloodline. They couldn't rent their places, but could let other people use them. They couldn't sell their shares without first offering them to the corporation.

This unique arrangement worked out well. After more than sixty years many of the same families enjoy the original cabins and this unspoiled piece of the Upper Canyon. Little has changed in this still-pristine semi-wilderness where some of the owners have their own springs for ice cold drinking water. The largest tree in Ruidoso is located here although it was struck by lightning a few years ago. It had to be cut down and it lies next to the river as a monument to the past. This Douglas fir was known throughout Ruidoso as the Big Tree, and when it was officially measured in 1958, it was nineteen feet, one and a fourth inches in circumference.

During the Depression, people were buying lots and building cabins in Hollywood, New Mexico, a little settlement on the eastern edge of Ruidoso. A post office was established in 1926 by George Friedenbloom who also operated a general store. Peggy Snell Shaifer (at right) remembers visiting Hollywood in the 1920s when her family drove up from El Paso. She remembers huge signs along the highway reminding motorists of lots for sale. Today, Hollywood still has a thriving post office, serving its patrons well as a branch of the Ruidoso post office.
(Courtesy Peggy Shaifer)

In 1936 Ike Wingfield resigned as Ruidoso's postmaster and his good friend, a well-liked entrepreneur named Jack Hull was appointed the next year. Hull was to leave a strong imprint on Ruidoso as an early contributor to the community's growth; some called him "Mr. Ruidoso." He was born in Parkersburg, West Virginia in 1887 and came to Ruidoso in 1923 from Roswell. Hull never lived in Texas but was probably acquainted with more Texans than many candidates for office in dozens of Texas counties.

Hull's daughter, Marie Rooney, lives in Ruidoso and has vivid memories of the family driving the rough road from Roswell up to Ruidoso. Marie remembers that "in 1920 and '21 we camped out on the river where the Ruidoso State Bank is now. Across the street where the Plaza Center is located was the Town Pump, on what they called Carter's Forty Acres. Everybody could fill up their buckets at the pump.

"Other families camped as we did, in tents, and we all learned to love Ruidoso. Later, after my

The Ruidoso Lodge provided fine accomodations in early Ruidoso. From the looks of the cars, this picture was taken in the 1920s. The Lodge is still in business, west of the post office and near the first bridge in the Upper Canyon. (Evelyn Estes Collection)

Since it has been absorbed by Ruidoso Downs, you have to look fast to spot Hollywood today. This photo of Bennett's Garage was taken about 1930.

father became postmaster, he built a bowling alley just west of the post office at the end of today's Pine Tree Square. It was a social center in the late thirties."

The Hull family's first commercial venture was called Ye Olde Pyne Tavern, a restaurant located in what is now a vacant lot at the entrance to the Upper Canyon. It was one of the earliest tourist accomodations. In conjunction with the tavern, Hull built four little rent cabins with pine slab siding for fifty dollars each. Marie remembers that the restaurant "didn't have water in those early days, and water served in the dining room came from the river. Cooking for the restaurant was all done on a wood stove."

Jack Hull's accomplishments in making Ruidoso a special place to visit or to live year-round are legion. He aided in securing a Chamber of Commerce, a Lions Club, Ruidoso High School (in the late forties), and a Boy Scout Troop. He helped organize the Ruidoso State Bank, and acquired CCC (Civilian Conservation Corps) camps during the Roosevelt administration for improving roads and parks. Among other things, he helped incorporate the village in 1945.

Ruidoso's original Main Street was renamed Sudderth Drive in honor of John Sudderth, another prominent Ruidoso resident and highway commission chairman who was successful in getting the muddy road paved from end to end.

Marie Rooney remembers a number of the businesses from the thirties that lined the street. She recalls:

The Ruidoso Golf Course (with sand greens) extended from the north of what is now the Public Library down to near the Junction at Highway 70. Horace Carter was one of the first developers. In 1925 he sold forty acres in Carrizo Canyon that adjoined the Mescalero Reservation to the New Mexico Military Institute as a summer camp. It is now Carrizo Lodge. Farther on up today's Sudderth was the Midway Garage. Then, all bars and nightlife: the Mint Bar, Central, Keck's Place and others. Also the Pueblo Theater, now The Aspen Tree Bookstore north of Brunell's Department Store.

On the left side of the street was Coke's Shooting Gallery, Fred Riley's Cafe, Davis Bowling Alley and

Bar. I think a lot of these places had slot machines. I know the Mint did. The Covered Wagon Curio store was along this stretch. It's still there and claims to be the oldest curio store in Ruidoso. Further on up was Wingfield's store, and next to it was the Britt Drug Store, post office and then my father's bowling alley. There was also a pool hall connected to the bowling alley. Montie's Riding Stables were just past today's Traffic Circle."

Roswell's Robert Keyes is a modern-day mountain man who has seen country around Ruidoso known only to God and *National Geographic*. Keyes is an inveterate explorer in the Sacramento Mountains and probably the best trout fisherman who ever wet a leader in the Ruidoso River. Back in the thirties, it was a bad day when he didn't catch his limit by noon, and he was miles away from town on the North Fork of the Ruidoso high in the Reservation. That was when the limit was twenty-five fish per person. Even in late July or early August he brought back trout packed in snow from the high reaches of the river since snow remained under overhanging rocks into mid-summer. In 1947 after he returned from Europe in World War II, he and his wife, Alerta, an English war bride, built a cabin by themselves on Keyes Drive.

In the early twenties Keyes' family spent summers in Ruidoso and owned the fourteenth cabin built in the Upper Canyon. He laughs when he describes the automobile trips from Roswell to Ruidoso. They were rides up a corrugated, rock-riddled dirt road—all-day trips in 1924. The family forded the Hondo and Ruidoso rivers fourteen times each way in their wooden-spoked open-air Dodge. Sometimes they had to wait for water to recede after rains upstream. They carried three extra tires each trip for insurance against blowouts. The radiator normally boiled over when they reached Border Hill where the mountains intrude into the Pecos Valley plains. Everybody but the driver got out and pushed.

Lots of folks started at daybreak in order to eat lunch at Bonnell's Ranch, which had become a popular stopover for weary travelers. The White Mountain Inn in the Ruidoso valley was a favorite spot for motorists to spend the night while traveling from Roswell to Ruidoso. But the days of passengers pushing their cars up hills were numbered.

New Mexico State Highway Department's records show that the strip of U.S. 70 from Roswell to the Lincoln County Line was graded and gravel-surfaced between 1923 and 1933, then oil treated by 1935. The entire highway from Roswell to Ruidoso was oil treated by 1938 and cars were zipping along.

Meanwhile, the Keyes family kept a string of horses in a corral on their place and rode up and down the Ruidoso, even chasing wild mustangs on Sierra Blanca. Robert remembers the first airport which was near the second hole of the old golf course. That course extended almost to the Junction. There have been three airports altogether. The second one was located at Cree Meadows, but proved to be a terrifying experience on landings and takeoffs because of down drafts and short runways. The current airport, built in 1986, is located on Fort Stanton Mesa. Keyes remembers riding horses on the Alto Road, a scary trail, especially in the rain. Keyes points to a spot on what is now Mechem Drive and says:

Right after turning onto Mechem from Sudderth, was a fenced entrance to Cree's pastures. There was a cattle guard so cars could go through to Alto five miles north. You had to open his gate if you wanted to go through on horses or wagons. From there on to Alto the land was all used for cattle grazing, just tall grass from what is now the Blue Spruce RV Park all the way to Alto. Cree had a sign offering a huge area for $10,000. The sign was there for a long time. Today part of the pasture is Cree Meadows Golf Course and The Links of Sierra Blanca.

Wingfield ran his cattle here but the land still belonged to the Crees. It was all good grazing land because the forest wasn't there then. The trees you see there now aren't very old. Small pines, once kept down by grazing cattle, have sprung up and altered the landscape. Even Peter Hurd's painting of his house down at San Patricio shows a fairly barren hill in the background. You look at that hill now, it's almost covered with timber. I remember when there weren't any trees around Sunset on the Roswell road. There's more pine trees and vegetation now than there was sixty years ago.

The little creeks around here add quite a bit of water to the Ruidoso. Cedar Creek goes underground for a while and then runs through Gavilan Canyon. Paradise Canyon Creek and Cedar Creek all drain into the Ruidoso River in the downtown area. Eagle Creek comes out of the mountains and enters into Alto Lake.

During the Depression, people were buying lots and building cabins in Hollywood, New Mexico, a little settlement at the eastern edge of Ruidoso. Although a post office was established in 1926, Hollywood was destined to be nothing more than a good-sized real estate development. Not many movie stars in dark glasses strolled its main street, but its thriving post office still serves its patrons well as a branch of the Ruidoso Post Office.

The first postmaster was George Friedenbloom, who operated a general store and had come from Hollywood, Florida. So he named the post office in honor of his hometown. There are still about a dozen post offices throughout the United States with the name Hollywood.

Peggy Snell Shaifer, who now lives in the Texas Hill Country recalls early-day Hollywood:

In the late 1920s my mom and dad and I and sometimes friends would drive from El Paso to Hollywood. We were friends of Mr. and Mrs. Friedenbloom. Mr. Friedenbloom was the postmaster. His property was pretty extensive, and I remember huge signs along the highway reminding motorists of lots for sale.

The post office adjoined their home, and after breakfast Mr. Friedenbloom would let me count the money and "help" him sort mail. Big deal for a little kid. I loved it. In the early 1930s I remember driving into Ruidoso with friends and we would shop at the general store [Wingfield's]. We would go to Weldon's riding stables to ride for an hour. It cost fifty cents an hour and it was really a treat. We were always amazed that the horses knew when the hour was up, then turned and trotted back to the stable.

Years later when I was a junior at Austin High School in El Paso, Marianne Kissel and I went back to Hollywood where we spent two weeks with the now-widowed Mrs. Friedenbloom. There was still a water pump at the kitchen sink, chickens in the pen and a two-seat privy out back.

There was a big general store across Highway 70 that sold peppermint sticks and post cards and fresh fruits and vegetables and lots of other stuff. The store smelled like leather and kerosene. It was neat. But the clerk had

Great Western Days was celebrated in the summer of 1930 in Midtown Ruidoso. Sitting on back of truck at far right is Della Wingfield. (Evelyn Estes Collection) Below, Ike Wingfield's general store and Ruidoso post office about 1930. This is now the location of Pine Tree Square on Sudderth Drive. (Herb Brunell Collection)

a roving eye and gleam which we didn't like. So we always left as soon as we made a purchase, and never got to look at all the Indian pottery in the back room.

You have to look twice to spot Hollywood today, since it's been absorbed by Ruidoso Downs. But there are still people who have lived here more than a half century. Two of them are C. L. "Bones" Wright and his wife, Joetyne, who own a lumber company on Highway 70, next door to the former Hollywood post office. Wright moved to Hollywood after World War II. Joetyne would have been born there but since there were no doctors or a hospital in Ruidoso, her mother journeyed to Roswell. Joetyne says:

My mother brought me here when I was two weeks old. We lived in a little one-room log cabin with a dirt floor. It had paper—called red rosin—on the walls to cover up the air holes. And it was full of centipedes. My mother was deathly afraid that a centipede would fall in my crib but that never happened.
My dad was Elger Miller and my grandfather was F.A. Miller. His headquarters for ranching operations was where the racetrack is today. He came here in the 1880s from Colfax County, New Mexico, when he was fourteen years old and went to work as a cowpuncher for the Crees at the VV Ranch.
Later, Dad and my grandfather had forest permits for a cattle operation of about two hundred and fifty cows. Their horse lot was up Cedar Creek which later became the old ski run. Where Innsbruck Village is today, they had a gathering corral. We gathered, branded and butchered and either drove cattle down to around Hollywood for winter pasture or took them up to the high country for summer pasture. Most of that country belonged to the Crees and most of the settlements were not where Ruidoso is now because it was too hilly. There were some settlements up Eagle Creek and around Nogal long before Ruidoso.
Today's race track location was part of our upper field, where we grew alfalfa. We also had a cornfield there too.
In 1933, my dad became postmaster of Hollywood and we lived in back of the post office. The building is still there next door to our lumber yard. A man named Craig who had a sawmill here planted two beautiful little blue spruce trees on each side of the post office, and they are still there over sixty years later, huge but looking sort of sad probably because of the highway automobile exhaust.
I went to grade school here at what they call Stetson

School, a four-room adobe building. People today would have a fit, since it had the center adobe wall propped up with 2 by 4s because it was about to fall down. The only heat we had was a pot-bellied stove. We never missed school because of snow. We went to school in an old sort of truck that had a chicken house put on it for a top. Fond memories.

When Peggy Shaifer and her parents and hundreds of other families from El Paso discovered Ruidoso in the late twenties and early thirties, the trip north through the Tularosa Basin was formidable. The Basin is a great pocket of sand, sun and sparse vegetation about thirty miles wide and two hundred miles long. Historian C. L. Sonnichsen once described it as "a parched desert where everything, from cactus to cowmen carries a weapon of some sort, and the only creatures who sleep with their eyes closed are dead. In all the sun-scorched and sand-blasted reaches of the Southwest there is no grimmer region. Only the fierce and the rugged can live here—prickly pear and mesquite, rattlesnake and tarantula."

This is what El Paso motorists faced in the late twenties and early thirties as they headed for the mountains. The pavement ended at the Texas-New Mexico line, and from there on, their old cars plowed through a hundred miles of sand and alkali flats before reaching Alamogordo and Tularosa. This route later became U.S. 54, but in these early years it was only a series of trails through miles of red sand dunes crowned with the lethal thorns of mesquite bushes. The dunes were (and still are) quite close together, so cars moved along at ten to twenty miles an hour twisting and turning around each dune. The children were usually relegated to the back seat, and since they didn't know when the next dip or turn was coming, it was like a carnival ride.

Motorists aimed their vehicles north, following closely the railroad tracks laid at the turn of the century by Charles B. Eddy. They just pointed toward the fuzzy outline of Sierra Blanca, a hundred miles away. The mountain was easy to see because air pollution was almost unheard of. Air conditioning meant opening windows, and motorists carried canvas water bags on bumpers

In 1936, this was the main road from Ruidoso Junction into downtown Ruidoso. The wide open pasture is now home for a number of Ruidoso's churches. (Herb Brunell Collection)

for inevitable over-heating stops. They followed tire tracks of preceding cars through the red sand until they reached an area where tracks were covered by blowing dust, or where another car had gotten stuck. Then they turned off the beaten path and improvised a road of their own. Part of the road was more than a mile wide.

My sister Romaine usually survived the ride through the desert until we reached the altitude change at Round Mountain. And then would come her plaintive whisper, "I'm gonna throw up!"

Romaine recalls: "The problem actually began long before we reached Round Mountain. The ninety miles of U.S. 54 from El Paso to Alamogordo was an eternity of unannounced dips in the road —there must have been hundreds of them. It was always hot and dusty and the only thing to look at was the road signs advertising CLABBER GIRL. To this day, I get queasy thinking

about that urpy trip every summer. But there was some relief when we reached Alamogordo. We often stopped for an ice cream cone at the wonderful old drug store where we sat at the marble counter."

It was an all-day trip, starting early in the morning and arriving in Ruidoso in the evening. The cool air and smell of pine trees was the reward.

The plight of pilgrims journeying to New Mexico's mountains began to ease somewhat in 1926. The State Highway department graded and gravel-surfaced the road from the Texas state line to Orogrande between 1926 and 1931. By 1936 the road was oil treated to Alamogordo, and by 1948 U.S. 54 was paved all the way.

In the thirties, Ruidosoans still didn't have indoor plumbing or around-the-clock electricity. Water for drinking and bathing came either

116

directly from the river or from seeping springs. In 1926 a man from El Paso named Joe Mogel built the first electric light plant to service Ruidoso. It was a little Fairbanks-Morse electric plant down by the river below today's Pine Tree Square near Sudderth and Mechem.

The plant shut down and the lights went out every night about nine o'clock, then came on again the next morning. Everybody had a houseful of kerosene lamps which they fired up when the lights went out. But most people took the inconvenience in stride, since there was no TV and precious few radios. In Ruidoso it was early-to-bed time.

Then along came a gem of a man named Bill Hart. He was originally from Lubbock where he got into the power business while a student at Texas Tech. Hart recalls:

I got the idea to put in a power plant in Ruidoso from two Fairbanks-Morse salesmen. We came over here and looked Mogel's little plant over, then went to El Paso to see him and he says, "Yes sir, I want to sell it." The way it finally ended up, we agreed on a price and submitted it to him. And he said, "Well, I got somebody else that wants it too, so wait and see." In the meantime we got in the car and came to Ruidoso. Before we got here I got a weather report that Ruidoso had a major snowstorm. This was September 3, 1936. We had three feet of snow.

The storm broke everything down, roads closed, it was awful bad. So I got on the phone and called this guy in El Paso and I guess by that time he'd heard about the storm and he knew what the condition was. I made him another offer and he accepted it. We started rebuilding everything the first few days of September in 1936, so that's what got me started in the power plant business in Ruidoso..

The very night I came in from El Paso in the snow, I got in about 11 o'clock and drove up in front of the power plant. I got my suitcase out and heard that old Fairbanks engine miss a lick. And I knew what was happening. It was time for them to turn off the lights, so I went running down there and told the guy, "Leave 'em on a little longer. Give me time to get in the house."

So he turned it back on for another hour or so and I moved into the basement under the office building. From then on we ran it twenty-four hours a day. We had interruptions of course but they weren't turn-offs.

I remember during the wintertime for the next three

or four years, hunting was awful good back up there in Cedar Creek and this ol' boy was working for me and we were both avid hunters. So we'd take off about daylight and hunt all morning as long as we could hear that engine back in town. We'd hunt turkey and deer up there. If we heard that engine die out then we beat it down there to start it back up. You could hear it—putt, putt, putt—for five miles easily.

A few years later we had another big storm in April or May and it broke the trees down all the way to the Reservation line. Trees that were no bigger around than your arm bent over and touched the ground. Acres of 'em. And they took the wires down with 'em. Well, I had a 2,300 volt power line all the way to the Reservation. Way up there. I was serving those early cabins like the Johnsons, McDaniels, Martins, Malones, Grays, Keyes, and many others.

Anyway, I hired this kid who had come into town just out of school and he wanted to be an electrician, a lineman. He got up there on those trees, handling that 2,300 volt electricity and got knocked out of a big tree. We thought we'd lost him but he came out of it.

I called the company The Ruidoso Power and Light. It wasn't all that lucrative for me though. I just couldn't keep up with the growth of Ruidoso. I put in another engine every year for five years and each time I had to mortgage everything I had. I sold out in 1945 to the Community Public Service, which was the forerunner of the Texas New Mexico Power Company.

I could see that building was going to continue and in about 1940 I went downtown there and put in a water system for the town. I had about a half mile of water lines in the middle of the street with customers on both sides. This was the first water line they had. We called it the Ruidoso Water Company. I had a well down by the river behind what used to be a skating rink and we piped it right up to the street.

At the upper end, George McCarty and his wife had this grocery store. Well, George had a well drilled behind that grocery store, so we tied the two together and he gave me that well. And then I had water comin' in both ends of the pipeline. I expect you could still find the well there now, but it may have been covered up. In 1974, I was a Lincoln County commissioner and we put in a water system over in the town of Lincoln.

Bill Hart, now retired and living in Roswell, will be remembered as the man who turned on the lights and water in Ruidoso.

Adios Bonito City

The most valuable commodity in the West was, and still is, water. Land without water rights for a farmer was no land at all.

Settlers and gold miners who moved into the meadows and forests of Bonito Canyon in the early 1880s were blessed with a plentiful supply of water from the Rio Bonito that raced down the mountains year around. The homesteaders called their little community Bonito City, a rather grand name for the cluster of log buildings that housed a saloon, post office, schoolhouse, church, general store, a hotel called The Mayberry House, and a number of comfortable residences.

The haunted Mayberry House. (*El Paso Times*)

Set amid lofty peaks twelve miles northwest of Ruidoso, apple orchards and livestock of the Bonito settlers flourished in the seven-thousand-foot meadows at the edge of the forests. Trout fishing was excellent in the Bonito River.

God was in his heaven and all was right with the world, or so it seemed when two events took place that would cause this serene and pleasant community to literally disappear. The centerpiece of Bonito City was the two-story log hotel called the Mayberry House operated by Mr. and Mrs. John Mayberry. They had three children; John, Eddie and Nellie. On the night of May 5, 1885, the Mayberry House leaped into the record books with one of New Mexico's most bizarre crimes.

Earlier that evening a number of miners ate supper there and left. Only two guests had rooms, Dr. R. E. Flynn from Ohio and a youth named Martin Nelson seemed to be pleasant and inoffensive roomers. All were in bed by ten o'clock. About one in the morning, Nelson arose and knocked on the bedroom door of the two Mayberry boys. John awakened and opened the door, at which point Nelson fired two rifle shots, killing him instantly. He then turned on the seven-year-old Eddie who was screaming in bed. Nelson killed him with a single blast.

Dr. Flynn, hearing the shooting, rushed from his room and was shot through the head. John Mayberry, after hearing the screams, was making his way up the dark stairs from the first floor when a shot through the heart dropped him on the landing. Blood was everywhere. Mayberry's daughter, Nellie, appeared and was shot through the side and left for dead. She later recovered.

Mrs. Mayberry ran upstairs, where Nelson shot her in the chest but failed to kill her. She stumbled downstairs with blood streaming all the way to her feet, leaving bloody footprints visible on the stairs years later. She fled to the nearest cabin for help, but Nelson followed, executed her, and threw her body into an irrigation ditch. Pete Nelson, the saloonkeeper (no relation) appeared on the scene, grappled with the youth but was no match for the murderer. Mark Nelson shot him to death and left his body bleeding in the sandy street. The next victim was the storekeeper, Herman Beck, who came out to learn the cause of the gunshots. Nelson killed him with one bullet.

Bonito's terrified citizens locked themselves in their homes until morning while Nelson roamed at large, finally climbing up a nearby mountain.

Next morning, as Charlie Berry, Rudolph Schultz and Don Campbell were standing in the street discussing the murders, they sighted Nelson returning down the mountain. He saw the men, brought up his rifle to fire, but was an instant too late. Berry felled him with a bullet through the heart. Nelson's last shot went harmlessly into the air as he fell.

Total casualties were eight killed, including the murderer, and one wounded. It was years before the people of Bonito City recovered from the shock, and for fifteen years nobody set foot in the log hotel. Folks said it was haunted, told stories of shrieks and groans in the dead of night, of seeing lights flicker from room to room, or hearing muffled shots. Those who peeped though the dusty windows could see the bloody footprints left by Mrs. Mayberry's feet. The murderer was buried at Bonito with his head pointing down. Folklorists say this custom was to prevent the buried person from walking as a ghost.

Gradually Bonito City died. The final blow came when the railroad arrived on the desert below and took a business-like approach to acquiring water rights in the Bonito Valley.

Since the turn of the century when Charles B. Eddy built his El Paso and Northeastern Railroad through the Tularosa Basin to Carrizozo and beyond, he was beset with the age-old lack of water in the West. But fate intervened in the form of the Phelps Dodge copper interests. Its Copper Queen mine in Bisbee, Arizona was booming and needed coal for smelting operations. The best option was to bring coal to Bisbee by rail from the Dawson coal fields in northeastern New Mexico. Eddy's railroad provided the perfect artery, but the stumbling block, of course, was finding sufficient water for steam engine boilers.

High in the mountains, the Rio Bonito provided the solution. Engineers agreed that plenty of pure water could be piped downhill to the railroad. The first problem: acquire the land and water rights from the Bonito homesteaders. Convinced the plan would work, Phelps Dodge bought the rail line in 1905, changed its name to the El Paso and Southwestern, and Eddy walked away a multi-millionaire.

The settlers didn't really want to sell their land and water rights, but most of them did. Few realized the sacrifices they were about to make, since there were no provisions to keep water for their own use. Generally the price was fair, although Mrs. Ben Robinson reportedly sold one hundred acres plus water rights for $8,000.

After the land sales, most settlers packed up and left Bonito Canyon and moved to towns nearby—like Nogal, Carrizozo and Capitan. Some worked on construction of the water pipeline which began in 1907. In four months pipeliners laid fifty miles of line ranging from six to sixteen inches in diameter. It was wooden pipe, made with two-inch wide slats of pine held together with flat steel bands. The pipe leaked constantly, but it did the job—sort of. Some disgruntled settlers shot and chopped holes in the line, and years later it was replaced with steel pipe.

The line originally extended from its intake on the Bonito River to Nogal Lake where the water was stored before moving down the mountains. Nogal was a natural mountain lake containing water year around. The water line serviced the railroad at Carrizozo as well as the town. It extended on north more than a hundred miles through Corona, Vaughn and the little town of Pastura in Guadalupe County east of Albuquerque. By 1914, water from the Bonito River became insufficient, and the railroad tied in another pipeline from Eagle Creek about three miles west of the town of Alto.

By 1924, the Southern Pacific acquired the railroad, and since the Nogal Lake reservoir was no longer adequate for the pipeline operation, the company constructed Bonito Dam in 1930 on the site of old Bonito City. Bonito City is now under seventy-five feet of water in

Bonito Lake. Water goes to Alamogordo and Holloman Air Force Base; the attractive Bonito lake provides a popular fishing spot for area residents and visitors.

Tampering with nature, even in the interests of progress, has its side effects. When Bonito Dam and Lake were first proposed, water users as far away as Roswell objected to the railroad diverting water from the river. They claimed their artesian wells would be dangerously depleted and filed suit against construction of Bonito Dam, but they got nowhere.

George Coe, who rode with Billy the Kid in the Lincoln County war, had this to say about diversion of the Bonito River water in 1934: "What became of the water that once ran joyously down the Bonito? It did not dry up, but it is not there….We are told for a paltry sum the settlers sold their water rights along the stream, and the water is impounded in huge reservoirs and is a valuable asset to the owners as a revenue-producer. A valley of beauty and prosperity has been reduced to a desert waste….The marked change in the scene in the last few years is most depressing. Rio Bonito no longer enchants the passer with its laughing water. Splendid orchards and flower gardens lie deserted and decaying…. There is a pathetic insolence in the way mere man dares ruthlessly to ravage Nature's rarest gems."

But nature's wounds have healed considerably during the past half century. In 1954 the Southern Pacific phased out its steam locomotives in favor of diesel engines making mountain water unnecessary. The city of Alamogordo quickly picked up the Bonito system and agreed to supply Holloman Air Force Base, with Bonito Lake as its reservoir. Six years later the last pipeline water was phased out in towns the railroad formerly supplied.

There are still times when the Bonito practically dries up below the reservoir. However during wet years, in spite of large quantities of its water destined for Alamogordo, the Bonito makes a sizeable contribution to the Ruidoso where the streams join to become the Hondo

The Rio Bonito tumbles down rocky ledges after leaving Bonito Dam. (Pancho Mangan)

River. The Bonito still serves water to Fort Stanton whose mission is to help the developmentally disabled. From 1896 until the 1960s it was a hospital for tuberculosis patients, and is now officially known as Fort Stanton Hospital and Training School. Several miles upstream from this quiet community the creek plunges into a rocky gorge making a downright lovely waterfall. God would seem to be back in his heaven.

Attractive Bonito Lake (above and left) provides a popular fishing spot for area residents and visitors. Bonito City, which once boasted a hotel, post office, saloon, schoolhouse and general store disappeared when the dam was built in 1930. It now lies under seventy-five feet of water in Bonito Lake. (Pancho Mangan)

The Cottage Eat Shop about 1940. Della Wingfield built this popular eatery at the intersection of Main and Alto roads, now Sudderth and Mechem. Building at right was Jack Hull's bowling alley, which is today a service station at the west end of Pine Tree Square. (Evelyn Estes Collection)

Business section of Ruidoso in the 1940s, looking east. Illegal gambling was at its height; bars and package stores lined both sides of the street. Some downtown favorites were the Ruidoso Bar, Mint Bar, Central Bar and Davis Bar. (Herb Brunell Collection)

10
Ruidoso Comes of Age

T WAS 1940. Europe erupted into war the previous year, the Great Depression had ended and Americans went back to work. They provided a steady flow of war materiel to help the British turn back the German Luftwaffe in the Battle of Britain. Dust bowl families ruined by drought and depression—the Okies and Texans and lots of New Mexicans—strapped mattresses and their worldy goods to the tops of old Model A's. They loaded the kids in the back seat, and headed for California to work in the yawning caverns of Americans defense plants. It would be only another year until America plunged into the conflict after the Japanese attack on Pearl Harbor.

Less than three months before the United States went to war, Ruidoso experienced its worst natural disaster, The Flood of 1941. Mother Nature went on a rampage and turned the normally rippling Rio Ruidoso into a raging torrent. The month of September had been rainier than usual. Long time Ruidoso resident Clayton Bennett remembers that it rained three weeks, night and day and the Ruidoso, Bonito, Cedar Creek and Eagle Creek were running full.

The coming drama was climaxed by two solid days of even heavier downpour, and by the evening of September twenty-second, the Ruidoso reached flood stage. The ground was saturated. During the night, people heard a deafening roar upstream as the surging water from the heavy deluge on the slopes of Sierra Blanca sent boulders as big as ice boxes bumping and crashing down the streambed. The water continued to rise. The river was pitch black with logs, mud, forest debris, and wreckage from flooded cabins. The flood badly damaged irrigated fields on the Ruidoso, Bonito and the Hondo.

Twenty years later writing in the *Ruidoso News* Dr. Burt F. Jenness, an early-day cabin owner in Ruidoso, described some of the drama of the first of two floods which occurred about a week apart:

People sat up all night checking the flood level, ready to move if the water reached the cabin foundations. By daylight, the flood had reached its peak but the devastation continued. The thunderous roar of the river and the sound of boulders pounding on other boulders increased.

All bridges were out and many residents were cut off from the village for a week. For days wrecked cabins [some say as many as seventy-five] were swept down river by the flood water as they gave way and broke apart at intervals. A few cabins were washed down intact or broke up in the current and were never seen again. Fortunately many cabins were vacant after Labor Day as most vacationers had left, and though

Three weeks of drenching rains turned the placid Ruidoso River into a raging torrent in September 1941.
Main Road in the Upper Canyon was severed, forming two streams which remained for years.
(Courtesy Robert Keyes)

During the flood, some cabins were washed down intact or broke apart in the current and
were never seen again. (Courtesy Robert Keyes)

property losses were heavy no lives were lost in Ruidoso. However, a resident of Ruidoso and Roswell, E. C. Trieb, was drowned when his car was washed off a bridge in the Hondo Valley.

Expert horseman Montie Gardenhire, owner of Montie's Riding Stables, rode the river on horseback every day for several weeks rescuing residents from their flooded cabins. Ike Wingfield, the town's most prominent citizen, and many others including Bill Hart who reestablished electric service, personally helped in mopping up after the flood. In one instance, Montie was attempting to cross the flooded stream on horseback when both he and his horse narrowly escaped drowning as the horse, plunging into the current, had to swim to reach a footing on the opposite bank.

Joetyne Wright, who has lived in the Hollywood area all her life recalls the flood waters being worse there than farther upstream because of the input from Cedar Creek, Bonito Creek, Eagle Creek, Carrizo Creek, Gavilan Canyon, and every other canyon that poured into the Ruidoso. She recalls, "The water from Carrizo washed out all the trees in its wake. Big walnut trees along the Ruidoso were ripped out. I remember Dad's cows were washed down the river and their horns hung in the top limbs of trees. Down around the racetrack there was a sea of water rushing all the way from the main riverbed to the hill—about where the quarter horse track is today. It even flooded Roswell."

A hundred young men from the CCC arrived to remove debris. They literally changed the course of the river in many places and straightened miles of channel since the flood had done so much damage on alternate banks at the curves. Engineers predicted that another flood of these proportions would be unlikely in the widened and straightened channel. The Ruidoso, they said, would take care of two or three times the amount of water that ruined so much property that September in 1941.

Less than three months later, on December 7 most people in Ruidoso thought their biggest problem was bringing in a few armloads of fireplace logs and fixing Sunday dinner. That is, until they heard radio broadcasts that the Japanese had attacked Pearl Harbor in the Hawaiian Islands with more than three hundred and sixty carrier-based airplanes.

As America entered World War II, many Ruidosoans thought the town would dry up because of heavy gasoline rationing ordered quickly by Washington. But such was not to be. People in the Southwest could still manage enough gas to get to Ruidoso, but long trips were out of the question. Soldiers on leave began coming up to the mountains from Fort Bliss, Texas, Biggs Army Air Field, Roswell Army Air Field, Alamogordo Army Air Field and other military installations. The field at Alamogordo was conceived as a training base for British bomber crews during the war. Top brass soon discovered a flaw: "This weather is too good," they said. They moved the operation to more European-like climes on the U. S. East Coast.

Not all the soldiers came to the mountains for rest and relaxation. Mounted troopers like the 8th Cavalry from Fort Bliss used New Mexico's deserts and mountains for maneuvers. Gordon Mooney of El Paso remembers being drafted in April 1941, taught to ride horseback, and by summer his regiment, the 8th Cavalry, marched to Cloudcroft. Mooney puts it this way: "We rode in a column of two's and since I was somewhere in the middle of the column, I ate dust for days. At the end of each day I looked like somebody had poured a sack of flour on me. We finally trailed into the mountains about where Timberon would be today. The Sacramento River was running full, and we all took off our campaign hats and high boots and jumped in the icy water. The horses loved it too.

"The regiment camped in a big meadow right outside of Cloudcroft and after a few days we mounted up and headed out of the mountains back through the dust to Fort Bliss."

Fort Bliss was the home of the famous 1st Cavalry Division and more than seven thousand horses were stabled there. But the horse soldiers were playing out their last role. The division became mechanized and turned in its horses in 1943.

By then, people from Austin, Dallas and the rest of Texas began to hear about Ruidoso, and the War literally put the village on the map. Visiting servicemen and wealthy oil people from Midland and Odessa, Texas arrived in Ruidoso with money jingling in their pockets. They were looking for some serious action and a number of Ruidoso entrepreneurs stood ready to help them part with their money. By the early forties, the Great Depression was a fading bad memory. Now there was enough money floating around to risk gambling with it, and Ruidoso became one of several spots in New Mexico with wide open but illegal gambling. It lasted until the late 1940s.

The main attraction in town was the Central Bar located at the west end of the Midtown strip. A two-story building exists there today, with the upside-down Wild Snail sign atop the second floor. Next to the Central was the Mint. In the same area along Main Street (now Sudderth) were the Ruidoso Bar, Vegas Bar, the Buckaroo and Keck's Bar—among others.

Several bars had walls and doors adjoining each other, so people could enter one establishment and try their luck conveniently in three of them without going outside. Keck's had large-stake poker games going on upstairs almost around the clock. The others resembled something right out of Reno with dozens of slot machines, roulette wheels and other paraphernalia guaranteed to separate the tourists from their money.

The illegal system worked well for the most part. Bar owners paid off the proper politicians, who would occasionally bring in police to raid the casinos. Gaming establishments conveniently shut down, law officers left town, and within a few days it was business as usual. Not a bad arrangement.

Bill Hart remembers one not-so-perfect method the gamblers employed to get early warning of a possible police raid:

There was one ol' boy by the name of Roger Schenk. Big fat fella, and he was a veteran of World War I. He came in here looking for a place to live and he found a vacant cabin that wasn't rented. He got the job of being the lookout for the gamblers. They had a shoe shine chair in front of the Central and he spent most of his time sitting up there reading the paper. If he saw a police car come up the street he'd tap on the wall or get word to 'em. They'd have time to shut down the games. That went on for years.

Every month he got a veteran's compensation check from the government. As soon as he got that check he'd go in and play Coon Can. His gambling game was Coon Can. Ted Johnson was head of the Central Bar. Ol' Roger would hit him up and tell him, "Ted, let's start up that Coon Can game. I got my check." Well, ol' Johnson was so busy he didn't have time to fool with it. But after awhile he'd say, "Come on Roger, let's get it over with." So they'd start playing and might play all night. Johnson would end up with the government check, then he'd have to loan Roger money to live on.

One evening ol' Roger got to reading his newspaper. He dozed off and forgot to watch very close. Police cars, three of 'em, drove right up in front and parked in the street. Got out, got their guns out, and raided the bars. And went right by ol' Roger before he woke up. The police took some slot machines and loaded them in their cars. Then Johnson came out on the street and gave Roger the worst dressin' down he ever got. Sittin' right there and not tellin' 'em they were fixin' to raid the bars. 'Course all ol' Roger could do was stutter; he couldn't remember what happened.

Joetyne Wright remembers that "I just liked the slot machines. I bought my lunch with what I won. And there were slot machines everywhere. Any cafe or bar, it didn't matter. I was sixteen. I could also go in and buy a drink any time, even on Sundays. The Ruidoso Bar was the tough one. You could find a fight there any time you wanted to."

Open gambling went on in Ruidoso all through the War, but the gaming was doomed to defeat. And Bill Hart remembers exactly how it happened because he was an eye witness. He recalls:

We had this grocery store across the street from the big bars. We had closed up and my wife liked to play roulette. Lots of times she'd take her purse and go up to the Buckaroo, two doors up. It was a very popular gamblin' place. But on this particular night after we closed the store I told her, "Something's fixin' to happen over there and I don't know what it is." There were just too many people across the street. So along about eleven o'clock here comes another bunch, this

Three Rivers Petroglyph Site on the west side of Sierra Blanca is an outstanding example of prehistoric Native American Indian rock art. More than forty thousand individual carvings have been found here. (Rio Grande Historical Collections, NMSU Library)

time police and sheriff's officers. And they raid the whole town.

Some of the gamblers had brand new equipment they just put in. Cedar tables and chairs and things. And the state police took out axes and chopped 'em up. Then they put 'em all in the street, right outside our door and set 'em on fire. Big bonfire right in the middle of the street.

That last big raid spelled doom for Ruidoso's gambling era. For lots of tourists and towns-people, it was fun while it lasted, but it was time to start developing a solid town, as residents began building year-round homes and investing in real estate projects.

Much of the real estate development in Ruidoso is tied directly to the Three Rivers Ranch on the west side of Sierra Blanca. Most people in Ruidoso see the mountain from the east side. Skiers are more acquainted with the north side where patches of snow linger until August. From Alamogordo and Mescalero it is usually viewed from the south. But the peak's western slopes are

seen by considerably fewer people. Motorists traveling U.S. 54 get a view of Sierra Blanca looming above the desert ten miles east of Three Rivers, which was the rail station for the ranch. The Three Rivers Station consisted of a depot, a store, a one-room schoolhouse and a boxcar.

A big red-faced Irishman from County Cork named Pat Coughlin first fell in love with the Three Rivers ranch country in 1873. He came by way of the U.S. Army. He had previously raised cattle in Texas, and within a few years Coughlin had acquired control of much of the range at the foot of Sierra Blanca. The Three Rivers name comes from three mountain streams—Three Rivers, Indian Creek, and Golandrina Creek. They come together and drain the western slope of Sierra Blanca, then meander through the ranch's fertile acres, and disappear into the Tularosa Basin.

On the east the ranch is bordered by the Shanta Indian community, an isolated part of the Mescalero Reservation. Here also is the land that Susan McSween Barber ranched when she was known as the Cattle Queen of New Mexico. Her first husband, Alexander McSween, was shot to death outside their burning home during the climax of the Lincoln County War. Pete Crawford, an ex-Buffalo Solder who worked for Mrs. Barber, once described Susan McSween Barber as "a tall one who wore shotgun chaps, always carried a six-shooter, and was a match for any man."

Pat Coughlin accumulated considerable money—by rustling other people's cattle. He systematically bought up water rights and parcels of land until he owned most of what C. L. Sonnichsen described as his Magic Valley, more than a hundred thousand acres. Pat got in trouble with the law buying stolen cattle from Billy the Kid, then selling the cattle as stock raised at Three Rivers. Years of defending himself in court for rustling left Coughlin broke and defeated, and in 1906 A. B. Fall acquired the ranch. He had been enchanted with the grandeur of Three Rivers since he first saw it in 1889. He later bought the adjoining property that had belonged to Susan McSween Barber.

By this time, Fall was the most influential man

Brunell's, a long-established clothing store, as it looked in 1946. Ruidoso was coming of age during the Post-War years. (Herb Brunell Collection)

The Ruidoso Club House (below) was a main center of attraction during the 1940s. It was located at today's intersection of Sudderth and Mechem. (Courtesy Marie Rooney)

in southern New Mexico, politically and financially. Money flowed to him from his law practice that gained him further interests in mining, railroads and lumbering. And he plowed much of it back into Three Rivers Ranch. In 1912, Fall went to Washington as one of the first two new senators from New Mexico, which had just achieved statehood. Although he now spent more time away from his beloved ranch, he entered into a major expansion with his son-in-law Mahlon Everhart who had married Fall's daughter Caroline. Everhart was in a partnership with his uncles, the Thatcher brothers, wealthy bankers and ranch operators in Pueblo, Colorado where Mahlon managed the ranches. The Hatchet was their main brand in Colorado, where they had a large ranch outside of Pueblo. They also used the brand in New Mexico—in Ruidoso, Hachita and near Three Rivers.

Everhart and the Thatchers bought the patented land and water rights of the old Bar W Ranch, whose cattle ranged over a vast territory in the northern part of the Tularosa Basin west of Carrizozo. The Hatchet Ranch adjoined Three Rivers, and after a merger with Fall, the combined ranges increased to over a million acres.

Three Rivers Ranch was a wonderful place for Fall's children and grandchildren. Emadair Jones, prominent Ruidoso resident and one of Fall's granddaughters remembers childhood days when her parents took them to the ranch and turned them loose for the summer:

It was lots of fun and we always enjoyed it and looked forward to it. Actually, I spent most of my youth around my grandparents. The Hatchet Ranch adjoined Three Rivers at the railroad and ran west all the way to the San Andres Mountains. The cattle had different brands, but they ran them together. My childhood ambition was to ride over the mountain with the cowboys when they brought the cattle to Ruidoso to graze in the summer. The closest I ever got was to ride up the Three Rivers side to meet them when they brought the cattle back in the fall.

My mother was A. B. Fall's eldest daughter, Alexina. My father was C. C. Chase. He was managing properties for his uncle, Colonel William C. Greene, in Mexico when he and my mother met. Greene had far-flung mining, cattle, timber and railroad interests in Mexico, and A. B. Fall was Greene's lawyer. My parents lived and worked in Cananea, Mexico until my grandfather persuaded them it was not safe there for Americans during the Mexican Revolution. So Chase managed Three Rivers and one of Greene's ranches at San Rafael, Arizona. My father later became customs collector at El Paso.

I was born in El Paso at the Paso del Norte Hotel and went through high school there, and then New Mexico State and the College of Mines. Meanwhile, Thatcher and Everhart were holding land in Ruidoso that had been patented back in 1884. It was along the river and in the Upper Canyon, Gavilan Canyon, Upper Cedar Creek and other places.

Finally, my uncle and the Thatchers realized that Ruidoso had more potential as a summer resort than for cattle grazing. They hired my father to survey, subdivide and be local agent for the leasing of Thatcher and Everhart land in Ruidoso. Later the Ruidoso Realty Company was formed when Thatcher and Everhart sold the land to Mae Rule. Mae's husband, L. T. Rule was a vice-president in the Thatcher bank in Pueblo. My father continued as local agent and started leasing land in Ruidoso to people who wanted summer cabins.

When World War II ended, I came up to Ruidoso to help my father, and just stayed. After the town was incorporated I ran for village clerk. And lost by one vote. I was so glad! But what was funny, one of the main instigators of my running was Edna Boyce Rigby and she was out of town that day. She went to El Paso and didn't vote. But I was fortunate that I didn't win. I don't think I really wanted it.

Daddy had tried to get Thatcher and Everhart to buy some Cree land but they weren't interested. Thatcher never did want to sell lots. Just lease them. This is funny. They'd lease some beautiful lots for five or ten dollars a year. When Daddy died I took over and at the time, the leases were fifteen years renewable. Well, I raised the rates from ten dollars to fifteen dollars and some people jumped up and down screaming, telling me how terrible it was. Finally the land owners decided to sell and do more developing in Ruidoso. When I married, my husband Tom Jones became the agent.

A. B. Fall had lost the Three Rivers Ranch after his political and financial troubles that took place during the 1920s and 30s. The ranch was broken up and sold several times. The prime part of the ranch, twenty five thousand acres stretching from Eddy's railroad tracks on the west (now the

Southern Pacific) to the timbered foothills of Sierra Blanca was acquired in 1941 by Thomas Ryan who was the next to be captivated by the area and who lived on it from 1946 to 1972.

Ryan was in the Air Force at the time of his purchase. After the war he spent the next twenty-six years at Three Rivers improving the ranch and becoming an excellent neighbor and builder of the area. He conceived the idea of a Kid's Rodeo and held it annually for ten years, drawing thousands to the ranch arena. He called it the A.B. Fall Arena. The generous Ryan built a hunting lodge and issued an open invitation to survivors of the Bataan Death March, many of whom were Hispanics and native Americans from New Mexico, to hunt on the ranch.

Ellyn Big Rope Lathan, who lives in Mescalero, once worked for Tom Ryan when she lived in the isolated Mescalero Shanta Community bordering the Three Rivers Ranch. Her great-grandfather was Shanta Boy, a well-known and respected Apache.

Ellen remembers the famous Billy the Kid Rodeos held at Three Rivers, particularly the time her brother Loren won the calf riding. "I still have a home in Three Rivers and I go there as much as I can," she says.

Virginia Klinekole, whose late husband was Bruce Klinekole, a survivor of the Bataan Death March, is the last of the Shanta family to continue living at Three Rivers. As a member of the Tribal Council, she makes the ninety-two-mile round trip to Mescalero to attend meetings and visit relatives and friends.

The hacienda that Ryan built for ranch headquarters is three miles up the road from the railroad tracks at Three Rivers. The ruins of Susan Barber's house is five miles farther in what Tom Ryan describes as the best of Three Rivers Ranch country. Today the biggest attraction is the Three Rivers Petroglyph National Recreation Site, five miles up the valley from U.S. 54. Here are thousands of intricate rock pictures, scratched and picked in the rocks by prehistoric Indians more than a thousand years ago.

About the petroglyphs, Ryan says, "The petroglyphs were on my land, but I gave the

government the whole area. Further on up near the foot of Sierra Blanca I also gave a hundred acres to the Forest Service which they made into a public camping ground. In the summertime it's always full of people.

"You can walk from this park to the top of the saddle on Sierra Blanca. I used to ride a horse up there all the time and you could go right to where the ski area is today. From up there you could look down and see all this Three Rivers country. It looked like a big oyster shell spread out below you."

As the years went by Ryan was still involved in other ventures, and in 1972 he decided to get out of the ranching business. He moved to Mesilla, New Mexico where he now lives with fond memories of Three Rivers. When the ranch was up for sale, a mutual friend introduced Ryan to well-known El Paso contractor Charles Leavell. Perhaps Leavell would be interested in Three Rivers. Tom Ryan remembers it this way, "Charlie flew up here and I drove him all around and near the Indian Reservation. The country looked good. And Charlie says, 'How much do you want for this outfit?' I said, 'I want $100 an acre for the patented land.' And he says, 'How many acres you got out there?' I said, 'I've got fifty thousand of which twenty-five thousand are patented acres.' He said, 'I'll pay that.' I said, 'Charlie, you just bought yourself a ranch.' Made a deal. Right quick."

Charles Leavell bought Three Rivers in 1972 for his organization, the C. H. Leavell Company. He sold it five years later and the ranch has gone through several ownerships since the late 1970s. Leavell says that "When I sold Three Rivers I saved out one hundred acres and gave it to the Lee Moor Children's Home so they could use it as a summer camp. They still use it and take twelve or fifteen children up there at a time." Three Rivers Ranch is presently owned by Carl McMillan who served in the defense department during the Bush administration. McMillan continues to make major improvements on the ranch.

During the Depression two young Tennesseeans, George McCarty and Joe Palmer,

Horseback riding (left) was a favorite diversion during the 1940s. (Frank Mangan Collection) Below, looking west toward Sierra Blanca. Downtown was crowded during the War Years as people from surrounding desert towns scraped together enough gas ration stamps to get to Ruidoso and back. (Herb Brunell Collection)

Capitan and Smokey Bear

In 1950, at the beginning of the dry late-spring fire season a devastating forest fire swept through seventeen thousand acres in the Capitan Mountains. The fire was presumably started by a careless camper. Lincoln National Forest timberland near the town of Capitan raged into a flaming ruin.

Clinging to a charred tree, a small black bear was found by a crew of firefighters. The motherless cub, badly burned and hungry, was taken to the home of a local rancher, then flown to Santa Fe for medical care. The late Elliot S. Barker named the cub Smokey, and Barker was intrumental in making the bear an international symbol of forest fire prevention.

The Piper Aircraft Corporation christened a special plane in Smokey's honor and flew the cub in style to the Washington D. C. Zoo. Above, Smokey and his handler, New Mexico Assistant State Game Warden Homer Pickens prepare to take off in the private plane from Santa Fe in 1950.

To honor Smokey, the town of Capitan built the Smokey Bear Motel and a log cabin museum. In 1976, Smokey Bear Historical Park was established there. In the Capitans, you can still see the scars of the fire in which the poster bear came to life—where so many animals and trees perished. Upon his death, the body of the original Smokey was brought back to Capitan for burial in the park.

were looking for brighter futures. Joe headed for New Mexico and discovered Ruidoso in 1930. Even under the national gloom Joe could see opportunities there, so he wrote his brother-in-law George McCarty to come out and look the place over. George and his wife Lucille arrived in 1931 and opened a little grocery store on Main Street.

Palmer was more interested in land development, but he and McCarty formed a partnership. Together they acquired two forty-acre plots where they started developing lots and were moderately successful. They formed the White Mountain Realty Company.

More than sixty years later, George's son Bill McCarty is still a major player in developing Ruidoso. Bill recalls:

Dad was in the grocery business during the Depression but he got interested along with Joe Palmer in developing land and lots. So they started keeping their eye on the Cree estate. The Crees were ranchers—from Scotland. They ran several thousand head of cattle around Ruidoso. Their headquarters were located about halfway to what is now the Sierra Blanca Airport. This was the Cree's old VV Ranch. In the late thirties or early forties the Cree land came on the market. Well, my uncle Joe Palmer and my dad met the Cree estate people at the O Bar O Ranch about five miles north of Nogal. Joe and my dad were interested primarily in seven thousand acres of deeded land that the Crees ran cattle on. They purchased it, as I understand, for eighteen dollars an acre.

This deeded land was the most usable property around Ruidoso. It was primarily out in the flat country, not on the hillsides. The edge of the rolling hills was developable-type land—like the old airport which is now the golf course. What became the Palmer Gateway was one of the flatter and most usable areas of Ruidoso.

Anyway, they purchased this land and started White Mountain Development Company in the early forties. They took in a partner named Mark Hamilton and developed, you might say, all of the Palmer Gateway, part of the Hollywood area, right on up to the Midway area of Ruidoso. They sold off several tracts, called Ponderosa Heights, to Lloyd Davis, Sr. They also sold off Paradise Canyon.

They put in a golf course on a cow pasture in Palmer Gateway where the hospitals are now located. I was about ten years old at the time and big enough to carry a golf bag, so I caddied for thirty-five cents a round, for nine holes. The course was native grass and sand "greens" mixed with motor oil. It went all the way to the Junction. You had to shoot right off that hill towards Highway 70. After the golf course didn't work out too well, Joe and George started developing land out on the north part of Ruidoso around the present-day Cree Meadows Golf Course. Even after they bought out the Crees, they still had a cattle operation and ran cattle on Cree Meadows. They developed lots out to the north edge of the village limits. You might say they were the largest developers of land in Ruidoso.

White Mountain Development Company donated the airport site to Ruidoso, free and clear. They also donated land for a number of churches in Palmer Gateway. And they've always given discount deals to anybody that's trying to do something for the community —leading to the growth of the town. They developed thousands of lots. Emadair Chase's folks also developed a lot of land and were one of Ruidoso's pioneer developers.

I remember some of the early-day land deals. White Mountain sold lots and a house for $900. We're talking a lot of dollars when money was real money. Early days, they'd sell lots for $300. Now we sell a lot for $25,000 and its about the same amount of money.

We had a false economy in the boom time of the late seventies and early eighties. We knew that couldn't last. It was unreal; people went wild. I think everybody in Ruidoso is so much better off now than they ever have been. Anybody who wants a house can get one. Everybody who wants to work hard can have a job or a little business. If they work hard, they can make money.

Ruidoso's had a good steady growth except for that boom time, and that set us back a few years. Property that somebody wanted $100,000 for was not realistic. That $100,000 went to $50,000 which it should have been in the first place.

As far as the original Cree land goes, out of the seven thousand deeded acres Palmer and my dad started with, we still have a thousand acres left. Joe Palmer and George McCarty devoted their lives to the development of Ruidoso in an orderly fashion. They worked hard all their lives, and never did have much money when they died. But they were happy because they got to live in Ruidoso—a place they both loved.

The Wonderful Navajo Lodge

Some people still get misty-eyed at the mention of Ruidoso's old Navajo Lodge. For more than two decades it was The Place to stay, particularly during the years at the end of the Depression, through World War II and beyond. The Lodge was in the heart of Ruidoso and the choice spot for entertainment since it was the only place that could handle large groups—dances, parties and political meetings for a few people or several hundred. There was always a fire in the fireplace that complemented the huge beamed ceiling and Pueblo style architecture.

It all started back in the twenties when Bob and Edith Boyce built a dining hall and a few small cabins near the river. Edith was the daughter of Frank Coe of Lincoln County War fame. She and her husband had a lease on some of the Cree lands and were running cattle on what later became the present Cree Meadows golf course.

Emadair Jones recalls that the Boyces acquired some land from Thatcher and Everhart in 1924 to build the small cabins. They were square rooms with wooden walls half way up, and screen the rest of the way. There were canvas rolls to be let down for privacy or to keep out the weather. Sometime later (in 1938, according to the *El Paso Herald-Post*), the Boyces built the large adobe structure that was a Ruidoso landmark for many years. The Boyces' son Bobby picked up adobes for the new structure in La Luz, the village at the foot of the Sacramentos. Bobby hauled adobes up the mountain to Ruidoso in a Model T pickup, and the loads were so heavy he had to turn around and back up the hills. But the handsome structure was completed to become the social center of Ruidoso.

College bands came up in the summer to play for dances on weekends. One favorite was Ned Bradley's orchestra. Kurt Massey often played the fiddle. He was the brother of Louise Massey who gained national fame during the 1940s with the song "In My Adobe Hacienda."

During the War, T. C. Delaney and his wife Betty came to Ruidoso to manage the Navajo. Ray Reid of Ruidoso Downs played for dozens of dances, and he talked Bob Wills and his Texas Playboys into performing at the Navajo Lodge. It was a wonderful time, the age of Tommy Dorsey, Benny Goodman and the big swing bands during the war. The sounds of Glenn Miller poured out of the juke box with "Chatanooga Choo Choo," "In the Mood," and "Moonlight Serenade."

Peggy Snell Shaifer is one of those who shares the nostalgia of those golden days at the Navajo Lodge. "Buddy Boyce was tall, dark and handsome," she says. "The Boyces ran the Lodge. Betty Jean Williams and I were madly in love with Buddy, who was either in his late teens or early twenties, and looked right through us. Killed our souls, so we decided we didn't need him anyway.

"When the lodge hired Texas Tech medical students who were instrumentalists and played in the band on Saturday nights, Betty and I thought that things were beginning to look up for us. But that, too, was short-lived. Betty's parents figured two little girls were getting too smart for their britches and the one-sided romancing stopped very abruptly."

Over the years, the Navajo attracted public figures including governors Edwin Mechem, Dick Elliot, John Miles, Tom Mabry and many other politicians. Famous war correspondent Ernie Pyle stayed for a week during the war. Pat Garrett's widow stayed there and her daughter Pauline was a frequent visitor.

The colorful landmark finally outlived its time and was torn down in 1975. It was located on the north side of Sudderth Drive across from today's Sun World Bank.

The Navajo Lodge was the social heart of Ruidoso during World War II and beyond. (Herb Brunell Collection)

The original Navajo Lodge in the early 1920s. Guest rooms were the little cabins behind the cars. The later Lodge replaced the cabins. The large building at right was used as a dance hall until the 1950s. (Evelyn Estes Collection)

Mescalero Apache Cultural Center highlights this scene of the Dance of the Mountain Gods.
Masked Crown Dancer is in center. (Frank Mangan)

11

The Mescalero Apaches

THIS WAS AMERICA IN 1913, the year before World War I swept across Europe. Americans crisscrossed the country in Pullman cars, flew airplanes, and built skyscrapers while Henry Ford put America on wheels with his assembly line Model T. To most people the Indian Wars were something they'd read about in history books, unpleasant events in another lifetime.

But on April 13, 1913, an incident took place in the tiny village of Tularosa, New Mexico causing some citizens to rub their eyes in wonderment as they viewed what seemed to be a contradiction of the twentieth century. A special train steamed into the station carrying 187 Chiricahua Apaches just released from imprisonment at Fort Sill, Oklahoma to join their kinsmen on the nearby Mescalero Apache Reservation. The Chiricahuas had been prisoners of war for almost thirty years, exiled from Arizona to Florida, Alabama, and Fort Sill, Oklahoma. Their ordeal had begun in 1886 when the last of Geronimo's Apache warriors surrendered to General Nelson A. Miles in a place called Skeleton Canyon just west of the Arizona-New Mexico line.

The Apaches were the last native Americans to resist the white man in his quest for Manifest Destiny—full title to the center of the North American continent. Military experts have called the Apaches the toughest and most formidable guerilla fighters the world has ever known. One U.S. cavalry officer called them "the tigers of the human species."

From childhood the Apache learned quickly how to survive in his arid, thorny, unforgiving country. As a warrior the Apache was a relentless foe. He was able to fight and live off the sparse land while his pursuers, the U.S. Cavalry, were burdened with supply wagons and water through the most difficult terrain in America.

The Apaches were on their own turf and they knew every water hole and spring for hundreds of miles. The Indians flourished in a country where white men starved and died of thirst. If necessary, an Apache could ride a horse to death, eat it, and "borrow" another from a ranch. Historian Charles Lummis, writing about these warriors said, "The Apache could wear out in physical endurance the most enduring of his white foes. Hunger he could stand twice as long, and thirst four times as long as the best of them."

Some of the Apaches' enemies, whom they called White Eyes, were not white at all, but black "buffalo soldiers" of the 9th and 10th cavalries. These black troopers were only two decades away from slavery in the South, and many had enlisted in the army on the western frontier to escape the post-Civil War racial strife. As individuals they were also tough, smart, big-muscled soldiers. They knew how to ride and work and fight. But in the end, even these hardy troopers could conquer the Apaches only by sheer weight of numbers.

By the early 1880s, the other Indian tribes—like the Sioux and Cheyenne—who had massacred Custer and parts of the 7th Cavalry at the Little Big Horn, had been overwhelmed and subdued. In New Mexico the Mescalero Apaches were finally living in comparative peace (and poverty) on their mountain reservation. West of the Rio Grande, the Warm Springs Apaches and a large number of Chiricahuas had ceased to resist and were languishing on a reservation at Fort Apache, Arizona. In October, 1880 the great Apache war chief Victorio and his followers were slain by Mexican soldiers at Tres Castillos, Chihuahua, two hundred miles south of Mescalero. The famed Apache leader Mangas Coloradas had been killed by U.S. soldiers in 1863.

By 1886 only Geronimo's decimated band remained free, fighting impossible odds. At the end, Geronimo's force was composed of sixteen warriors, twelve women and six children. Deployed against them were five thousand U.S. troops (one fourth of the entire U.S. Army), as well as some three thousand Mexican soldiers.

Two armies couldn't defeat this little band, but time was running out for Geronimo, and he knew it. He agreed to lay down his arms and surrender, which he did on September 4, 1886. In the subsequent talks, he interpreted General Miles's statements to mean that the Chiricahua families would be united in a beautiful reservation in Florida, then return home to Arizona in two years.

But there was to be no reservation. Geronimo and a small group were put on a train and shipped to Fort Pickens on Florida's Gulf Coast. The tough, audacious warrior would never see Arizona again.

After Geronimo's surrender, four hundred Chiricahuas and Warm Springs Apaches who were living peacefully at Fort Apache were suddenly placed under guard by General Miles. The army moved them a hundred miles to the railroad line and shipped them to Florida. By any measure, this was one of America's most disgraceful acts. To make matters worse, the callous Miles rounded up his faithful Indian scouts and exiled them to Florida with the others. The Indian Wars in the Southwest were over.

Most of the prisoners were confined at Fort Marion in St. Augustine. It was an old Spanish fort, a wretched place for them. Sanitation was woefully inadequate. The damp climate and mosquitoes caused extra misery to Apaches already suffering the degradation of being prisoners. They never knew what their ultimate fate would be when, if ever, they would return to their dry deserts and green mountains. They began to die in alarming numbers. Few of them would ever see their homeland again.

In 1887 the government transferred the melancholy Apaches to Mount Vernon Barracks in Alabama and some of the children were sent to Carlisle Indian School near Harrisburg, Pennsylvania where thirty of them died. Another unexpected move came in 1894 when the government shipped the Indians to Fort Sill, Oklahoma. They camped temporarily in brush and canvas tents but at least they were back in more familiar open country. New Mexico was now only six hundred miles away, and citizens there petitioned federal authorities including the President about the latest move. The Apaches, they said, were too close to their old haunts, creating a danger to the Southwest. Old wounds were slow to heal.

By the turn of the century, Geronimo was earning money making public appearances while a prisoner. He was featured in Pawnee Bill's Wild West Show and doing a brisk business selling bows and arrows and autographs. He sold the buttons off his shirt for twenty-five cents each, but he carried a supply of replacements, a sad commentary on the charismatic Geronimo who was billed as the Tiger of the Human Race.

Geronimo died in 1909 at Fort Sill. His old warriors such as Nana, Chihuahua and Loco also died in captivity, and the government's hostility

Chiricahua Apache prisoners of war. Geronimo and his tiny band of warriors agreed to lay down their arms in 1886, then were put on a train and shipped to Florida. They were released in 1913 from Fort Sill, Oklahoma after almost thirty years in captivity. Front row, Geronimo sits fourth from left. At his right is the famous Apache Chief Naiche who lived out his old age at Mescalero. (Aultman Collection, El Paso Public Library)

began to soften. The Apaches were no longer considered a threat. The United States began to see the madness of keeping them from becoming productive citizens. And coincidentally, the army wanted to convert Fort Sill into an active field artillery base.

The wheels of bureaucracy turned slowly toward releasing the Apaches, who themselves were actively campaigning for freedom. The Mescaleros in New Mexico had a record of generosity toward exiled Apache bands and offered to share their reservation with the Chiricahuas. Freedom was long overdue and much of the

credit for the move to Mescalero was due to one of Geronimo's right-hand men, his nephew Asa Daklugie. Daklugie had been one of the Chiricahua children sent to Carlisle Indian School. Many years later, the late Eve Ball of Ruidoso interviewed Daklugie for her book *Indeh*. The aloof, aged Indian was by then the dominant patriarch of the Mescalero Reservation and he seldom condescended to talk with inquiring white people. Only after four years of persuasion by Mrs. Ball would he speak with her at length. Then, he spoke freely and eloquently. In one interview he described his first days at the Indian

Mescalero Apache camp. Photo probably taken before the arrival of Fort Sill Chiricahuas in 1913. Camps such as this were not permanent, but seasonal. (Aultman Collection, El Paso Public Library)

Mescalero Apache horsemen in early twentieth century. (R. G. McCubbin Collection)

Last of the Apache traders, Buck Prude, holds the hand of his son, Andrew. This Ruidoso Store and post office was located near the Mescalero Reservation border about the turn of the century. The Prudes served the Apaches as traders for more than forty years. (R. G. McCubbin Collection)

School and how he became saddled with the name Asa.

"The first thing they did was cut our hair," said Daklugie. "I had taken my knife from one of my long braids and wrapped it in my blankets, so I didn't lose it. But I lost my hair. The bath wasn't bad...but while we were bathing our breechclouts were taken and we were ordered to put on trousers. We'd lost our hair and lost our clothes. With the two we'd lost our identity as Indians."

Carlisle's rules dictated that students have a given name, and Daklugie recalled how the Apache children received theirs: "They marched us into a room and our interpreter ordered us to line up with our backs to the wall. I went to the head of the line...then a man went down it and starting with me he began: 'Asa, Benjamin, Charles, Daniel, Eli, Frank.' Frank was Mangas's son. So he became Frank Mangas and I became Asa Daklugie. I've always hated that name." He soon began calling himself "Ace" Daklugie and the name stuck.

To say that Daklugie had little use for the white man is an understatement. He told Mrs. Ball, "My father was a good man; he killed lots of White Eyes." He also told her how the term White Eyes originated, as did a Lipan Apache named Philemon Vanego. Vanego said that what impressed them most about white people was the whites of their eyes. "We don't have that," he said. "Our eyes are coffee-colored where yours are white. That is how you got your name White Eyes."

The Lipans were sometimes called the "Texas Apaches" since they roamed east of the Pecos River into the Great Plains and southward through Texas and Mexico. At one time, Vanego's band escaped the U.S. soldiers, headed south to Mexico and settled near the tiny village of Zaragosa across the Rio Grande from El Paso, Texas.

Before the Mescalero arrival of the Chiricahuas from Fort Sill, a band of Lipans were allowed to come to Mescalero from Mexico where they had suffered severely in the Texas wars. The infusion of other tribes, even small numbers like the Lipans and the greater numbers of Chiricahuas were welcomed by the Mescaleros because it added to their total strength, and the reservation could easily absorb the newcomers. The Mescaleros felt that an increase in population would help them keep their lands. From Fort Sill, about two-thirds of the Chiricahua survivors moved to Mescalero while the others stayed in Oklahoma, freed from government restraint. Their descendants live there today.

The source of the name "Mescalero" is the mescal plant, a cactus that served the tribe as a principal source of food. Mescalero means literally "mescal maker." The mescal is familiar to desert dwellers—known to most as the century plant, a large agave with thick gray-green leaves, each ending in a dangerous needle-sharp point. Apaches would locate a mescal field, cut the heart out of each plant, then roast the cabbage-sized centers in rock-lined pits for three or four days. The resulting sweet mescal would then be eaten or made into a sort of candy-like hardtack and stored indefinitely. Mescal on the reservation has become scarce since most of the fields were harvested from arid mountain slopes years ago.

In 1873 the Mescalero Reservation was established by executive order of President Ulysses S. Grant, to be located at Fort Stanton, New Mexico. But the seeds for the long-sought reservation were planted back in 1865 at the infamous Bosque Redondo Reservation near Fort Sumner. There nine thousand Navajos and Apaches had been interned for several miserable years. On the night of September 3, 1865, every Apache who could walk vanished from captivity at Bosque Redondo.

After their breakout, the Apaches were again at war with the United States.

By this time, President Grant was sincerely intent on pacifying the hostile tribes and helping them become self-sufficient. In 1869 the government sent word to the fragments of the Mescalero tribe informing them that if they would come in they would have a reservation in the area around Fort Stanton, part of their original homeland. Little by little the Apaches came in and made peace. But as usual rations were short, clothing was not enough to keep them warm. In 1875 the reservation was extended into the Sacramento Mountains, where at least the Indians could hunt wild game as they had done to survive in the old days.

L.G. Murphy and Emil Fritz (who became combatants in the Lincoln County War) were the post traders at Fort Stanton, busily bilking both the government and some seven hundred Apaches out of rations and farming equipment. In protest, an honest Indian agent, W.D. Crothers, moved the Indian Agency to South Fork on Tularosa Creek at Blazer's Mill. This was the beginning of today's Mescalero headquarters.

But greed and corruption were hard to stop. Historian Herb Seckler writes that "in 1881 it was found that the 'Nogal Mining District' contained rich mineral wealth but lay inside the Reservation boundaries. Anglo miners were not to be denied. They appealed to the U.S. Army which in turn forwarded recommendations to Washington requesting that the lines be changed and the mining claims be placed in the public domain. The commissioner of Indian affairs convinced himself that the Indians were willing to give up the Nogal area for a strip of land to be added to their eastern boundary. The boundaries were revised in 1882 and the miners had their claims."

Meanwhile in 1883, another change was to take place for the Mescaleros, much to their dismay. The Jicarilla Apaches who had occupied a reservation in northern New Mexico, were ordered to move in with their cultural kinsmen, the Mescaleros. The move was doomed to failure from the first, as the two tribes did not get along. The Mescaleros resented the Jicarillas who now

Mescalero Apaches circa 1900 pose for traveling photographer from Vance, Texas. (R. G. McCubbin Collection)

outnumbered them two to one. Within four years, the government relented and allowed the Jicarillas to return to their traditional homeland near the Colorado line. Besides, the reservation property was considered almost worthless at the time. It wasn't until the twentieth century that oil and gas were discovered and the true value of the Jicarilla land was revealed.

The Mescaleros numbered only about four hundred after the reservation was established. The Chiricahua and Lipan bands didn't officially become members of the Mescalero tribe until the tribe was organized formally in 1936. Government rations had been cut off back in 1902, but receipts from cattle, timber and other jobs on and off the reservation brought in payrolls.

Today more than three thousand members of the tribe live on the reservation. Most tribal families live at or near the community of Mescalero but there are still outlying settlements at Three Rivers, Elk Silver, Carrizo, White Tail and Mudd Canyon. Since nobody is required to stay on the reservation, a number of families and individuals relocated over the years away from Mescalero. But soon, most wanted to return to their wild green mountains and clear icy streams. They missed the seclusion and beauty of their homelands and the mystical White Mountain which soars twelve thousand feet into the blue New Mexico sky. The lowest altitude on the reservation, incidentally, is over a mile high—at Three Rivers. Almost all the land is covered with

Mescalero Indian village circa 1900. These were the lean years before the infusion of Fort Sill Apaches. The Mescalero tribe was down in numbers to only a few hundred. (McGaw Collection, El Paso Public Library)

timber; pine, fir, spruce, aspen, white oak, piñon and juniper. With the exception of a few privately owned acres, all of it within reservation boundaries—over 460,000 acres—is owned by the tribe. Individual Indians are granted the right to use specific tracts called "assignments" but title and control remain with the tribe.

The Mescaleros are governed by a Tribal Council of eight members plus a president and vice president which operates under a constitution designed roughly after the constitution of the United States.

There is still a misconception that the federal government doles out checks to the Mescaleros. They work for a living just like anybody else, and they pay taxes just like anybody else. One tribal member smiles and says, "The IRS gets to us on the reservation too."

Today, driving along U.S. 70 which bisects the Mescalero Reservation you can see what has motivated the Apaches to remain on their homelands. The tribe knows its responsibility as guardian of this land so that it can support future generations of its people. They treat their country with great care. Nature has not been harmed.

Berle Kanseah, a member of the Tribal Council, is one who knows the traditional Indian ways as well as the modern ways. This soft-spoken man was born on the reservation and has lived to see times change from the old days to a diversified business after more than three decades of leadership under Tribal President Wendell Chino.

Kanseah has the proper credentials to speak about Mescalero. His grandfather was Geronimo's nephew and was on the warpath with him in the last battles of 1886. Jasper Kanseah was the youngest warrior in Geronimo's band, only fourteen years old when they finally surrendered to General Miles and were shipped to Florida. "My father was a Chiricahua born at Fort Sill," says Berle Kanseah. When they moved to Mescalero, my dad married my mother who was a Mescalero. I guess you could say I'm kinda half and half."

Festivities on the 4th of July

Colorful parade kicks off the annual Fourth of July ceremonial at Mescalero. The four-day festivities celebrate the coming of age of girls approaching womanhood. Brush arbors and tepees cluster around the rodeo arena overlooking the Mescalero community. (Frank Mangan)

When the Fort Sill Chiricahuas first arrived at Mescalero, Ace Daklugie took a good look at the whole area and received permission to locate his people at White Tail, about sixteen miles east of the Mescalero community. At 8,000 feet altitude, it was a choice location, with plenty of wild game, timber, ample water, wild flowers and lush meadows. Says Kanseah: "That's where I grew up and went to school. We had a two-room school-house with sometimes one teacher, sometimes two if there was a man and wife team." Kanseah chuckles when he remembers that "you learned to live a hardy life out there, but you didn't know you were having a hard time growing up. You just conditioned yourself to accept it. It's such an easy time now—compared to those days."

For more than three decades the little community of White Tail succeeded in ranching and farming but as families grew people had to find other jobs. White Tail dozed in its splendid isolation as one by one people relocated near the Mescalero headquarters.

Describing his life on and off the reservation, Kanseah recalls:

For high school I went off the reservation to the little town of Tularosa. We were bussed the seventeen miles to Tularosa every day. I got interested in history and I think it's important to preserve. But it's difficult. When I went to the public schools in Tularosa I didn't hear anything about the Apaches. Geronimo may have been mentioned somewhere along with Sitting Bull, who was a Sioux. And depending on where the history teacher was from, we learned about her area. Our teacher was from the East and she covered Hiawatha more than anything. But she was a good teacher; it was just that there wasn't any material. So we were into other people's history.

After high school I entered the service, U.S. Army. I remember my parents saying 'You're old enough now. Your grandfather was a warrior to protect his family and land. It's different now, but you are coming of age. Are you going to join the army?' Simple as that. I enlisted. Went in and served my time, 1960 to '64. Did it with some pride. I have some reservations and feelings about it. But I still did it with pride. That's how we were taught.

I spent all my time in Germany and Europe with the armored infantry. Those were the Cold War years and I had the opportunity to see the other countries over

there. It was a valuable experience for me.

After the service years, I came right back to Mescalero. My wife and I got married while she was in school. We both grew up at White Tail; her background is also Chiricahua—from the prisoner of war families. She started college at Highlands University in Las Vegas, New Mexico, transferred to New Mexico State, graduated and got her Masters Degree there.

Three of our kids are grown up. We have one boy in the service. He's with the Marines right now. Two are working at Mescalero. Our daughter is the youngest and still in school.

At our present place we have sixty-six acres. Hopefully we can begin to turn over some of our land to our children as we move back to our original home, White Tail, and set up out there again. I want to rebuild all that. We've got seventeen cultivated acres and about twenty or thirty more which is pasture land back in the trees on the hillside. I might raise some livestock. We just want to go back where it's quiet, nice and peaceful. Nobody lives out there any more but two families. The old school building is still there.

Mescalero's Jonathan Adams, left, heads up the big game hunting program which adds to the tribe's coffers. (Peggy Mangan Feinberg) Below, Ellyn Big Rope Lathan is curator of the Museum and Cultural Center. She works at maintaining the tribe's identity and past history. (Frank Mangan)

For thirty years Kanseah has been involved in the tribe's timber industry, a desire he had when he first returned from the army. He works for the Bureau of Indian Affairs Branch of Forestry that deals with timber stands of the reservation, the tribe's principle source of income. The Mescaleros are capable of harvesting nineteen million board feet of lumber a year and they operate on what is called a sustained yield (allowing the forest to continue growing). Generally, any tree under fourteen inches in diameter is left to gain optimum growth. By this selective method the Apache lumberjacks open up areas so that stands can better achieve saw size. It's a thinning out process.

Grazing land on the reservation supports from four thousand to eight thousand head of white-face Herefords owned by tribal members through the Mescalero Apache Cattle Growers Association. In addition, the tribe operates various enterprises such as Ski Apache, Inn of the Mountain Gods, a mercantile store, and a number of recreational facilities. The 250-room Inn of the Mountain Gods is a showplace resort with luxurious rooms, fine dining, a lounge, piano bar and a 150-acre lake for fishing, sailing and canoeing. There is a championship golf course, an eight-court tennis complex, gun club, riding stables, a big game hunting program and a video gaming casino.

Headquarters of the tribal government are located in the Mescalero community, as is the

Inn of the Mountain Gods is a 250-room luxury hotel. The resort includes, among other amenities, a championship golf course, tennis complex, riding stables and a video gaming casino. (Peggy Mangan Feinberg)

Mescalero's nationally-known Hot Shots fight forest fires all over the country. They maintain a grueling fitness routine, staying in top condition for their dangerous assignments. (Peggy Mangan Feinberg)

Apache girls in traditional buckskin dresses march in parade honoring tribal members who fought in America's wars. (Frank Mangan)

Below, two examples of colorful Apache beadwork. These antiques were traded by Mescaleros to Ruidoso residents early in the twentieth century. Beadwork is still done today; much of it used during annual puberty ceremonies. (Courtesy Robert Keyes)

Mescalero Elementary School, hospital, the Bureau of Indian Affairs, the Mescalero Apache Cultural Center, the Bureau of Sports Fisheries and Wildlife, and the U.S. Public Health Service. These provide employment for tribal members. Five churches are on the reservation.

Miles away from Mescalero community the tribe runs several recreational areas—open to the public. Eagle Creek RV Park is on the north boundary of the reservation, with two lakes nearby. Silver Lake recreation area is on the south boundary of the reservation, with trailer hookups and an adjacent mountain lake. All waters are stocked with trout from the National Fish Hatchery at Mescalero.

A limited number of permits are available each year to the public for hunting elk and bear. Permits are also available for fishing the north, south and middle forks of the Ruidoso River. Mescalero's Jonathan Adams, an outdoorsman-expert on big game heads up the hunting program. Adams and his guides and horse wranglers organize a number of bull elk hunts every year. "We average about twenty hunters on each trip," he says. "Elk are the most popular and we take only mature bull elk which are seven or eight years old and weigh up to a thousand pounds. On other hunts, we try to take two to three hundred cow elks off the reservation each season. That way we can maintain the herd. If you have too many animals they begin to die of disease and starvation."

By the late 1960s, elk were almost extinct on the reservation, and the tribe reintroduced them with 162 animals. Now there are about forty five hundred Rocky Mountain elk scattered within the boundaries. Many of them live above timberline on Sierra Blanca in spring and summer, then migrate down to the juniper and piñon in winter. "Black bears are also popular to hunt," says Adams. "They roam all over the reservation. We're not doing any antelope hunting right now. Our last antelope hunt was in '87 when we noticed a decrease in numbers during aerial surveys. We need to get the herd a lot stronger. The herd lives on the eastern part of the reservation down on the plains area toward Roswell—lots of grass, rolling hills, big meadows, piñon and juniper trees. Most of it is fenced off by the Cattle Growers Association but the animals pretty much run free." Consequently, the tribe's outdoor recreation program for the public is in basic harmony with Native American values and traditions.

Visitors to the reservation today hoping to see Indians in buckskins and blankets are likely to be disappointed. They'll see lots of black cowboy hats (since many Mescaleros are ranchers), Levis, cowboy boots, baseball caps, long hair, short hair, skirts and bobby sox. High school kids dress pretty much like other high school kids.

Sweeping changes have occurred in the Apache way of life in the last two generations. The tribe has survived stresses that might have destroyed people with less fortitude. Although changes have eroded an ancient cultural heritage, they have not come without benefits.

Berle Kanseah sums it up well: "The tribe is striving to get an education for anybody who wants the opportunity to eventually take over tribal management positions. We're moving along, more kids in college the last two years. They're graduating from high school. But we have dropout problems and the use of alcohol and drugs. I think it's rampant over the whole country and it happens on the reservation.

Our tribe remains very traditional. We still practice our tribal ceremonials, partly open to public viewing during the annual July 4th celebration at Mescalero. This is the puberty ritual of the coming of age of girls who are approaching womanhood. It takes place four days and five nights. We offer part of that to the public so they can see who we are, what we're all about. Other tribes from across the country make it a point to visit our ceremonial. Surprisingly, they tell us that we are about the last tribe that is practicing its traditions like in the old times."

During the festivities, brush arbors and tepees cluster around the rodeo arena on the mesa overlooking the community of Mescalero, buzzing with childrens' games, prizes and ceremonial dances. Among them, the dramatic Dance of the

Mountain Spirits takes place around the fire at night. A colorful parade kicks off the festivities. Booths sell everything from crafts and jewelry to Indian fry bread and tacos. Kanseah grins and says, "We have a big old time during the 4th of July."

Although the Mescaleros have become a model for other tribes, the future remains in a delicate balance. Mark Chino, a criminal investigator for the Bureau of Indian Affairs, sees the vital importance of the tribe maintaining its identity—and consequently its success. He envisions two keys to the future. One is to continue the solid investment in the tribe's enterprises as well as seeking new methods of generating revenue.

"Also," says Chino, "we're looking at ways to expose youngsters to Apache culture. The language is difficult to learn, and as the years go by, fewer Mescaleros speak it." But Chino predicts a resurgence of teaching Mescalero tradition beginning as early as pre-school.

Located on the Mescalero Reservation, Sierra Blanca remains a sacred mountain to tribal members. Many follow the age-old ritual of going to the peak and meditating to refresh their spirits and minds. The Mescaleros consider three other mountains as sacred: Three Sisters, Guadalupe Peak and Oscuro Peak. (Anne Brunell)

12
Skis, Boots and Poles

Skiers can take the Gondola Lift to the 11,400-foot Gazebo or go to the 11,500-foot Lookout in Apache Bowl and enjoy the 200 mile panoramic view. (Riker Davis)

BACK IN THE THIRTIES and forties the summer people made a mass exodus from Ruidoso after Labor Day. They packed up their kids and pets and almost everything including bedding, closed their cabins, and headed back to the flatlands for the winter. Few cabins were winterized or had indoor plumbing. Icy winds gusted through the cracks in the pine slabs that shrunk a little each year as the wood dried.

For weekend tourists and summer cabin owners there was not a lot of incentive to linger in the mountains. Most part-time residents didn't miss the subtle qualities of ice-crystal days and the unique light of New Mexico mountain winters. After Labor Day even the wooden sidewalks rolled up. You could have run a bobsled down the middle of Main Street and the chances of maiming anyone were practically nil. Local residents knew how to prepare for cold weather however. They stoked their fireplaces and settled in for the fall and winter at a leisurely pace. Although many breathed a sigh of relief having the village to themselves, something was missing.

Ruidoso was for most folks a three-month town. Yet more and more people were making it their permanent home. They needed year-round businesses to ensure a steady tourist income through the winter months. And this came in the form of long wooden skis.

Ruidosoans Bill Hart and Carmon Phillips were among the first to explore the possibilities of commercial skiing in Ruidoso. They were joined by, among others, Dr. W. D. Horton and Ray Izard. As early as 1938 Hart was already skiing in what later became Cree Meadows Golf Course. Dianne Stallings of the *Ruidoso News* noted that Hart's friend Montie Gardenhire (owner of Montie's Stables) would ride out on his horse, drop a rope to Hart and pull him on skis around the flat portions of the valley. This was the ancient art of "ski-joring." It still happens on private or limited ski courses. Not exactly Aspen, Colorado.

Since the snow melted too rapidly on the flats, the higher elevation and pine-shadowed hillside of upper Cedar Creek, several miles north of town, seemed a likely spot for winter sports. Cedar

Creek Canyon soon became Ruidoso's first official ski run. The short downhill slopes were exhilarating but struggling back in deep snow was punishment enough to ruin your day. To make it easier on the skiers, a primitive lift was made from an old automobile engine and a tow rope. Not high-tech, but it worked.

During the forties and fifties, local skiers improved the area which attracted hundreds of visitors on winter weekends. But since the season was short, only about two months, a group of enthusiasts looked longingly upward to the shimmering slopes of 12,000-foot Sierra Blanca.

Bill Hart remembers the first excursions ever made carrying skis to the present location of Ski Apache. Hart, Montie Gardenhire, Carmon Phillips, and Warren Barrett rode horseback with skis on their shoulders into what was known as White Mountain Park, a green meadow high on the north side of Sierra Blanca Mountain.

Carmon Phillips recalls that "Bill and I were up there having a wonderful time skiing. When we started coming out we got caught in the dark. We skied down real slow, poles out in front to keep from running into trees. When we felt something in our path we'd just drop down in the snow. Finally the moon came out about the last quarter of the distance and made it easier. I never want that to happen to me again."

Hart adds, "On the way down we finally got to where ol' Alfred Hale was growing potatoes. At the upper part of the potato patch there was half a mile where there wasn't a tree in the way, just an open mirror. The moon was coming up and that snow was the purtiest thing you ever saw. I guess it was about one o'clock in the morning when we plumb gave out and got off that mountain. The other guys were still waiting for us and we headed back to town. But that was about the first pioneering ever done on skiing at White Mountain Park. That's exactly where the Ski Apache lodge is today."

Back then, the region was part of the White Mountain Wilderness area set aside by the Forest Service. This meant you couldn't build a road into it, but you could ride horseback or pack in. It also meant you packed out your own trash. Sierra Blanca Peak was, and still is, on the Mescalero Apache Indian Reservation. The Forest Service ultimately released a portion of the primitive area for winter sports. In cooperation with the Apache Tribe, the efforts of Senator Clinton P. Anderson and mountain explorations by Lincoln National Forest Ranger Pete Totemoff, a ski resort project was about to become reality. All it needed was an entrepreneur with deep pockets to revitalize the Ruidoso community and gamble a large sum on the ski run.

During the 1940s and 1950s skiiing enthusiasts developed this ski area in Upper Cedar Creek. A primitive rope tow shortened the time it took to climb back to the top of the runs. (Herb Brunell)

Enter Robert O. Anderson. Anderson was a successful oil man from Roswell whose faith and money galvanized numerous New Mexico ventures. He formed the Sierra Blanca Corporation and brought in a brilliant ski expert named Kingsbury Pitcher from Aspen, Colorado. For the next several years Pitcher rode horseback around White Mountain Park studying the feasibility of a ski resort. He liked what he saw, and what he saw was more than six feet of snow in April 1959. Pitcher became president and general manager of the Sierra Blanca Corporation. But with all its beauty, plus snow, plus excellent terrain, the site had to be more accessible to skiers.

White Mountain Park was two thousand feet higher than the nearest highway out of Ruidoso, and a road was needed to get to the site. In 1961 crews blazed a rugged trail with hairpin curves, edged by sheer cliffs, switching back and forth through the forest. Funds from Robert O. Anderson and the State Highway Department built the pioneering trail. Construction began on the resort facilities. The next year saw the completion of a road, plus a handsome laminated wood-spired lodge designed by Victor Lundy. In 1958 the critics proclaimed Lundy as America's outstanding architect.

Sierra Blanca Ski Resort, climbing the north side of Sierra Blanca Peak, opened for Christmas in 1961. Its three T-bars carried twenty six hundred people an hour to the top of the ski run. Lift tickets sold for three dollars.

In the summer of 1962 a gondola, the first four-passenger mono-cable in North America was installed. At seventeen hundred vertical feet, it is more than a mile and a half long. The second season attracted twenty five thousand skiers, and today the gondola is still the only one in New Mexico.

In 1963, Robert O. Anderson merged his oil properties into Atlantic Richfield. He sold the Sierra Blanca ski resort, the Santa Fe resort, and his share of the Buttermilk ski area at Aspen which he had acquired several years earlier.

When Anderson divested himself of the operations, Kingsbury Pitcher bought the Santa Fe ski resort which took him out of the Sierra Blanca

picture, although he remained on the board of directors. Anderson sold the Sierra Blanca ski area to the Mescalero Apaches. The leadership of Tribal President Wendell Chino has guided the tribe's ownership ever since.

Before Kingsbury Pitcher left Sierra Blanca, he contacted his friend Roy Parker who had managed a Colorado ski resort and who had a long, successful ski background. Pitcher asked him to manage the Sierra Blanca project. Parker accepted the new challenge and headed for New Mexico. Parker remembers it this way:

In 1964 I flew down to Alamogordo and arrived about ten at night. In the morning I looked out the window of the Travelodge. The back of the motel faced south. This is kinda funny. I saw nothing but desert through the curtains and I wondered what the devil I was doing here looking for a ski area!

Later, driving toward Ruidoso, I noticed the transition from semi-desert, to brush, to trees. By the time I got to Mescalero and Apache Summit, I was in a ponderoso pine forest—this requires a minimum precipitation of twenty to twenty-five inches a year. When I got to Ruidoso, then drove up the mountain to the ski area at 9,700 feet, I knew it was an ideal site.

I took over as manager of Sierra Blanca in 1964 and I've been in love with this mountain ever since. When the Sierra Blanca Ski Resort was sold to the Mescalero Apache Tribe in 1963, Wendell Chino, president of the Tribe, was far and away the key player. My relationship with Wendell Chino has been very successful, he has left me pretty much alone in the management.

The first time the resort had a losing year, since Roy Parker took over, was 1968 but some years have been close, with bad snow. During the off-season at the ski run, about thirty-five Apaches are employed maintaining the slopes, forests and machinery. During winter months, about a hundred forty Apaches work at the ski run. About 75 percent of the complex is on Forest Service land and about 25 percent is on the Reservation.

In the 1984-85 winter the resort hosted an all-time record of 274,000 skiers and was renamed, appropriately, Ski Apache. It is the state's second busiest ski resort and with its gondola and lifts, Ski Apache can move more people than any New Mexico ski area.

Ski Apache's laminated wood-spired lodge was designed by Victor Lundy who was proclaimed America's outstanding architect in 1958. (Riker Davis)

From the gondola, skiers reach a dazzling white wonderland called Apache Bowl. At 11,500 feet altitude, it is the highest destination on the mountain. Only a part of Apache Bowl is on the Reservation; up to seven feet of snow cover it from November until mid-April.

From some places in Ruidoso, you can spot what looks like a tiny dark shack perched on the wind-blown ridge atop Apache Bowl. What you are looking at is a three-story forty-foot high terminal. The lift goes inside the building and unloads its cargo. The building houses a snack bar, the drive machinery and an electric generator.

An enclosed gondola takes skiers to another destination, the Gazebo. At 11,400 feet, this ride has become a winning tourist attraction as even non-skiers can ride up in the wintertime. This

gondola operates seven days a week. You can buy a ticket to the top and enjoy a two-hundred-mile view that includes White Sands 7,000 feet below. Thousands of non-skiers ride the gondola, make the trip to the Gazebo, enjoy the sights, have lunch, and return at their leisure.

Some folks remember when the twelve-mile unpaved climb to Sierra Blanca proved too thrilling and are still nervous about negotiating the ski run road in wintertime. "Not to worry," says Parker, "I live in Ruidoso and have driven that route every day for twenty-eight years. In the summertime, it takes me about twenty-five minutes to get from my house up to the ski run.

"By ten o'clock on winter mornings, the paved road is clear 85 percent of the days. Even in heavy snow winters like 1991-92, we only had about

Ski Apache is the southernmost major ski area in the United States. It ordinarily has temperatures ten to fifteen degrees warmer than those at resorts in northern New Mexico and Colorado. (Riker Davis)

Tanya Thomas, left and Heather Hauberg from El Paso are part of the kaleidoscope of color splashed against the sparkling snow. Ski outfits have become clothing designers' dreams—lightweight, colorful and warm. (Courtesy Heather Hauberg)

twenty days when tire chains were needed. By mid-morning on those days, the roads had been plowed and salted. There was snow along the sides but all the pavement was showing."

The season at Ski Apache traditionally begins at Thanksgiving. As a backup for Mother Nature, the resort has an arsenal of snow-making machines. The system pumps thousands of gallons of tiny water drops into the freezing nightime air, creating heavy snowfalls on the lower slopes.

Ski Apache's biggest days are always at Christmas time. The biggest day on record is seventy-six-hundred lift tickets. In the course of a normal winter, five or six thousand skiers show up on a Saturday. Being the southernmost major ski area in the United States, Ski Apache ordinarily provides temperatures ten to fifteen degrees warmer than those at resorts in northern New Mexico or Colorado. During early spring in the mountain's mild sunny weather, it's not unusual for individuals to ski in short sleeved shirts and shorts. Sunblock is a must.

Ruidoso merchants depend on Ski Apache's success. No small part of the expense for skiers is the choice of proper equipment—skis, boots, poles and natty warm clothing. A typical bright sunny day around Ski Apache is a kaleidoscope of color splashed against the sparkling snow. Ski outfits, frequently purchased in town, have become fashion statements in hot pink with black, scarlet, purple, brilliant turquoise, lime green and endless combinations. These are clothing designers' dreams, and their products are both lightweight and warm. And expensive.

Mac and Sunny McDougal run a popular Ruidoso ski and sports shop, Ski West Sports. The McDougal's have a sign outside the store reading "We Love Texans." McDougal explains why:

Ruidoso is dependent on customers from out of state, so naturally the Texans are very important. I imagine you'd have to say that about 70 percent of our business comes from Texans. Chihuahua has found us, but most Mexican visitors are coming from Mexico City. There's no skiing at all in Mexico, and we're the

Sierra Blanca is the southernmost glaciated peak in the United States. This rocky, U-shaped valley on the northeastern side of the Peak is a classic example of what geologists call a glacial cirque. The upper end of the cirque reaches nearly to the summit. It is a half mile wide and nine hundred feet high. The sun never hits this spot during the winter, and the snow is estimated to be sixty to eighty feet deep in the cirque. (Riker Davis)

Peeled logs for this new lodge at Ski Apache were all cut on the resort's property.
Dining is cafeteria style, with some tables outside on the deck, enabling people to dine
while watching skiers come down the slopes. (Frank Mangan)

closest major ski area. Mexicans are fascinated by snow; they love the atmosphere of skiing. And they spend money to participate. It seems to be a prestigious sport and they want to be involved. From Mexico City, they fly to El Paso or Juarez where some have cars and they just drive on up to Ruidoso.

We get a lot of skiers now from all over Texas: Dallas, Fort Worth, Houston, San Antonio—as well as El Paso, Lubbock and Midland-Odessa. Also there are quite a few from Oklahoma and even Louisiana and more and more people are finding us from Arizona and California. They don't have to wait in long lines, and the skiing is hassle-free. We need to be aware that convenience is what people want. The competition is still Colorado and the more we can do to make easy access to Ski Apache the better it is.

But the ski scene isn't for everyone. The *El Paso Times* reported that Texas Governor Ann Richards spent a weekend in Ruidoso during racing season and said "I like that little town." But she probably won't return to the mountains for a skiing trip. Richards was quoted: "I spent about two hours on my rear end on the baby slope one time and I thought: 'Here it is, I'm staying at this nice place and there's a fireplace and I've got a great book over there and I'm laying on my back in ice with my feet up in the air and sticks on them—surely this does NOT make sense.'"

Trees of the Lincoln

Traveling upward to the top of Sierra Blanca from the plains and deserts that surround Lincoln National Forest takes you through six of the seven known life zones: Lower Sonoran, Upper Sonoran, Transition, Canadian, Hudsonian, and Arctic Alpine. Missing only is the Tropical Zone. Each of these zones has dozens of varieties of trees and shrubs, but there are always representative (and most common) plants for each belt. They're called "forest indicators."

The Lower Sonoran Zone, at an altitude of about 3,000 to 5,000 feet, is studded with desert plants: yucca, chaparral, mesquite and grease-wood (creosote bush). The Upper Sonoran Zone, ranging from 5,000 to 7,000 feet is the piñon-juniper woodland. Small scattered trees with grassy savannas in between are usually located in the foothills. This zone is still arid but it supports some of New Mexico's finest ranching and grazing land. The piñon is the state tree of New Mexico.

The Transition Zone is marked by tall ponderosa pines. They grow in open stands from about 6,500 feet to 8,000 feet and receive considerably more moisture than trees in the lower zones. This zone of ponderosa pines includes some of the most valuable timberlands in the forest. It is also the habitat for deer, black bear, mountain lion, wildcat, coyote and turkey. Rattlesnakes seldom venture above 7,000 feet.

As the altitude rises into the Canadian Zone, from 8,000 to 10,000 feet, the forest receives additonal rain and snow. This promotes the heavy growth of Douglas fir, aspen, and blue spruce creating a true Alpine environment.

The Hudsonian Zone is between 10,000 and 11,500 feet and supports the high altitude Engleman spruce and the wind-shaped and twisted bristlecone pine. The Hudsonian receives the heaviest snowfall, and the nearly constant wind at this altitude causes the upper reaches of the forest to be stunted and dwarfed.

At around 11,500 feet the timberline reaches the Arctic Alpine Zone. The trees gradually become smaller until they cannot grow at all, and Alpine tundra takes over the rocky slopes. When summertime nears its end in Ruidoso, springtime is just beginning above timberline near the top of Sierra Blanca. Among the boulder-strewn upper slopes, dwarf arctic and alpine plants and colorful flowers burst forth for their own short summer, carpeting the peak.

The different climatic tree zones are not always distinct, tending to blend and intermix with each other. This mixture depends upon soil conditions, temperatures, moisture and other factors. Both plants and animals adapt to the various mountain conditions. For example, on the warmer, drier slopes of canyons (the southern sides that face the sun), an occasional prickly pear cactus or yucca thrives at an elevation normally reserved for ponderosa pines. Across the same canyon are tall stands of ponderosa and Douglas fir, due to the cooler and moister climate in the deep shade.

A good example of this exists in the top reaches of Ruidoso's Upper Canyon. The ponderoso pines that thrive in downtown Ruidoso diminish farther up the canyons as they are replaced with thick stands of Douglas fir. Closer to the Mescalero boundary, the Upper Canyon is much heavier forested, moister and cooler. Patches of snow still cling to the hillsides weeks after it has melted and disappeared in other parts of town. Similar conditions exist in Cedar Creek Canyon. One of the most magnificent groves of giant Douglas fir left in the area is near the upper end of the Forest Service road. Around Ruidoso you can pick the climate you prefer by checking the altitude and the sunny or shady side of a canyon.

The high altitude of Sierra Blanca Peak has created a classic example of what geologists call a glacial cirque, a rocky U-shaped valley which gashes the northeastern side. The upper end of the cirque reaches to near the summit. It is a half mile wide and nine hundred feet high. This is the southernmost glaciated peak in the United States.

Roy Parker, Ski Apache's general manager, who sees this side of the mountain every day winter and summer says, "It takes till the middle of June, the high solstice, for the sun to get in there. We don't know how deep the snow gets, but I suspect it's anywhere from sixty to eighty feet. In the winter there is no melting whatsoever because the sun never hits it."

The headwaters of the North Fork of the Ruidoso are close to the ski resort. The largest of these water sources is Ice Spring, a mile west of Ski Apache. Roy Parker says, however, the main drainage into the North Fork comes from the snow melt in the cirque basin. The two streams merge below the ski area and provide first-rate trout fishing all the way down the mountain canyons into Ruidoso and halfway to Roswell.

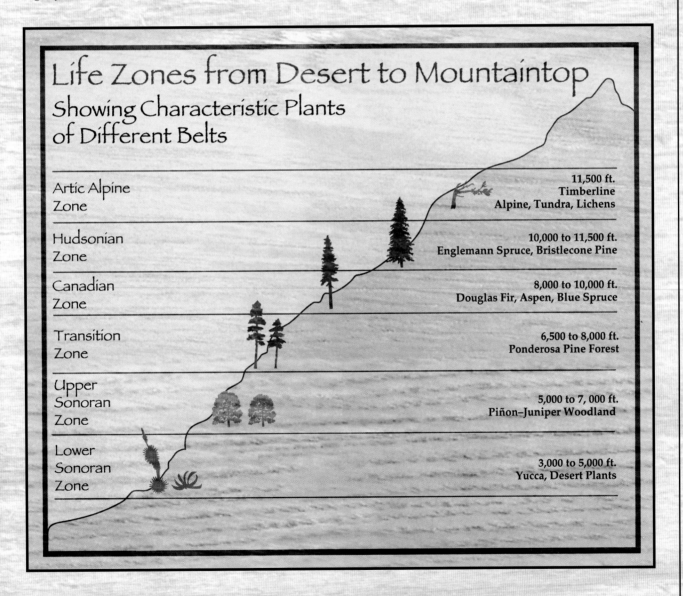

Life Zones from Desert to Mountaintop
Showing Characteristic Plants of Different Belts

Artic Alpine Zone	11,500 ft. Timberline Alpine, Tundra, Lichens
Hudsonian Zone	10,000 to 11,500 ft. Englemann Spruce, Bristlecone Pine
Canadian Zone	8,000 to 10,000 ft. Douglas Fir, Aspen, Blue Spruce
Transition Zone	6,500 to 8,000 ft. Ponderosa Pine Forest
Upper Sonoran Zone	5,000 to 7,000 ft. Piñon–Juniper Woodland
Lower Sonoran Zone	3,000 to 5,000 ft. Yucca, Desert Plants

Racing season at Ruidoso Downs begins in May and ends on Labor Day. It is the home of the world's richest quarter horse race, the All American Futurity. (Courtesy Mark Doth)

13

They're Off and Running

DURING WORLD WAR II dice rolled, roulette wheels whirred and slot machines clattered as they disgorged coins to lucky patrons in downtown Ruidoso. Wide-open illegal gambling flourished. The gamblers called it fun, and the bar owners called it good business. Even so, the participants glanced warily over their shoulders for unannounced deputy sheriffs.

The village of Hollywood, New Mexico bordered the eastern edge of Ruidoso. Here on a grassy meadow called the old Miller cornfield, ranchers from Texas, New Mexico and Oklahoma matched and raced their fastest horses. Fifty thousand dollars often changed hands on the outcome of a two-horse race on a rough strip cut through the cow pasture.

The law paid little heed since participants in Miller's cornfield seemed to be just a bunch of good old boys, ranchers, cowboys and spectators milling around and enjoying a Sunday afternoon of racing. It was simply the age-old challenge, "my horse can outrun your horse." They loved their action face-to-face. Winner take all.

New Mexico racing historian Jerry Knott remembers that the strip was located near the present home stretch at today's Ruidoso Downs. The finish line was fourteen feet higher than the starting point but nobody seemed to mind. Near the straightaway was an open area along the Rio Ruidoso that was popular for Sunday picnics, where kids could catch trout with their hands. Indians from Mescalero occasionally crossed over the rickety wooden bridge and camped along the river. A rodeo arena had been on part of Miller's property and crudely-built bleachers still existed as well as a number of rodeo chutes.

But match races replaced rodeos for folks who felt it was more exciting to watch lightning-fast quarter horses run. Crowds increased to several thousand. Horse owners walked around with a hatful of money to bet against each other, and they asked no odds. It was easy to wind up broke in Miller's meadow.

Meanwhile, Ted Johnson and Tommy Hicks who owned the Central Bar and the largest gambling businesses in downtown Ruidoso helped visitors leave behind money that was vital to the town's economy. But Johnson could foresee the day when the State would deprive him of this revenue. What the town needed in the meantime, he reasoned, was a real race track with pari-mutuel wagering where visitors and townspeople could bet on the horses during the day, then spend their evenings at the downtown gaming tables. After all, the Oil Patch people risked their money in the oil fields and gambling was part of their nature. They would bet on almost anything; if two birds were sitting on a limb, somebody was willing to bet which bird would fly off before the other. It was this free wheeling attitude that gave racing its spark of life in Ruidoso.

A group of local businessmen, with help from Giles Williams from the little town of Bovina in the Texas Panhandle, hammered on an addition to the original rodeo bleachers. They also built a two-story jockeys room constructed of rough lumber. The grandstand was not very grand, comforts were few, but it was an improvement over the old bleachers. Spectators had a roof to keep off rain that occasionally pelted them during thunderstorms. Fans enjoyed top-quality quarter horse racing; exciting, extremely quick contests lasting only about twenty seconds. The track would eventually attract the fastest horses in the world. And just as Ted Johnson predicted, in the late 1940s the State shut down illegal gambling in New Mexico.

Organized racing began in Ruidoso in 1947 when the New Mexico Racing Commission granted permission to operate a track with pari-mutuel wagering. The track was called Holly-wood Park for nearby Hollywood, New Mexico in the same valley that had been Miller's cornfield. Jerry Knott writes in *My Horse Can Outrun Your Horse* "the grandstand was a crudely built struc-ture following the slope of the land and there were still rodeo chutes in the center field. The parking lot was Miller's horse pasture. Steep juniper-covered hills rose up back of the track and to the south and east there were mountains bristling with ponderosa pines." Because of an identity conflict with Hollywood Park in Inglewood, California the track changed its name to Ruidoso Downs in 1952.

Before pari-mutuel betting became a reality at Ruidoso, the wagering was handled by oddsmakers, better known as bookies. They offered odds which they personally arrived at by compiling information on each horse such as breeding, past performances, workouts and

jockeys. The bookmakers then walked back and forth in front of the bleachers. Fans came down and placed bets with the bookies who held the money and gave them a receipt from their "books." There were three or four bookmakers at the Ruidoso track and they worked unbelievably fast. They also had to be extremely honest.

The arrival of the pari-mutuel system did away with bookies although today's racetracks still have their own oddsmaker who figures the odds on each horse. These odds can change every thirty seconds depending on whether more or fewer people bet on a particular horse. Up-to-the-second odds are relayed by computer to the infield boards in front of the stands, and the odds continue to change up until a race begins. At the pari-mutuel windows mistakes are rare, even in this frantic scenario of putting each race together.

Meanwhile during the 1950s, the village of Green Tree dozed quietly across Highway 70 from Ruidoso Downs. H. V. "Heck" Johnson had developed the townsite in 1933 and named it Palo Verde. Johnson sold lots and water rights from Hale Spring at the base of the mountain just to the south. The spring produced such an abundance that new residents irrigated gardens and or-chards, and two sawmills operated with water from the spring. Within a few years Palo Verde's population grew to about five hundred. The remains of an ancient irrigation ditch, ten feet wide and six to eight feet deep and a large burial ground indicate that the area was once a good-sized Indian settlement. Perhaps a prehistoric people who preceded the Apaches.

When Palo Verde residents applied for a post office in 1946, the government approved it but stipulated that the name be changed to Green Tree, the English equivalent of Palo Verde. There were already enough Palo Verdes to cause confu-sion. So Green Tree it became. Within a decade, Ruidoso Downs grew from virtual obscurity to a nationally-known institution. The track's manage-ment persuaded Green Tree residents to change the town's name to Ruidoso Downs so the facility would have a postmark. In 1958, citizens voted to make the name change official. Today, the village of Ruidoso Downs is a lively collection of motels, condos, cafes, homes and businesses—many of them racetrack-related.

The world's first $1 million horse race took place at Ruidoso Downs. Its birth is traced to a meeting in the Hilton Hotel bar in Albuquerque in 1953. A half-dozen horsemen had stopped by for a drink or two, and the conversation turned to horses. These men had some top mares in foal and they compared notes as to who had the best breeding line. They decided the only proof would be a race two years later, matching the then unborn colts. In racing parlance this is called a "futurity," referring to future foals. They proposed a winner-take-all race at Ruidoso Downs which was later won by a two-year-old horse named Segura Miguel. This event formed the concept of the famous All American Futurity.

To enter a futurity, an owner pays a fee to nominate his horse for a future race. He also makes "sustaining" payments to keep the horse eligible during the year-and-a-half before the race. So, with a large number of horse owners' nomination fees and Ruidoso Downs making a sizable contribution, the pot develops easily into the magic number of well over a million dollars.

The American quarter horse has been around since this country's beginnings. The animal was bred from aristocratic bloodlines of the Spanish Barb, a horse noted for endurance and speed. This was the ancestor of the tough Spanish horses brought to America by the conquistadors. On the East Coast, breeders in the American colonies crossed long-running English horses with smaller, stocky Spanish horses, producing the first true American breed, the quarter horse. It became the standard animal on western cattle ranches, eager to start, stop, turn quickly and respond instantly to the slightest movement of a cowboy's reins. The quarter horse could run at high speeds for short distances, much like an Olympic sprinter in a one-hundred meter dash. Owners trained this American breed for "quarter racing," one-quarter-mile of raw speed on a straight track.

By the mid-1950s quarter horse racing at

Ruidoso Downs was extremely popular, thanks in part to an unusual character with a genius for promotion. His name was Eugene V. Hensley and he became the power behind the All American Futurity. It dwarfed most other purses in racing history.

Hensley had been a successful liquor distributor in Phoenix. He came to New Mexico and in 1952 bought controlling interest in Ruidoso Downs. He knew nothing about racing, but he was a natural-born salesman and he used his persuasive talents to bring America's top quarter horses to Ruidoso. He picked up a long string of detractors along the way from minority stockholders to the IRS. Hensley also had plenty of fans in his corner. Dick Alwan, long-time publicist at both Ruidoso Downs and Sunland Park, says, "Thanks to the spadework and promotional ingenuity of Gene Hensley, the guiding light of Ruidoso's early days, the track bridged the gap from the leaky-roof cicuit to a going operation."

Jerry Knott was pari-mutuel manager at Ruidoso Downs from 1952 until he retired in 1986 and his thoughts on Hensley echo those of Dick Alwan. Knott says, "Eugene V. Hensley made Ruidoso Downs. He gave quarter horse racing its national recognition when he put the All American Futurity on national TV and had the All American written up in *Sports Illustrated*. Now people in the East who had never heard of quarter horse racing and who had never heard of the little resort town of Ruidoso know all about the richest horse race in the world."

The first All American Futurity was run on Labor Day in 1959 and has been the highlight of the summer racing season every Labor Day since.

The All American, as well as other futurities, are races exclusively for two-year-olds, the rookies of racing. There are now two other high-dollar futurities at Ruidoso Downs; the $400,000 Ruidoso Quarter Horse Futurity and the $600,000 Rainbow Futurity. The $2.3 million All American remains one of the richest anywhere and it is still the world's finest quarter horse race. How rich? By comparison, the 119th running of the Kentucky Derby in 1993 featured a total purse of $985,900

with the winner receiving $735,900. The winner of Ruidoso's All American Futurity receives a cool million dollars every year.

Walt Wiggins, the renowned photo journalist (originally from Roswell) was responsible for many national stories on the All American. He had access to *Life, True, Argosy* and other magazines and was known and respected in the publishing world. After Wiggins visited Ruidoso Downs, he and Hensley became friends. Gene convinced him to take over public relations for the track and together they went on the road personally promoting Ruidoso Downs and the All American. Hensley entertained lavishly, with private parties in his office where free liquor flowed like the Rio Ruidoso. He kept little record of his expenses to the chagrin of the stockholders and the income tax people.

Gene Hensley also called on the promotional talents of Ray Reed. Reed is a ruddy-faced quintessential cowboy who has been involved with the track since the beginning and still maintains an office there representing the New Mexico Horsemen's Association. Ray is also the organizer of the Lincoln County Cowboy Symposium held each October in Glencoe, New Mexico. He remembers riding broncs in the local rodeos where the track's infield is now. And he later drove thousands of miles with Hensley seeking top horses to run at Ruidoso Downs. The colorful Reed recalls that "when it was time to start promoting the next year, Gene would tell me to bring the pickup over. We had a white Chevrolet and it had ALL AMERICAN RICHEST RACE IN THE WORLD painted on the front. He'd load that pickup with bottles of whiskey and I'd take 'em to the right people all over the United States."

Shortly after Hensley acquired control, he decided the track needed a clubhouse, a country club at the races. He and a group of stockholders organized it as the Jockey Club in 1953. They constructed it above the grandstand where members could overlook the finish line in more than comfortable surroundings. Original stockholders

Pine-clad mountains form a backdrop for the twelve-thousand seat facility at Ruidoso Downs. Although racing fans come to Ruidoso to bet on the horses, they enjoy the added bonus of cool summer weather. The track has facilities to stable seventeen hundred horses. (Pancho Mangan)

who joined the club paid $500 for lifetime memberships. Memberships currently sell for around $30,000 when one becomes available. During the height of the oil boom in the 1980s, memberships went for as much as $90,000. The elite Jockey Club is the only one of its type not controlled by the racetrack, but is solely owned by the members.

The futurities are just part of the racing agenda at Ruidoso with stake races for three-year old quarter horses like the $250,000 Kansas Derby, the $500,000 Rainbow Derby and the $750,000 All American Derby. And although quarter horses put Ruidoso on the racing map, thoroughbreds are favorites among fans who find longer races more exciting. The thoroughbred is much different than the quarter horse. Developed from Arabian horses, this breed is usually heavier and more high spirited and sensitive. It has powerful lungs and long muscular legs and can cover a mile in about a minute and a half. Many polo ponies are part thoroughbred.

Thoroughbred racing is a way of life for Margaret Varner Bloss and her partner Margaret DuPont of El Paso. Bloss is a former U.S. national badminton champion in singles, doubles and mixed doubles. DuPont and Bloss breed, raise and race their horses in New Mexico at Ruidoso, Sunland Park, Albuquerque and Santa Fe.

Bloss and DuPont don't bet on their horses, but when one wins, they get 60 percent of the total purse which is determined by the amount of money bet on a race. The owners actually receive just 40 percent since the jockey and the trainer each get 10 percent—paid by the owner. When a horse comes in second, owners get 20 percent of the purse. For running third owners get 10 percent; they receive 5 percent for fourth and 2 percent for finishing fifth. So all is not lost even if a horse doesn't win, place or show. The track makes its profit from pari-mutuel commissions on each race, as well as from concession stands and admission tickets.

"To horse owners, trainers are very special.

"You can underline the word *very*," Margaret DuPont says. "How well a horse runs depends, of course, on the animal, but if the ability is there it is up to the trainer to bring it out."

Horses are stabled at the track where they are running. Ruidoso Downs, for example, has facilities to stable seventeen hundred horses. Trainers take each horse for a daily workout to keep them in top shape. They exercise their charges each day to get them in condition to peak physically at race time. This kind of training applies to quarter horses as well as thoroughbreds. It's a job of skill and patience; expert trainers handle horses gently but firmly and teach them to bolt from the starting gate when it swings open.

"Thoroughbreds run different distances at Ruidoso but the most popular is one mile," says Bob Haynsworth, a director of Ruidoso Downs. "Since the track is one-mile around, the horses start in front of the grandstand and finish in front." Haynsworth has owned and raced horses since 1958 and was manager of Sunland Park Racetrack for four years in the early 1960s. He says, "Jockeys are hired by the horse owner, usually three days before a race. They normally wear the colorful silks of the owner. My own colors, are white with red checkerboard sleeves." Owners' silks are kept in the Jockeys Room at the track.

Since its first season in 1947, Ruidoso Downs has had its share of ownership changes. In 1988 R. D. Hubbard and his partner Dr. Ed Allred acquired the track. Hubbard is a Fort Worth businessman who has invested heavily in Ruidoso and become a dedicated philanthropist in the area. Through the R. D. and Joan Dale Hubbard Foundation, contributions include the Museum of the Horse at Ruidoso Downs and gifts for the arts, schools and the Space Hall of Fame in Alamogordo. Hubbard has a large home in Ruidoso overlooking The Links, a handsome golf course he developed at a cost of $4.7 million. He is also chairman of the board and CEO of Hollywood Park race track in Inglewood. He built Woodlands race track in Kansas City and owns the Multnomah Kennel Club in Portland.

Under Hubbard, Ruidoso Downs moved ahead even after the wild oil boom and bust of the 1980s which had a crushing effect on Ruidoso. Hubbard spent over $3 million improving the racetrack and grounds, giving it a complete overhaul in 1989. He bought out his partner, Ed Allred in 1991. Yet, even with this life-saving infusion of capital, competition for the discretionary income pie remains a disturbing factor at Ruidoso.

Mark Doth, marketing director of Ruidoso Downs says, "If you check the tracks's parking lot, the vast majority of license plates will still be white (from Texas). But, the arrival of legalized racing in Texas is heavy competition. You've got Bandera Downs outside of San Antonio and Trinity Meadows at Dallas-Fort Worth. Then Texas legalized a state lottery in 1992. Another thing is the Indian casino here at the Inn of the Mountain Gods, the video games. I've talked to people up here from San Antonio or Dallas-Fort Worth. They spent money as they drove, stopping at convenience stores to buy lottery tickets; then instead of spending two days at the track, they stayed one day at the Mescalero casino and one day at the track. Everything just cuts the pie up that much smaller so we have to be very competitive for our gambling dollars."

But in spite of stiff new competition, Ruidoso can bank on the popularity of horse racing in the pines. As Doth says, "We have no trouble capitalizing on great summer weather and we still see plenty of San Antonians. They come up here to escape the heat and lots of them have condos or second homes. The same goes for people from Dallas-Fort Worth. But we feel a lot of pressure in the scramble for horses from the new Texas tracks. The more tracks there are, the fewer horses you can draw from. But people come to Ruidoso Downs to gamble on the races and have a vacation at the same time."

Where do most of the racing fans come from? "Midland-Odessa, Lubbock, Amarillo and Abilene," says Doth. "And of course El Paso will always be a strong market. Again it depends a lot on the weather. If it's hot in El Paso we could have about 10 percent of our fans from there.

Whereas from Midland-Odessa and Lubbock we might have 60 to 70 percent. And then on a daily basis we always attract fans from the surrounding communities like Roswell, Ruidoso and Alamogordo." Racing season at Ruidoso begins in early May and ends on Labor Day. Vivacious Kathy Soliday, a waitress at the Log Cabin Restaurant quips, "You know when the season is over in Ruidoso, all the license plates turn back to yellow."

In 1989 intertrack wagering began at Ruidoso and has created a happy increase in betting dollars. Ruidoso Downs races are simulcast to other New Mexico tracks where fans can place bets on the Ruidoso races while watching them on a TV screen. Typically, Ruidoso simulcasts its races to Sunland Park, New Mexico (adjoining El Paso), San Juan Downs at Farmington, La Mesa Downs at Raton, The Downs at Santa Fe and the State Fair Races at Albuquerque.

Ray Sanchez, former sports editor and race handicapper for the *El Paso Herald-Post*, says many racing enthusiasts tend to be their own worst enemy at the pari mutuel windows. Ray once wrote a novel called *The Gods of Racing* because, he says, "I have always been fascinated

by the mysterious forces working against the bettor. Why do people change their minds or ask for the wrong tickets or not bet on a horse they really like?" Sanchez insists it's more than coincidence that every time you make a decision at a race track it's wrong. He thinks someone up there, or down there, is watching, ready to take advantage of your every mistake. For example, you go up to the ticket window fully convinced that say, horse number 3 will win. Seconds before placing your bet, you hear somebody behind you comment that number 4 is almost certain to win. What do you do? You change your mind and bet on number 4. Who wins the race? Number 3, of course. Sanchez says this sort of thing happens to every racing fan. No question about it, there are mysterious gods hovering around. They're called the gods of racing.

Although people go to Ruidoso Downs to gamble, there is an added bonus to watching the horses run. And that is people-watching. In the twelve-thousand-seat facility, fans' attire runs the gamut from the Old West to the New West and everything in between.

Pin stripe suits and alligator loafers make only a small splash here, but there are lots of women's big hairdos, skintight jeans and silver cowboy boots. Watching the odds on the infield boards are old cowboys wearing sweat-stained western hats, big belt buckles and muddy boots. There is a mixture of trendy, inlaid multicolored walking boots and plain Texas style stovepipe boots that reach to just below the knee.

There are rodeo bronc riders, goat ropers, wealthy ranchers and their wives and kids. Most are decked out in wide-brimmed straw hats, Levis or Wrangler jeans. Some are dripping turquoise and silver jewelry, just right in this place. To this mix, add the outfits of some summer tourists resplendent in tank tops, shorts and hundred dollar pump-up basketball shoes. You've got a veritable sea of sartorial splendor. At the very least, it's a mixture of western Americana.

14
Ruidoso Style

THE ACCIDENT OF GEOGRAPHY changed Ruidoso from a tiny dot on the map of southeastern New Mexico to a resort-style community of five thousand residents, swelling to thirty thousand on special summer weekends. For decades parts of southeastern New Mexico have been known as Little Texas. The reason: the gods of geography placed West Texas on two sides of New Mexico. Through the years, Texans wandered across the state line and stayed. Many, lured by fabulous stories of tall mountains and cool streams, had their hopes dashed when they crossed into New Mexico. What they saw were more sandhills and cactus. Somebody forgot to tell them that the Texas plains are pretty much like New Mexico's.

These Texas pilgrims pushed on, finally discovered Ruidoso Country, and continued coming to play and stay. Consequently the predominant speech patterns in Ruidoso have a decided West Texas accent. Many children born in Ruidoso grow up talking like their mommas and daddies. Some folks say if you scratch the surface of a Ruidosoan, you may find a Texan under there somewhere—even if their descendants go back a half century or more. So Ruidoso has its share of good old boys and good old girls. It has a folksy charm, a trust and a country sense of humor lost long ago in much of America.

Ruidoso's growth began in earnest in the 1920s and has continued at a fairly steady pace, with one exceptional spurt, the Texas oil boom. During the early 1980s the Texans arrived daily looking for a place to invest a seemingly endless stream of new money. Thus, the frenetic activity in Ruidoso was tied directly to the oil boom. Nobody could have predicted an Arab embargo which was the underlying cause. In 1973 oil sold for $3.98 a barrel. With the Arabs cutting the supply, a domestic drilling frenzy began, and during the rest of the decade the price zoomed straight up. By 1980 a barrel of oil cost $32, and there was talk of it going to $50.

People got extremely rich overnight. The Texans brought to Ruidoso a wave of capital that caused the town's prices to skyrocket. They did some serious wheeling and dealing and built condos faster than you could say grits and gravy. The line of investors seemed to stretch from here to Dallas and Houston. The cost of summer cabins almost doubled causing some natural resentment among the Ruidoso citizenry. It was reminiscent of the way the British viewed American GIs during World War II: "They're over-paid, over-sexed, and over here."

But times change. The boom went bust and by 1986 oil was selling for $10 or $11 a barrel—or less. Many of the new rich lost everything and

Midtown Ruidoso glistens after a light snowfall. The upside-down Wild Snail sign is a familiar sight in this part of the village, the center of illegal gambling in the 1930s and '40s. (Frank Mangan)

pulled out of Ruidoso. More than three hundred Texas banks failed. Local citizens settled back to normal lives. But some of the out-of-state investors became enamoured with the cool mountains and kept summer homes. Some even retired in Ruidoso and are today's solid citizens.

Before his retirement in 1983, Chuck Chesbro was a jet pilot flying for El Paso Natural Gas out of Houston. His flights took him to London, Paris, Algiers and Munich as well as cities in Japan and the Far East. In 1989 Chesbro and his wife Eva bought a retirement home in Alpine Village and are now a dedicated part of the Ruidoso community. Chuck is on the board of the Alpine Village Water Association, and both he and Eva are active in church and civic work. Says Eva: "We like the slow-paced lifestyle," and she adds with a chuckle, "even though Ruidoso gets called the dumpster capital of the world. This is a laid-back, clean-blue-jeans-on-Saturday-night kind of

town." Besides enjoying the seclusion of a home in the forest, Chuck Chesbro is a serious skier. "Where else around here," he asks, "can you go skiing in the morning less than thirty minutes from home and play golf in the afternoon?"

Another who came to Ruidoso in the 1980s and left an imprint was Bill Hostetter. He was a kind and extremely talented man, one always fascinated by the weather. Specifically the weather in the Ruidoso area. A retired meteorologist from the U. S. Weather Bureau, he and his wife Lois moved to Ruidoso in 1983. During his years with the Weather Bureau he spent much of his career in South Texas, the Texas Hill Country, and San Antonio. He moved to Ruidoso from Houston.

After retirement he wanted to continue working in the same field in which he had spent so much of his adult life. "With my job," said Hostetter, "I figured I could live anywhere I wanted because there was a demand for people

with my background. We did a lot of looking around and easily chose Ruidoso because there's just no place like it. I like the four well-defined seasons and the cool summers." Until his death in 1993, he worked as Ruidoso's consulting meteorologist. This kept him on the telephone much of the time checking with other weather stations, answering calls from the media, and recording Ruidoso's weather conditions.

One of his primary jobs was recording accurate levels of precipitation. According to Hostetter, to get the average, you combine the measured rain with sleet and snow (snow is measured independently by melting it). In Ruidoso, fifteen inches of snow equals about one inch of moisture. The average precipitation in Ruidoso (snow, sleet and rain) is 23.26 inches.

To get the most accurate count, you can't depend on just one rain gauge at say, the FAA tower at the airport. That location receives less moisture than the rest of the area because it's situated in a different weather pattern on the Fort Stanton Mesa. The official weather station is located at the Ruidoso Police Department.

The farther down the Ruidoso River you go the less rainfall you get. Glencoe, twelve miles east for example, gets less precipitation because of its lower altitude and being farther from the weather-making slopes of Sierra Blanca. But Glencoe gets a heavy river runoff from the rains in Ruidoso.

Hostetter left voluminous weather record books and computer data, enough solid weather information to boggle the mind. For example: 1941 was the wettest year New Mexico ever had. Whitetail on the Mescalero Reservation had 62.45 inches of precipitation. The snowiest winter on record occurred in 1974-75 when over 100 inches fell. This measurement was taken at the old airport, where

Dark clouds build up minutes before a New Mexico summer thundershower begins. Photo above was taken in front of the Herman Oteros' home in Capitan. (Frank Mangan) Below, Cree Meadows is Ruidoso's oldest established golf course. It is one of many locations named after the Scotsman James Cree, Ruidoso's first large landowner. (Ruidoso Valley Chamber of Commerce)

Outlaws gather. Little Billy the Kids and Pat Garretts take the stage at Cedar Creek Park during Billy the Kid–Pat Garrett Days. (Courtesy Charles Stallings, *The Ruidoso News*)

The Links golf course is now. Ruidoso's driest month is April with average precipitation of only 0.69 inches. The monsoon season starts about June 17 when warm moist air moves in from the Gulf of Mexico and Lower California. The rainy season is July and August with an average precipitation of over eight inches for the two months. During summertime, it's not unusual to see smoke curling slowly from cabin fireplaces—especially in the heavily forested, cooler and damper areas along the Rio Ruidoso in the Upper Canyon.

The sunny warm days of April with the greening grass, blooming fruit trees and explosion of dandelions inevitably stir the instincts of Ruidoso gardeners, but weather records indicate caution. The average date for the last spring freeze is June 2 and there is a 10 percent chance that it could freeze as late as June 28. In 1978 it froze on August 7. The first fall freeze usually occurs about September 21.

This is not to say that Ruidoso's winters are extreme. With an average of 243 days of sunshine during the year, a winter storm can, in one day, cover the village with snow. But it seldom remains long on the ground. Usually the sun will come out the next day and melt most of the snow. This is because of the proximity to Ruidoso of warm desert air. It brings a rapid return of sunshine,

preventing problem accumulations of snow. The average high temperature during winter months (December, January, February, March) is 52 degrees. High spring winds and sandstorms aren't the pesky problem they can be in the surrounding deserts and plains—a plus for Ruidoso. But occasionally it can get weird.

A freak mixture of storms occurred one night in March, 1991. Gale-velocity winds blew in from the western deserts across White Sands National Monument forty miles away. The force of the winds picked up tons of the white sugar-like gypsum sending it thousands of feet in the air and into the mountains. At the same time Ruidoso, at seven thousand feet, was getting rain and sleet from the same direction. When the mixture hit Ruidoso the world turned white. Next morning, black cars were literally white. Cabins and homes facing west looked as though they had been spray-painted with a coat of whitewash. Windows were impossible to see through. It took days for folks to scrape and wash off the unwelcome paint jobs.

Twenty miles down the road from Ruidoso the tiny village of San Patricio attracts art lovers from all over the country. The Rio Ruidoso flows leisurely out of the narrow canyons and tall pines into a wide valley backed with piñon dotted

John Meigs (left) of San Patricio is an established painter and collector who owns a rambling adobe treasure of art and antiques called Fort Meigs. (Peggy Mangan Feinberg) Below, Anne Stradling brought the Museum of the Horse to Ruidoso Downs in 1992. It houses the largest collection of horse-related items in the world. (Ruidoso Valley Chamber of Commerce)

hillsides. The slower moving and not-so-noisy river irrigates apple and cherry orchards and small farms on its way through San Patricio to its junction with the Rio Bonito and the Hondo Valley.

This is what some call Hurd Country, since San Patricio was the ranch home of the late Peter Hurd, who gained world recognition as a landscape and portrait painter. The handsome Hurd-La Rinconada Gallery is the centerpiece of San Patricio where works of Peter Hurd are on permanent display.

Visitors to the gallery also are treated to the art of Hurd's widow, Henriette Wyeth Hurd and their son Michael Hurd and daughter Carol Hurd (Mrs. Peter Rogers) as well as the paintings of Andrew Wyeth and N.C. Wyeth, all members of one of the country's most acclaimed art dynasties.

John Meigs, longtime friend of Peter Hurd, is an established painter and collector who owns a rambling adobe treasure of art and antiques across a tree-lined dirt road from the Hurd-La Rinconada Gallery. Meigs displays hundreds of paintings, photographs, graphics and thousands of books in his twenty-two room hacienda and gallery which welcomes visitors from all over the country.

Meigs recalls that when he started at San Patricio he purchased a three-room raw adobe house for a hundred dollars. Little by little the inveterate collector added on more rooms to

Ruidoso area golf courses offer a cool treat for local citizens and visitors from nearby desert communities. The surrounding scenic beauty adds spectacular new dimensions to the sport. (Ruidoso Valley Chamber of Commerce)

display and house his growing collection. Says Meigs, "Peter Hurd started calling this place Fort Meigs. Then when I kept adding on, Hurd called it *Old* Fort Meigs and as the place got bigger and bigger, he re-named it *Historic* Old Fort Meigs."

There is an intense, powerful quality of light in the San Patricio valley and it attracts a growing number of fine artists and sculptors. The village of Ruidoso, however, is the place where most artists and sculptors sell their work. Art galleries line Sudderth Drive in the downtown area and the largest is Fenton's. It is owned by husband and wife team Dan and Peggy Fenton, both from West Texas ranch families.

Peggy Fenton's blonde hair is usually topped with a wide-brimmed Stetson matching her stylish western outfits. Her blue eyes fairly sparkle with enthusiasm when she describes the art scene in Ruidoso.:

At one time we had five galleries including one in Ruidoso. Danny always knew Ruidoso was the best location, but he didn't want to live here. These trees bugged him real bad. And it really did take some adjusting for him. I was careful and chose a place to live that was not in the Upper Canyon with a lot of trees where we might be closed in if the weather got too bad. So we decided to live over on Cree, the golf course area. Nice and open. It was also near the gallery.

So we moved to Ruidoso, and the oil crunch hit big time. When we arrived the Texans were busted and moving out. Bad deal. Since the economy was in the shape it was in, Danny booked big shows in cities like Las Vegas, Denver and Oklahoma City. A lot of our framing business comes from California and Arizona, from people who liked our framing at the shows. You can't believe how much we get from California.

When everything was booming people would spend a thousand or two thousand dollars. But after the oil crunch they'd spend between three and four hundred dollars on a piece. There were over thirty galleries then, now there are about eighteen. But next to Santa Fe, we're still probably the best art town in New Mexico.

The arts received a major boost when race track owner R.D. Hubbard and his wife Joan Dale came to Ruidoso. In 1992, they were instrumental in bringing the Museum of the Horse to Ruidoso Downs, a showplace that would be a striking addition to any city in the country. Peggy Fenton calls it "extremely classy." And by any stretch of the imagination, it is. "The Museum of the Horse is Joan Hubbard's project and she's done great with it," says Fenton.

The museum was the brainchild of Anne C. Stradling, a wealthy easterner turned westerner, who was inspired by a love of horses, a passion for collecting anything that was related to horses. She and her husband put together the original Museum of the Horse in Patagonia, Arizona. The collection grew to more than ten thousand items. But concerned with her health and the museum's future she worked out an agreement with the Hubbard Foundation to renovate an old convention center in Ruidoso Downs and bring her collection to New Mexico.

Ann Stradling died in 1992, leaving Ruidoso the largest collection of horse-related items in the world. It includes pieces such as a conestoga wagon, an 1860 stagecoach, saddles, harnesses, bits and spurs and Indian artifacts dating from 1300 A.D. to the present. There are also items from ancient Greece and Rome, as well as original paintings by western artists Charles Russell and Frederick Remington.

Adding luster to the Ruidoso renaissance is the annual Ruidoso Art Festival, held the third weekend in July. The festival became an annual affair in 1972 and continues its lively aesthetic tradition bringing in quality art from throughout the country.

Every summer the sleepy frontier town of Lincoln with its Old West roots and rustic setting wakes up and puts on its best face for visitors who are making it a tourist destination. And of course, what's good for Lincoln is good for Ruidoso.

Lincoln has no bars, the shops don't sell rubber tomahawks, there's only one pay phone, on the porch of the Wortley Hotel. And there are no neon signs or sidewalk Coke machines. Visitors usually stay in Ruidoso and spend the day in Lincoln moseying around and absorbing the history that makes the town unique.

178

Cool Clear Water

The creeks run full in Ruidoso Country during spring run-off time. At left the Sacramento River tumbles down a canyon at Timberon, south of Cloudcroft. (Wally Sheid) Lower left, the Rio Bonito drops through a rocky gorge near Fort Stanton. (Donna Mangan) At lower right, the Bonito forms an attractive waterfall below Bonito Lake. (Pancho Mangan)

Horse-drawn carriages add a festive, Old West touch to downtown Ruidoso during the height of the tourist season. (Pancho Mangan)

For those who like their history undiluted by tourist trap-ism, Lincoln has the soft mellow look of Territorial New Mexico—a walk through time. This tree-lined, one-street hamlet was once the county seat of the largest county in the United States, the focal point of the Lincoln County War in 1878 and '79. It was also the site of Billy the Kid's famous escape from the jail in the Lincoln County Courthouse in 1881 where he cheated the hangman by slaying both his guards. Those bullet holes are still in the walls. Today the courthouse is a museum, administered by New Mexico State Monuments.

Every August, in an annual weekend celebration known as Old Lincoln Days, folks browse through arts and crafts and food booths scattered about town and are treated to entertainment such as marching horse cavalry soldiers, Apache Indian dancers, costumed mountain men demonstrating black-powder shooting, and oldtime fiddlers contests and parades.

The main event is always a favorite of the boots-and-belt-buckle crowd as they gather on wooden bleachers to watch "The Last Escape of Billy the Kid." The outdoor pageant with a volun-

teer local cast began in 1940, and except for an interruption during World War II, it has been an annual celebration.

There are several good reasons why the town looks pretty much as it did in the nineteenth century. Back in 1912 Lincoln was still the county seat with a population of about a thousand, sort of a market place for farmers and ranchers along the Bonito, Ruidoso and Hondo valleys. But when it lost the county seat to the new railroad town of Carrizozo, Lincoln's prosperity and businesses promptly folded. The population packed up and left, leaving only about sixty citizens. Lincoln went into a decline from which it never recovered.

In retrospect this was the best thing that could have happened to Lincoln. The result was survival through neglect, of a nearly intact nineteenth century town. It is now a National Historical Landmark. Lincoln resembles itself a hundred years ago. If it had retained the county government for another twenty or thirty years, the town would look completely different. The adobe courthouse would likely have been bulldozed and replaced with something more monumental.

In 1972 Lincoln became a historic district. A

Some of New Mexico's finest grazing land lies in the piñon-dotted rolling hills about fifteen miles north of Ruidoso. Handsome valleys near Alto, Bonito and Capitan were once part of the sprawling Cree Ranch at the turn of the century. Above, Craig Van Winkle and his son Chance move a small herd. At left is the Young Rider, Chance Van Winkle. He has his own brand. (Frank Mangan)

review board keeps a wary eye on alterations and new buildings that threaten a clash with the town's Territorial look. The board has enforced rules against chain-link fences, mobile homes and solar panels, among other things. No motels, no service station, no fast food.

Today Lincoln's citizens are keeping the twentieth century at bay thanks in part to the Lincoln County Heritage Trust and the Lincoln County Historical Society. The Trust was formed in 1976 by a group interested in preservation and restoration. Roswell oil man Robert O. Anderson served as a benefactor—along with the late artist Peter Hurd, western writer Paul Horgan and others.

Bob Hart is director of the Lincoln County Heritage Trust. He also supervises the Territorial-style Heritage Trust Museum which houses, among other things, displays of folklore and items relating to the life of Billy the Kid. Across the grass patio, the Historical Center Museum Store is well stocked with books on regional history, as well as local arts and crafts keyed to the nineteenth century.

Historical Center hosts dress in period costumes, adding a touch of nostalgia. According to Hart, Lincoln is at a crossroads. "The national media seeks us out, we don't seek them," he says, "and they've started to write us up. As a result, we're getting more folks who are searching for some sort of experience here. But there's a possible downside. If we take the wrong path then we turn ourselves into kind of a Disneyland. Other people are looking at Lincoln as a place to retire or open a business."

Even in the early twentieth century when Lincoln was almost deserted, Hart says "some progress took place. We eventually got electricity. We have a paved road now. But I think the town basically existed in a never-never land, an economic backwater. You see, progress is a two-edged sword. At what point does the village become too commercialized? Someone wanted to put a junkyard in town. That's not compatible. Somebody else suggested a used car lot. Also not compatible. But if someone wanted to put in a gallery—as long as they didn't put it in a geodesic dome or something which doesn't fit—then fine. It would probably amount to stronger support for the preservation effort."

Some folks moved to Lincoln because it was untouched by the twentieth century. They would just as soon see it remain this way well into the twenty-first century. Well, maybe with one more pay phone.

Lincoln County War chronicler Frederick Nolan says that today, Lincoln lives on for only one reason: Because it is Billy the Kid's town.

Mountain towns are little towns, and that's the way Ruidoso is. The village has spread out since it developed as a summer resort. The main street still meanders through six miles of pine forest, and arteries now reach out into side canyons dotted with summer homes. Motels, condos and resort hotels abound. There are some forty-five restaurants, more than a dozen churches, a civic events center and a first-rate health care facility, the Lincoln County Medical Center. Its award-winning newspaper, *The Ruidoso News* was founded by Lloyd P. Bloodworth almost a half century ago and remains committed to covering area events and people who live and work here. Subscribers live all over the world. The village has two radio stations, KRUI and KBUY. Television is available through Lincoln Cablevision.

There are tiny cabins hidden in the forest, as well as large homes ranging up to a half-million dollars or more, like many of those in the planned community of Alto Village. In 1965 M.H. Blaugrund of El Paso envisioned Alto Village as a resort community similar to developments he had seen in California. Alto Village, five miles north of Ruidoso, was named for the little ranch and orchard settlement of Alto. Today an eighteen hole championship golf course, swimming pool, clubhouse and restaurant are surrounded by seven hundred fine mountain homes.

Unique is a good word to describe Ruidoso. It has a charm, a fascination, a draw that is very difficult to escape. Some people have gone out on a limb and predicted that the village was on its way to becoming a little Santa Fe. True, Ruidoso

Church in the vale. This is the Community United Methodist Church, built in 1947. Clustered nearby are a number of Ruidoso's other churches, of which there are more than a dozen. (Frank Mangan)

sits at the same seven thousand-foot elevation with much the same climate and has its share of art galleries, artists and sculptors, but there the similarity ends. "Ruidoso is just itself," say Herb Brunell, Ruidoso businessman and photographer, "and really shouldn't be compared to any place else. I like it the way it is and I call it 'Ruidoso Style.' This town has its own personality."

In 1993 *Southern Living* magazine called Ruidoso "the premier resort town of southeastern New Mexico, a high-altitude escape from summer heat…unlike Santa Fe, Ruidoso has not become a haven for the rich and famous. It's more family oriented and casual." Fortunately, there is an absence of over-priced junk shops that blight so many once-magical spots.

Most towns experience a cultural trade-off when they grow up and come of age and Ruidoso is no exception. Joetyne Wright has roots here that go back to her grandfather who came to Capitan in the 1880s. Wright has fond memories of growing up in Ruidoso in the twenties, thirties and forties and she weighs the advantage of a town expanding from wood sidewalks and dirt streets. In some ways she's not too happy with the growth since she doesn't have as much privacy

any more. "I used to go where I wanted to," she says. "And it didn't matter if we were gone for a month, we just didn't bother to lock the house. Now we do. But that's everywhere—not only here. It's just the times.

"The modern advantages of Ruidoso's growing up are much better. I think back sometimes about how my mother had to drive me to Roswell seventy-five miles away, over icy roads for my daughter to be born. That was not fun. They had to take my dad at midnight to Roswell for an emergency appendectomy. I nearly died here because my own appendix ruptured before we got to a doctor. So things are much better. Medical facilities are great."

New Mexico customs and loyalties are strong and deep-rooted in Ruidoso although they are diluted by distance from much of the rest of this large state. Ruidoso has a free and easy personality of its own that can't belong to any other region. It is oriented to neighboring Texas, yet it belongs only to itself and to anyone who wants to enjoy living in this small-town atmosphere in the high mountains. It is a happy place.

183

Sources

INTERVIEWS

Jonathan Adams
Dick Alwan
José Andow

Bob Barron
Clayton Bennett
Helen Bennett
Margaret Varner Bloss
Bert Brunell
Herb Brunell
Wayland Burk
Ed Byington
Stacy Byington

Chuck Chesbro
Eva Dell Chesbro
Mark Chino
Wendell Chino
José Cisneros
Skip Clark
Bill Cornell
Terry Cornell
Shawn Cupid

Riker Davis
Alden Deyo
Jane Deyo
Mark Doth
Carolyn Driver
Walter Driver
Joe Dunlap
Margaret DuPont

Jim Eckles
Evelyn Estes

Mary Lou Faller
Andy Feinberg
Peggy Mangan Feinberg
Dan Fenton
Peggy Fenton

Joanne Vickers Gnauck
Mary Lou Gooch
Bill Green

Bill Hart
Bob Hart
Bob Haynsworth

Hazel Haynsworth
Caroline Herrera
Kayla Hightower
Maurice Hill
Una Hill
Ken Hosmer
Lyle Hosmer
Bill Hostetter

Tillie Jack
Emadair Jones

Berle Kanseah
Jo Kazhe
Paul Kennedy
Alerta Keyes
Robert Keyes
Greg Klinekole
Dorothy Bell Knapp
Tom Knapp

Ellyn Big Rope Lathan
Charles Leavell
Cordelia Lewis
Charles B. Little
Eleanor Lorentzen
John Lorentzen

John Magruder
Susan Magruder
Anna Belle Malone
Earl Malone
Frank "Pancho" Mangan
Bill Maxwell
Joy Maxwell
Ellis Mayfield
Susan Mayfield
Bill McCarty
Bob McCubbin
Ernest McDaniel
Robert McDaniel
Hattie Patterson McKean
Mac McDougal
Sunny McDougal
Millard McKinney
Tom McNight
Blaine McNutt
Ray McNutt
John Meigs

Leon Metz
Gordon Mooney
Wayne Morgan
Romaine Mounce

Herman Otero
Antonia Otero

Roy Parker
Seferino Peña
Louise Perkins
Martha Patterson Peterson
Carmon Phillips
Marilyn Poel
Sue Polk

Bill Rakocy
Gloria Rakocy
Ray Reed
John Romero
Anne Rone
Tom Rone
Marie Rooney
Betsy Bryant Rose
Thomas Ryan

Fred Salem
Ray Sanchez
Richard Sanchez
Peggy Snell Shaifer
Howard Shaw
Wally Sheid
Cara Mae Coe Smith
Kathy Soliday
Tom Starkweather

Tony Terry
Don Thurman
Sam Tobias
Herb Traylor
Cliff Trussell
Gene Turner
Ruby Turner

Craig Van Winkle
Josephine Via
Larry Walker
C. L. Wright
Joetyne Wright

BOOKS

Adams, Ramon F. *A Fitting Death for Billy The Kid*. (University of Oklahoma Press: Norman, 1960).

A'loge, Bob. *Knights of the Six Gun*. (Yucca Tree Press: Las Cruces, 1991). Arizona Board of Regents. *The WPA Guide to 1930s New Mexico*. Forward by Marc Simmons. (University of Arizona Press: Tucson,1989).

Ball, Eve with Nora Henn and Lynda Sanchez. *Indeh: An Apache Odyssey*. (Brigham Young University Press: Provo, 1980).

Ball, Eve. *Ma'am Jones of the Pecos*. (The University of Arizona Press: Tucson, 1969).

Ball, Eve. *Ruidoso: The Last Frontier*. (The Naylor Company: San Antonio, 1963).

Bannon, John Francis. *The Spanish Borderlands Frontier 1513-1821*. (The University of New Mexico Press: Albuquerque, 1974 and Holt Rinehart Winston: New York).

Barker, Allen. *The KId with Fast Hands*. (Author, Pine Grove, 1993)

Barrett, Boyd. *Trouble in Lincoln County*. Video cassette. (Ladder Films and Nash St. Media: Roswell, 1990).

Bell, Bob Boze. *The Illustrated Life and Times of Billy The Kid*. (Boze Books: Cave Creek, 1992).

Bender, Norman J. *Missionaries, Outlaws, and Indians: Taylor F. Ealy at Lincoln and Zuñi, 1878-1981*. (University of New Mexico Press: Albuquerque, 1984).

Billington, Monroe Lee. *New Mexico's Buffalo Soldiers 1866-1900*. (University Press of Colorado: Niwot, 1991).

Bonney, Cecil. *Looking Over My Shoulder: Seventy-five Years in the Pecos Valley*. With introduction by Peter Hurd. Francis L. Fugate, editor. (Hall-Poorbaugh Press, Inc.: Roswell, 1971).

Botkin, B. A. *A Treasury of Western Folklore*. (Crown Publishers, Inc.: New York, 1951).

Brent, William. *The complete and factual life of Billy The Kid*. (Frederick Fell Inc.: New York, 1964).

Calvin, Ross. *Sky Determines*. Illustrations by Peter Hurd. (University of New Mexico Press: Albuquerque, 1948).

Campa, Arthur L. *Hispanic Culture in the Southwest*. (University of Oklahoma Press: Norman, 1979).

Charles, Mrs. Tom. *More Tales of the Tularosa*. (Bennett Printing Company: Alamogordo, 1961).

Chesley, Hervey. *Trails Travelled Tales Told*. (Nita Stewart Haley Memorial Library: Midland, 1979).

Chilton, Lance and Katherine Chilton, Polly E. Arango, James Dudley, Nancy Neary, Patricia Stelzner. *New Mexico: A New Guide to the Colorful State*. (University of New Mexico Press, Albuquerque, 1984).

Cline, Don. *Antrim & Billy*. (Creative Publishing Company: College Station, 1990).

Coe, George W. *Frontier Fighter: The Autobiography of George W. Coe as related to Nan Hillary Harrison*. (Houghton Mifflin Company: Boston and New York, 1934).

Collier, John. *Indians of the Americas*. (Mentor Books: New York, 1947).

Crouch, Brodie. *Jornada Del Muerto: A Pageant of the Desert*. (The Arthur H. Clark Company: Spokane, 1989).

Cunningham, Eugene. *Triggernometry: A Gallery of Gunfighters*. (The Press of the Pioneers, Inc.: New York, 1934).

Curry, George. *George Curry 1861-1947 An Autobiography, edited by H. B. Hening*. (University of New Mexico Press: Albuquerque, 1958).

Dobie, J. Frank. *The Longhorns*. Illustrated by Tom Lea. (Little, Brown and Company: Boston, 1941).

Dobie, J. Frank. *A Vaquero of the Brush Country*. (Little, Brown and Company: Boston, 1946).

Ellis, Richard N. (ed.) *New Mexico Past and Present: A Historical Reader*. (University of New Mexico Press: Albuquerque, 1971).

Elmore, Francis H. *Shrubs and Trees of the Southwest Uplands*. (Southwest Parks and Monuments Association: Tucson, 1976).

El Paso Writers League. *Southwestern Mosaics*. Jo Gwyn Baldwin (ed.). (Boots & Saddle Press: El Paso, 1969).

Emerson, Dorothy. *Among the Mescalero Apaches: The Story of Father Albert Braun, O.F.M.*. (The University of Arizona Press: Tucson, 1973).

Fergusson, Erna. *Murder & Mystery in New Mexico*. (Merle Armitage Editions: Albuquerque, 1948 and Lightning Tree: Santa Fe, 1991)

Fergusson, Erna. *New Mexico: A Pageant of Three Peoples*. (University of New Mexico Press: Albuquerque, 1951).

Fitzpatrick, George (ed.}. *This Is New Mexico*. (Horn & Wallace: Albuquerque, 1962).

Fleming, Elvis E. and Minor S. Huffman (eds.). *Roundup on the Pecos*. (Hall-Poorbaugh Press, Inc.: Roswell, 1978).

Fleming, Elvis E. and Ernestine Chesser Williams with additional articles by Dr. Lynn I. Perrigo and Peggy L. Stokes. *Treasures of History II Chaves County Vignettes*. (Chaves County Historical Society: Roswell, 1991).

Fugate, Francis L. and Roberta B. Fugate. *Roadside History of New Mexico*. (Mountain Press Publishing Company: Missoula, 1989).

Fulton, Maurice G. *History of the Lincoln County War* (The University of Arizona Press: Tucson, 1968).

Fulton, Maurice Garland and Paul Horgan. *New Mexico's Own Chronicle*. (Banks Upshaw and Company: Dallas, 1937).

Gilbert, Beth. *Alamogordo: The Territorial Years 1898-1912*. (Starline Printing: Albuquerque, 1988).

Glover, Vernon J. *Logging Railroads of the Lincoln National Forest, New Mexico*. (USDA Forest Service: Southwestern Region, 1984).

Hammond, George P. and Agapito Rey. *Don Juan de Oñate Colonizer of New Mexico 1595-1628*. (The University of New Mexico Press: Albuquerque, 1953).

Hammond, George P. and Agapito Rey. *The Rediscovery of New Mexico 1580-1594*. (The University of New Mexico Press: Albuquerque, 1966).

Harkey, Dee. *Mean As Hell*. (The University of New Mexico Press: Albuquerque, 1948).

Heitzler, Gretchen. *Meanwhile, Back at the Ranch*. (Hidden Valley Press: Albuquerque, 1980).

Helbock, Richard W. *Post Offices of New Mexico.* (Richard W. Helbock: Las Cruces, 1981).

Hertzog, Peter. *A Directory of New Mexico Desperados.* (The Press of the *Territorian*: Santa Fe, 1965).

Hertzog, Peter. *Little Known Facts About Billy, The Kid.* (The Press of the *Territorian*: Santa Fe, 1964).

Hinshaw, Gil. *Lea, New Mexico's Last Frontier.* (The Hobbs Daily News-Sun: Hobbs, 1976).

Horgan, Paul. *Conquistadors in North American History.* (Texas Western Press: El Paso, 1982).

Horn, Calvin. *New Mexico's Troubled Years: The Story of the Early Territorial Governors.* With a foreword by John F. Kennedy. (Horn & Wallace, Publishers: Albuquerque, 1963).

Hough, Emerson. *The Story of the Outlaw: A Study of the Western Desperado.* (The Outing Publishing Company: New York, 190V).

Houston Jaycees. *Houston: A History of a Giant.* (Continental Heritage: Tulsa, 1976).

Hunt, Frazier. *The Tragic Days of Billy The Kid.* (Hastings House Publishers: New York, 1956).

James, George Wharton. *New Mexico: The Land of the Delight Makers.* (The Page Company: Boston, 1920).

Jenkins, Myra Ellen and Albert H. Schroeder. *A Brief History of New Mexico.* (The University of New Mexico Press: Albuquerque, 1974).

Jensen, Joan M. and Darlis A. Miller. *New Mexico Women: Intercultural Perspectives.* (University of New Mexico Press: Albuquerque, 1986).

Keleher, William A. *The Fabulous Frontier: Twelve New Mexico Items.* (The Rydal Press: Santa Fe, 1945).

Keleher, William A. *Violence in Lincoln County 1869-1881.* (University of New Mexico Press: Albuquerque, 1957).

Klasner, Lily. *My Girlhood Among Outlaws.* (The University of Arizona Press: Tucson, 1972).

Knott, J. E. *My Horse Can Outrun Your Horse.* (Mesa Publishing: El Paso, 1992)

Larson, Robert W. *New Mexico's Quest for Statehood 1846-1912.* (The University of New Mexico Press: Albuquerque, 1968).

Lavash, Donald R. *Sheriff William Brady: Tragic Hero of the Lincoln County War.* (Sunstone Press: Santa Fe, 1986).

Lavash, Donald R. *Wilson & The Kid.* (Creative Publishing Company: College Station, 1990).

Lavender, David. *The American Heritage History of the West.* (American Heritage/Bonanza Books: New York, 1988).

Lincoln Country Postmaster. *A History of Lincoln County Post Offices.* (Ruidoso News Plant: Ruidoso, 1962).

Link, Martin A. *Navajo, A Century of Progress 1868-1968.* (Navajo Tribe: Window Rock, 1968).

Lowe, Charles H. *Arizona's Natural Environment.* (The University of Arizona Press: Tucson, 1964).

Mauldin, Bill. *A Sort of a Saga.* (William Sloane Associates: New York, 1949).

Mauldin, Bill. *The Brass Ring.* (W. W. Norton & Company, Inc.: New York, 1971).

Metz, Leon C. *Border: The U. S. - Mexico Line.* (Mangan Books: El Paso, 1989).

Metz, Leon C. *City at the Pass: An Illustrated History of El Paso.* Illustration editor: Mary A. Sarber. (El Paso Chamber of Commerce, Windsor Publications, Inc.: Woodland Hills, 1980).

Metz, Leon C. *Turning Points in El Paso, Texas.* (Mangan Books: El Paso, 1985).

Metz, Leon Claire. *John Selman Texas Gunfighter.* (Hastings House Publishers: New York, 1966).

Metz, Leon Claire. *The Shooters.* (Mangan Books: El Paso, 1976).

Mullin, Robert N. *A Chronology of the Lincoln County War.* (The Press of the Territorian: Santa Fe, 1966).

Myrick, David F. *New Mexico's Railroads.* (rev. ed.). (University of New Mexico Press: Albuquerque, 1990).

Neal, Dorothy Jensen. *Captive Mountain Waters.* (Texas Western Press: El Paso, 1961).

Neal, Dorothy Jensen. *The Cloud-Climbing Railroad.* (Alamogordo Printing Company: Alamogordo, 1966).

Neal, Dorothy Jensen. *The Lodge 1899-1969 Cloudcroft, New Mexico.* (Alamogordo Printing Company: Alamogordo, 1969).

Nichols, John. *If Mountains Die.* Photographs by William Davis. (Alfred A. Knopf, Inc.: New York, 1979).

Nolan, Frederick W. *The Life & Death of John Henry Tunstall.* (The University of New Mexico Press: Albuquerque, 1965).

Parker, Morris B. *White Oaks: Life in a New Mexico Gold Camp 1880-1900.* (The University of Arizona Press: Tucson, 1971).

Pearce, T. M. (ed.). Assisted by Ina Sizer Cassidy and Helen S. Pearce. *New Mexico Place Names: A Geographical Dictionary.* (The University of New Mexico Press: Albuquerque, 1965).

Poldervaart, Arie W. *Black-Robed Justice.* (Historical Society of New Mexico Publications in History, Vol. XIII: 1948)

Priestley, Lee with Marquita Peterson. *Billy the Kid: The Good Side of a Bad Man.* (Arroya Press: Las Cruces, 1989).

Rakocy, Bill. *The Kid: Billy The Kid.* (Bravo Press: El Paso, 1985).

Raphael, Ralph B. *The Book of American Indians.* (Fawcett Publications, Inc.: Greenwich, 1933).

Raynor, Ted. *Old Timers Talk in Southwestern New Mexico.* (Texas Western Press: El Paso/Mesilla Book Center: Mesilla, 1960).

Ream, Glen O. *Out of New Mexico's Past.* (Sundial Books: Santa Fe, 1980).

Richardson, Rupert Norval. *Texas The Lone Star State* (2nd ed.). (Prentice-Hall, Inc.: Englewood Cliffs, 1958).

Rickards, Colin. *How Pat Garrett Died.* (Palomino Press: Santa Fe, 1970).

Seckler, Herb. *Hoofnotes from the Downs.* (H. Seckler: Bent, 1990).

Seckler, Herb. *Ruidoso Countryside: The Early Days.* Illustrated by Ken Hosmer. (Ruidoso: 1987).

Sell, Henry Blackman and Victor Weybright. *Buffalo Bill and the Wild West.* (The New American Library of World Literature, Inc. New York, 1959).

Shinkle, James D. *Fifty years of Roswell History 1867-1917.* (Hall-Poorbaugh Press, Inc.: Roswell, 1964).

Shinkle, James D. *Martin V. Corn: Early Roswell Pioneer.* (Hall-Poorbaugh Press, Inc.: Roswell, 1972).

Shinkle, James D. *Reminiscences of Roswell Pioneers.* (Hall-Poorbaugh Press, Inc.: Roswell, 1966).

Shinkle, James D. *Robert Casey and the Ranch on the Rio Hondo.* (Hall-Poorbaugh Press, Inc.: Roswell, 1970).

Simmons, Marc. *Ranchers Ramblers and Renegades: True Tales of Territorial New Mexico.* (Ancient City Press: Santa Fe, 1984).

Smith, Cara Mae. *The Coe's Go West.* (Complete Printing, Inc.: El Paso, 1988).

Sonnichsen, C. L. *The Mescalero Apaches.* (University of Oklahoma Press: Norman, 1958).

Sonnichsen, C. L. *Pass of the North.* (Texas Western Press: El Paso, 1968).

Sonnichsen, C. L. *Tularosa: Last of the Frontier West.* (The Devin-Adair Company: New York, 1960).

Stanley, F. *The Alamogordo (New Mexico) Story.* (Pep, Texas, 1963).

Stanley, F. *The Carlsbad (New Mexico) Story.* (Pep, Texas, 1963).

Stanley, F. *The Fort Fillmore (New Mexico) Story.* (Pantex, Texas, 1961).

Stanley, F. *The Lincoln (New Mexico) Story.* (Pep, Texas, 1964).

Stanley, F. *The Seven Rivers (New Mexico) Story.* (Pep, Texas, 1963).

Stanley, F. *The White Oaks (New Mexico) Story.*

Stratton, Porter A. *The Territorial Press of New Mexico 1834-1912.* (University of New Mexico Press: Albuquerque, 1969).

Tatum, Stephen. *Inventing Billy the Kid: Visions of the Outlaw in America, 1881-1981.* (University of New Mexico Press: Albuquerque,1982).

Timmons, W. H. *El Paso: A Borderlands History.* Illustrations by José Cisneros. (Texas Western Press: El Paso, 1990).

Traylor, Herbert Lee. *Tales of the Sierra Blanca.* (Pioneer Printing Company: Roswell, 1983).

Traylor, Herbert L. and Louise Coe Runnels. *The Saga of the Sierra Blanca.* (Old-Time Publications: Roswell, 1986).

Tularosa Basin Historical Society. *Otero County Pioneer Family Histories, Volume 1.* (Composing Services: Tularosa, 1981).

Tularosa Basin Historical Society. *Otero County Pioneer Family Histories, Volume 2.* (Composing Services: Tularosa, 1985).

Ungnade, Herbert E. *Guide to the New Mexico Mountains.* (2nd ed.). (University of New Mexico Press: 1972).

Utley, Robert M. *Billy the Kid: A Short and Violent Life.* (University of Nebraska Press: Lincoln, 1989).

Utley, Robert M. *Four Fighters of Lincoln County.* (University of New Mexico Press: Albuquerque, 1986).

Utley, Robert M. *High Noon in Lincoln.* (University of New Mexico Press: Albuquerque, 1987).

Weigle, Marta and Peter White. *The Lore of New Mexico.* (University of New Mexico Press: Albuquerque, 1988).

Westphall, Victor. *The Public Domain in New Mexico 1854-1891.* (The University of New Mexico Press: Albuquerque, 1965).

Wiggins, Walt. *Lincoln; New Mexico As It Was One Day: A Photographic Essay.* (Western Heritage Press: Roswell, 1975).

Williams, Jerry L. and Paul E. McAllister (eds.). *New Mexico in Maps.* (University of New Mexico Press: Albuquerque, 1981).

Wilson, John P. *Merchants Guns & Money: The Story of Lincoln County and Its Wars.* (Museum of New Mexico Press: Santa Fe, 1987).

Woods, Betty. *101 Men and 101 Women of New Mexico.* (Sunstone Press: Santa Fe, 1976).

ARTICLES

Bell, Bob Boze. "Billy the Kid." *Arizona Highways.* Vol. 67, No. 8 (August 1991).

Henn, Nora. "The House on Golden Hill Terrace." *Password.* Vol. XXXVII, No. 3 (Fall 1992)

Leo, John. "The North American Conquest." *U. S. News & World Report.* (May 13, 1991).

McMurtry, Larry. "How the West Was Won or Lost." *The Roundup Quarterly, Western Writers of America.* New Series Vol. 3, No. 4 (Summer 1991).

Price, Stephen D. and Bill Landsman. "Horse." *The World Book Encyclopedia.* Volume 9. (Chicago, 1984).

Roach, Joyce. "C. L. Sonnichsen: A Memorial." *The Roundup Quarterly.* Vol. 4, No. 1 (Fall 1991).

Williams, Ernestine C. "Fort Stanton." *Mountain Passages,* Issue 3 (Fall/Winter 1990-91).

NEWSPAPERS

El Paso Herald
El Paso Herald-Post
El Paso Times
Lincoln County News
The Ruidoso News

MAGAZINES

Car & Driver
National Geographic
New Mexico Magazine
The Quarter Horse Journal
Ruidoso Downs Media Guide
Smithsonian
Texas Monthly

Index

Fort Bliss, TX, 34, 49, 77
Fort Fillmore, NM, 34
Fort Griffin, TX, 61
Fort Marion, FL, 138
Fort Pickens, FL, 138
Fort Sill, OK, 137-139, 142, 144
Fort Stanton, NM, 31, 33-34, 36, 39, 41,
    47, 49-51, 53, 59, 100, 142
Fort Sumner, NM, 35-36, 56-57, 59, 61,
    63, 97
Fountain, Albert Jennings, 39, 57, 79,
    83-85, 88, 91
Fountain, Henry, 83, 85, 91
French, G. E., 109
Friedenbloom, George, 99, 110, 113
Fritz, Emil, 41, 46, 50
Fugate, Francis & Roberta, 56

Gadsden, James, 28
Gadsden Purchase, 28
Gardenhire, Montie, 125, 153-154
Garfield, James, 69
Garrett, Apolinaria, 88
Garrett, Elizabeth, 89
Garrett, Jarvis, 90
Garrett, Pat, 38, 54-61, 63-64, 67, 69-70,
    79, 86-90, 93, 95-98
Gauss, Godfrey, 59
Geronimo, 137-139, 144
Gilbert, Beth, 74
Gililland, Ed, 100
Gililland, Jim, 85-88
Gilliam, Jack, 33
Glencoe, NM, 16, 33, 53
Gonzalez, Florencio, 31
Goodnight, Charles, 36
Gould, Jay, 70-71
Grant, Joe, 63, 66
Grant, Ulysses S., 38, 142
Gray, Meldrum, 109
Greene, William C., 129
Green Tree, NM, 164
Grissom, C. W. & Janean, 57

Hale, Alfred, 100, 103-104, 154
Hamilton, Mark, 133
Hardin, John Wesley, 55
Hart, Bill, 100, 117, 125-126, 153-154
Hart, Bob, 65, 182
Hagerman, James J., 70
Harding, Warren G., 90
Hawkins, William Ashton, 71, 87
Hayes, Rutherford B., 47, 55
Haynsworth, Bob, 168
Hedgecoke, Coke, 103
Henn, Nora, 91
Hensley, Eugene V., 165-166
Herrera, Fernando, 51
Hicks, Tom, 163
High Rolls, NM, 74
Hill, Tom, 46
Hillsboro, NM, 88
Hindman, George, 49
Holloman Air Force Base, 14, 120
Hollywood, NM, 99, 110-111
Hondo River, 16, 21, 32, 39, 50

Horgan, Paul, 182
Horrell Brothers, 33, 38-39
Horton, W. D., 153
Hostetter, Bill, 172-173
Hot Shots, 148
Hough, Emerson, 70
House of Murphy, 41, 52-53
Hubbard, Joan Dale, 168, 178
Hubbard, R. D., 168
Hull, Jack, 108, 110, 112
Hurd-La Rinconada Gallery, 177
Hurd, Peter, 16, 93, 177, 182

Izard, Ray, 153

Jenness, Burt, 123
Jicarilla Apaches, 142-143
Jingle Bob (brand), 36
Johnson, H. V. "Heck", 164
Johnson, S. P., 109
Johnson, Sylvester, 95
Johnson, Ted, 163-164
Jones, Emadair, 26, 38, 129, 133-134
Jones, Heiskell, 37
Jones, Tom, 129

Kanseah, Berle, 144, 146-147, 150-151
Kanseah, Jasper, 144
Kearney, Stephen Watts, 27
Keleher, William, 87
Kemp, Maury, 67
Kerney, Kent, 87-88
Keyes, Alerta,
Keyes, Robert, 112
Kinney, John, 56
Kirby, Brandon, 95-95, 98
Kissel, Marianne,
Klasner, Lily, 39
Klinekole, Bruce, 130
Klinekole, Virginia, 130
Knott, Jerry, 163-165

La Luz, NM, 73
Larrazolo, Octaviano, 79
Las Cruces, NM, 14, 52, 83-84, 87-90,
    93-94
Lathan, Ellyn Big Rope, 130, 147
Lavash, Donald R., 41
Leavell, Charles, 130
Lee, Jim, 88
Lee, Oliver, 71, 79, 84-87, 90-91
Lesnett, Frank, 38, 97, 99
L. G. Murphy & Co., 40-41, 44-45
Lincoln County Court House, 42
Lincoln County Heritage Museum, 37
Lincoln County Heritage Trust, 54, 64-
    67, 182
Lincoln County War, 16, 21, 42-53, 69,
    93
Lincoln National Forest, 94, 160
Lincoln, NM, 13, 32, 34, 41-53, 76, 83
Lipan Apaches, 141-143
Little, Charles, 13
Loco, 138
Long Walk, 35
Lorentzen, Eleanor, 94

Loving, Oliver, 36
Lozano, Lorenzo, 55
Lubbock, TX, 93
Lucero, Felipe, 89
Luck, Barney, 105
Lummis, Charles, 137
Luna, Solomon, 79
Lundy, Victor, 155-156

Mabry, Thomas, 63
Mahill, Mollie, 33
Malone, Earl, 109
Malone, R. L., 109
Mangas Coloradas, 138
Martin, C. C., 95
Massey, Louise,
Mauldin, Bill, 74
Mayberry House, 118
Mayfield, Mrs. Davis, 102
Mayhill, NM, 33-34
Manzano, NM, 31
Martinez, Atanasio, 47
Martinez, Juan, 38
Maxwell, Pete, 61-62
McAllister, Paul, 79
McCarty, Bill, 133
McCarty, George, 117, 130, 133
McCarty, Lucille, 133
McDaniel, Ernest, 95, 108-109
McDaniel, Robert, 108
McDougal, Mac & Sunny, 157
McKinney, Collin, 61
McKinney, Thomas, 61-62
McLean, E. B., 90
McMillan, Carl, 130
McMurtry, Larry, 70
McNary, James G., 91
McNew, Bill, 85-87
McNutt, Blaine, 91
McSween, Alexander, 42-43, 46-47, 50-
    51, 66
McSween, Susan, 42, 45, 51, 127
Medler, Edward & Lillian, 94-95, 108
Meigs, John, 16, 176-177
Mencken, H. L., 90
Mescalero Apache Reservation, 13-16,
    18-19, 21, 36-37, 48-50, 58, 73, 83,
    88, 95, 99
Mescalero Apaches, 14, 23, 25, 28, 35-
    36, 137-151
Mesilla, NM, 28-29, 31, 34, 39, 57-58,
    83-84
Metz, Leon C., 29, 55, 63, 66
Middleton, John, 46-47, 49
Mier y Terán, Manual, 27
Miles, Nelson A., 137-138, 144
Miller, Darlis, 37
Miller, Elger, 115
Miller, F. A., 115
Miller, James B., 89
Mills, "Ham", 39
Mims, John, 100
Mogel, Joe, 100, 117
Montaño José, 41, 50-51
Mooney, Gordon, 125
Morton, Billy, 46, 63